Declarations of Independence:
American Cinema and the Partiality of Independent Production

John Berra

Declarations of Independence:
American Cinema and the Partiality of Independent Production

John Berra

intellect Bristol, UK / Chicago, USA

First Published in the UK in 2008 by
Intellect Books, The Mill, Parnall Road, Fishponds, Bristol, BS16 3JG, UK

First published in the USA in 2008 by
Intellect Books, The University of Chicago Press, 1427 E. 60th Street, Chicago,
IL 60637, USA

A catalogue record for this book is available from the British Library.

Cover Design: Gabriel Solomons
Copy Editor: Holly Spradling
Typesetting: Mac Style, Nafferton, E. Yorkshire

ISBN 978-1-84150-185-7

Printed and bound by Gutenberg Press, Malta.

CONTENTS

ACKNOWLEDGEMENTS

I would like to give thanks to a number of people, without whom this book would not have been possible. To Professor Fred Inglis, for his guidance, friendship, and support throughout what has been a challenging and fascinating process. To my wife, Meng Yan, for the love and stability she has brought to my life and for her ever-valuable external perspective on a very specific area of research. To my parents, Paul and Janet, my sister Rebecca, and my grandmother Doreen, for their continued encouragement of my chosen path. To Yan's parents, Meng Zhaoquan and Wang Tieli, for their acceptance of me into their family and culture. I hope that this text provides fresh insight into a socially prominent sector of cultural production, and I welcome any discussion that arises from its publication.

1

GENESIS: MODERN AMERICAN INDEPENDENT CINEMA AND ITS POSITION WITHIN AN INDUSTRY OF MASS PRODUCTION

'Independent *adj* **1** Free from influence or control of others. **2** not dependent on anything else for function or validity. **3** not relying on the support, esp. financial support, of others.'[1]

'Cinema *n* **1** A place designed for showing films. **2 the cinema** the art or *business* of making films.'[2]

It is debatable as to whether a genuine American 'independent cinema' exists in the new millennium, a debate which this study will enter into in due course. What is not debatable is that the term 'American independent cinema' not only exists, but carries with it a variety of meanings, associations, and expectations of both an artistic and commercial nature. A by-product of society's constant need to assign labels to, and invent categories for, all forms of cultural expression and enterprise, the term 'American independent cinema' has been used to describe both a mode of production, and a form a thinking, relating to the financing, filming, distribution and cultural appreciation of modern film. It is a term which is suggestive of the classic argument of the relationship between art and commerce, the patronage of the artist by the economically well-endowed sponsor, and yet also indicative of a thoroughly modern sense of artistic enterprise, as rapidly developing technology opens up a variety of opportunities for fledgling film-makers and ambitious entrepreneurs. The term 'American independent cinema' is also suggestive of a romantic vision of filmic productivity, alluding to work that exists within a great narrative tradition, yet is presented within the context of a modern art form, and has been created autonomously, without the interference of other parties. The question here is whether such a form of cultural production is sustainable. As Bourdieu dryly notes,

> At a given level of autonomy, intellectuals are, other things being equal, proportionately more responsive to the seduction of the powers that be, the less well endowed they are with specific capital.[3]

This is to say that, when art meets, or conflicts, with economy, the artist is more willing to compromise their ideals when faced with the lure of financial reward, or the overarching economic power of the corporate giants. Recent commentators such as Caves have argued that it is possible for autonomy and economy to co-exist:

> The basic structural characteristics of creative industries – their technologies of production and consumption – fiercely resist governance by anything approaching a complete contrast. Yet they have evolved distinctive and serviceable contract forms that seem to differ from deal-making patterns prevalent in other sectors.[4]

Caves is referring to the romantic ideal of the artist and sponsor, whose relationship is both mutually exclusive and beneficial and this is the root of the paradox that lies at the heart of film-making, and 'independent cinema' in particular. The main benefit of the motion picture is its status as a cultural product of mass consumption, but such cultural products can only be regarded as 'artistic' or 'independent' works if their creators are to be allowed absolute autonomy. In order for all the opportunities, particularly those of an economic nature, to be realized, compromises with regard to the autonomy of the artist, or director, may have to be enforced and endured. It is this tension between the needs or the artist and the demands of the market, and its most prominent suppliers, which will form the crux of this study.

1.1 The Aims and Objectives of the Study

(1) To disprove the popular assumption amongst commercial journalists and consumers of popular culture, that cinematic works that have been declared as, or critically assigned the status of, 'independent', are autonomous of corporate sponsorship, or influence from other forms of popular media. This study will systematically outline the theory that American 'independent' cinema is dependent on corporate sponsorship in the form of the Hollywood studios and this theory will be supported by economic and intertextual evidence, provided by references to specific feature films and how they have conformed to the system of mass production, in terms of their conception, technical construction, marketing, and distribution. In addition, this study will seek to place American 'independent' cinema within a theoretic framework to show its relation to, and dependence on, the corporate giants, before questioning if the nature of this relationship is actually one of co-dependency.

(2) To redefine what can be meant by the term 'modern American independent cinema' in the new millennium, through a discussion of its moral economy, methods of production and distribution, and the qualities of the films themselves. While the status of many films as being 'independent' from an economic standpoint may be found to be impossible to substantiate due to their ties with the corporate giants, it will be of interest to attach such films to moments of popular feeling and periods of industrial change, thereby setting them apart from the more commercial

cinematic offerings that are popularly associated with the Hollywood production line. This will be an analysis of what has become known as the 'independent spirit', a description that has recently been applied to film-makers who are considered to be true to their own cinematic visions, whilst also seeking sponsorship from corporate organizations.

(3) To establish whether creative autonomy can actually exist within the system of mass production. This will entail an analysis of Hollywood's absorption of the 'independent' sector through reference to film-makers, the qualities of their work, the conditions under which it is created, and how it has been received by the audience.

1.2 The Social-Economic Background of the Study

Although the economics of feature film production and of mass entertainment in general, have previously been discussed in detail in an academic context, the industry sector that is American 'independent' cinema has been generally overlooked by scholars who have focussed on this particular form of modern media. If that has been discussed at all, as in Garnham and Wasko, it has been as an aside or a footnote to a bigger picture, its economic and social practices only coming in discussion when they are aligned with those of the corporate giants. Garnham acknowledges the existence of independent production, but divides it into two categories, one that ultimately becomes the product of the corporations in that it 'gets picked up by the major distributors after completion',[5] and another that is aimed at 'specialized markets',[6] examples of which he cites as being 'nature films' and 'soft porn'. Wasko only occasionally references independent film production, focussing largely on Hollywood and its dominance of the entertainment industry. In keeping with her key theme, she mentions independent cinema in industrial, but never cultural, context and does so as a means of emphasizing the economic power of the Hollywood studios. She states that;

> While the film industry accommodates independent production, the majors ultimately set the agenda and reap the bulk of the rewards. Through their control over film distribution, as well as by pursuing various strategies to reduce risk, and protect and promote their products, the Hollywood majors have maintained their dominance of the US film industry, as well as much of the world's film business.[7]

This means that this study will be delving into subject matter that is, at least academically, non-established. There are three possible reasons for this. Firstly, a rigid definition of American 'independent' cinema is hard to pinpoint. Secondly, the term has only gained cultural significance since the early 1990s, meaning that its place in the popular consciousness is still in a formative state. Thirdly, it is arguable that American 'independent' cinema is still not finite, existing somewhere between being a form of technical production, and the idealized conceptual model for any *auteur* wishing to use film as their form of popular expression.

Until the early 1990s, 'independent cinema' was simply a term used to define a production company that was not affiliated with a major studio, whereas now the term carries with it a cultural, as well as economic, significance. Therefore, the majority of references to 'American independent cinema' are found in modern works of journalism, many of which have simply used the term as a shorthand method of implying certain aspects of, or attributes to, a particular cinematic work, shorthand references that can be found in both commercial journalism and more supposedly thorough texts on the subject, some of which will be referenced and discussed in this thesis. This study will seek to 'rescue' the term from such lazily non-specific usage, and place it with a theoretic framework, treating American 'independent' cinema as a method of production and a form of cultural expression, worthy of analysis within a social-political context.

This study will take 1969 as its starting point, although feature films completed and distributed prior to that date will be referenced. The year 1969 was the year that independent cinema came into both cultural and economic prominence, with the release of two films from opposite sides of the Atlantic. In the United States, Dennis Hopper and Peter Fonda released their biker odyssey *Easy Rider*, a cinematic road trip about two hippies riding across the country with a stash of cocaine concealed in their tanks; while in the United Kingdom, Ken Loach made *Kes*, an adaptation of the Barry Hines novel, *A Kestrel for a Knave*, which concerned a schoolboy who is neglected by both his family unit and the educational system. With their confrontational subject matter and distinctive aesthetic sensibility, each film played a major role in ushering in a new wave of cinema, an 'independent' cinema that was as much a means of social-political thinking as it was an alternative form of escapist practice. Both films traded studio shooting and rigid scripting in favour of real locations, improvised dialogue, episodic narrative, and reflective codas that would encourage discussion amongst critics and audiences alike. As Balazs explains;

> The camera carries my eye into the picture itself. I look at things from within the space of the film. I am surrounded by the characters of the film and enmeshed in its actions which I witness from all sides...my gaze and with it my consciousness is identified with the characters of the film. I look at the world from their point of view and have none of my own. Nothing like this kind of identification has ever occurred in any other art.[8]

These were cinematic works that sought to reach new levels of social-realism by integrating production method with subject matter, resulting in the absorption of the audience in an acute filmic depiction of reality. As Benjamin notes,

> Thus, the filmic representation of reality is incomparably more significant for contemporary man...since it offers, precisely because of the radical permeation of reality with mechanical equipment, an aspect of reality which is free of equipment.[9]

Such methods created a new form of film production, one that would come to be termed 'independent' for both its unique aesthetic approach, and its social-political thinking. With the benefit of hindsight, it is possible to view *Easy Rider* as a 'hippie fantasy', a marketable version of a youth movement that had already imploded, and to regard *Kes* as simply the forerunner of what has become known as the 'kitchen-sink' school of British cinema, wallowing in the plight of the working class for the 'benefit' of a middle-class audience. However, it is doubtful that without their formal experimentation and social polemics, audiences today would have an 'independent cinema', regardless of whatever form, tangible or ideological, it can be seen to exist.

While Hopper and Loach were granted creative autonomy with regard to the genesis of their films, they did not self-finance them, and were reliant on a corporate sponsor with a commercial interest in the end result. For a film that dealt with a counterculture movement, *Easy Rider* offered the Hollywood studios a glimmer of hope at a time when their grip on the mass audience was slipping. This was a cinematic revolution that came from economic necessity. Hollywood's profits were not only down in the 1960s, the studios were actually running substantial losses, $35 million and $52 million in the cases of MGM and Warner Brothers respectively. When *Easy Rider* became not only a cultural phenomenon, but the fourth highest grossing motion picture of 1969, with domestic box office revenues of $19 million, the studios recognized not only a valuable new market, but also realized which resources it needed to utilize in order to successfully tap into it.

Easy Rider is the first example of how the unprecedented commercial success of one particular film brought about such rapid change in the industrial hierarchy of the Hollywood system, and in its production practices. It also encapsulated a movement of popular feeling, as an audience eagerly latched on to the presumed ideals of the piece, as if they had almost willed it into existence as a means of reflecting growing social-economic change in society. Later 'independent' pictures, such as Steven Soderbergh's *Sex, Lies, and Videotape* in 1989 and Quentin Tarantino's *Pulp Fiction* in 1994 have threatened to have a similar effect, but the system has learnt from its experiences and has been able to absorb the more socially and artistically radical implications of such films, whilst still maximizing their economic potential. Such absorption has been achieved through an economic dominance of the feature film production and distribution in the United States, a dominance which will be explained firstly through theoretic framework, and secondly by reference to specific business practises. The stranglehold which the Hollywood studios have over the film business has contributed to the 'commercialization' of American 'independent' cinema, the gradual erosion of its values, the restrain of its cultural impulse, and the labelling of a 'movement' that has become an invaluable aspect of Hollywood's industry of mass production.

1.3 The Methodology of the Study and its Structural Framework
As the subject matter that this study will be exploring has been largely untouched theoretically, the method of enquiry will use certain existing literature as a starting point, before engaging in an intuitive form of intellectual practise. The study will work from the exterior of this 'field of power' to the interior, in order to provide a theoretic framework, shedding light on the political economy of American independent cinema. Bourdieu establishes a theory of the cultural field, placing artists and their work within the social

conditions of their production, exhibition, and acceptance. However, it is his positioning of the field of cultural production within the field of power that is most applicable to this study. He examines the uneasy but necessary relationship between those who posses economic capital, and those who posses intellectual ability, assessing the competitive tension between both parties, and how their relationship within the field of power is, to an extent, one of co-dependency.

For Bourdieu, forces that are financial and artistic are contained within the field of power, although the field that he terms 'literary and artistic' is in a particularly dominated position, due to its lack of hard economic or political capital, although the field's possession of such symbolic capital as culture and education enables it to find a place within the field of power. Thus, intellectuals and artists are members of the dominant social class but, within that particular class structure, they find themselves dominated.

This lack of economic capital entails that Bourdieu's cultural field is split into two opposing sub-fields, the field of 'restricted' production and the field of 'large-scale' production. Bourdieu's field of 'restricted' production is what modern critics may class as 'high art', in that it represents the composition of culture for other producers, either for them to appreciate or derive further inspiration from. This is a world that uses its lack of income as an example of its moral economy. Therefore, success in this field is not measured in prestige and recognition from other producers, adding to the cultural credibility of the artist. By contrast, the field of 'large-scale' production is what could be classed as mass production, in that it is produced for the largest possible audience, where success is measured purely in financial profit and acknowledgment comes in the form of popular awareness of the eventual integration of the product in the public consciousness.

This economic aim means that the cultural production that is conducted within the field is commonly of less artistic value than that which is conducted within the field of 'restricted' production, but that is not a concern as profit is the only ultimate objective. Therefore, the field of 'large-scale' production is a purely capitalist enterprise, one that seeks economic dominance, but can only achieve its goal through the participation, however reluctant, of representatives of the field of 'restricted' production, who possess both the artistic ability and cultural credibility that the field of 'large-scale' production requires to attract the mass-audience. In terms of today's audience that credibility is best represented by 'independent' film-makers, who are seen to be working against the system, although some of the most celebrated are actually working within it.

The American independent film-makers of today have become the new millennium equivalent of the trail-blazing novelists of the beat generation – young, talented, opinionated, and supposedly defying the corporate values of the economic giants through the methodology and content of their work. However, their opposition to any 'system' is enough to make them a part of it, especially when they are using vertically integrated marketing practices (film festivals, print media and television coverage, distribution patterns) to bring them success. With young novelists not as in vogue as in previous decades, and the music industry stifling artists with heady commercial expectations and a need to reach the overstretched teen market, film directors have become folk heroes for a generation bereft of their own Jack Kerouac, Bob Dylan or Arthur Miller. Instead, they have such film-makers as Quentin Tarantino, Kevin Smith, Steven Soderbergh, David O'Russell, and Paul Thomas Anderson, film-makers who work with the resources of major corporations to bring their visions to fruition. While most of these directors maintain their status as 'independent film-makers', they are engaged in willing relationships with major corporations and court a wider audience for their work as a means of enhancing their standing within the industry. Their 'independent' status is, therefore, somewhat questionable. Bourdieu insists that

> The field of restricted production can only become a system objectively producing for producers by breaking with the public of non-producers, that is, with the non-intellectual fractions of the dominant class.[10]

The position of these 'independent' film-makers within the field of power means that the term 'independent' is a misleading one. No film-maker or producer is truly 'independent', in that they cannot exist separately from the field of economic power, in this case represented by studios, distributors, exhibitors, and promotional media. While a creative autonomy may be achieved through self-financing, the need for art to connect to an audience entails that the film-maker is always in a compromised position. Even if an individual is able to raise the funds to shoot, edit, and prepare a final print of their film, there would be little chance that they would be able to afford to distribute and advertise their work. In the unlikely event of a grass-roots release, the work would be stranded in that the majority of cinemas in the United States are part of chains that programme their outlets nationally rather than individually, with even most art house cinemas being part of smaller chains or reliant on corporate sponsorship. This means that the autonomously created and distributed work would be overshadowed by other films that would reap the benefits of the positive relationship that art, or kitsch, can enjoy with economy when properly aligned within the field of power.

Cinema that is autonomous of the field of economic power is what Bourdieu would refer to as 'the field of cultural production, where the only audience aimed at is other producers', or 'art for art's sake', meaning that the economic failure of a work is a sign of its success. The lack of economic capital in specific areas, most notably those of marketing and distribution is symbolic of the independence of the work and a guarantee of its autonomy and, therefore, its integrity. As truly autonomous as these 'failures' may be, the works of modern cinema that are celebrated, as being 'independent' are works that have followed the same system of production as that of any Hollywood feature film product. That system is as follows:

(1) A writer/potential director attaches a narrative idea to a movement of popular feeling. This idea takes the form of a screenplay, and the originator of the piece contacts a producer who can bring their work to the screen.

(2) The producer then approaches various sources of funding to raise the money necessary to make the feature film.

(3) Filming commences, and proceeds in accordance with a schedule agreed by all parties engaged in the project in both a creative and financial capacity.

(4) Once filming is completed, the film enters into the post-production process with the raw footage being edited into a commercially viable form that audiences will accept primarily as a professionally produced piece of escapist entertainment, and possibly also as something with a higher social value.

(5) Marketing strategy is then applied through related mediums (e.g. – cinema trailers, television spots, print advertising, and celebrity endorsement) in order to heighten audience awareness of the now finished, and soon to be released, feature film.

(6) Distribution of the film to cinema chain and/or art house outlets for public consumption, based upon distribution arrangements made by the producer and financiers at various stages in the production process

This study will ally itself with the sequence of production, so that the study works from an exterior conception of the industry and of independent feature films to an analysis of the making and marketing of such feature films, to a discussion of their appeal to cinema-going audiences and status as examples of 'independent' cinema.

1.4 American Independent Cinema – Popular Perceptions and Industrial Realities

The image often associated with independent cinema is that of driven, resourceful, mostly young film-makers with stories to tell and axes to grind, working against the grain of corporate-sponsored cinema to bring their visions to fruition. It is an image that does not feature any major Hollywood stars, or soundstage shooting, or expensive special effects, or vertically integrated product promotions. It is instead an image which features gritty location shooting with an avant-garde approach, and little-known actors. Upon completion, the results of the labours of love of such cinematic crusaders are screened in decaying art house cinemas to an audience comprised of hip urban dwellers, whose interest in low-budget feature films effectively finances an underground 'movement', enabling independent film-makers to make more features in similarly economically stringent, but creatively autonomous, circumstances.

This is a romantic notion, the idea that independent cinema is a cinema made by individuals, as opposed to committees; a cinema that is made for an audience that appreciates and absorbs, rather than one that simply consumes and forgets. It is also a notion that many 'independent' film-makers and even some financiers wholeheartedly subscribe to. From an economic standpoint, the term 'American independent cinema' can be used to represent everything from horror pictures such as *Last House on the Left* and *The Blair Witch Project*, to socially conscious dramas like *Traffic* and *Dead Man Walking*, and avant-garde exercises in formal experimentation along the lines of *The*

Living End and *Gummo*. Economically, it is a term that is all-encompassing, encapsulating a variety of films, directors, themes, and genres. Culturally, the term is vague, as the independent sector has produced titles like *The Usual Suspects, My Big Fat Greek Wedding*, and *In the Bedroom*, films that fit into the Hollywood production mould, in that they conform to classic narrative structure and enjoy the attributes of 'star' casting and production value. The Hollywood system is undoubtedly more accommodating of a film like *My Big Fat Greek Wedding*, which offers escapist pleasures and exhibits the aesthetic sensibility of a television sit-com, than it is of *Gummo*, which does not belong in any particular genre and was made with a cast of non-professional actors, but all 'independent' cinema is at least recognized by the major studios. As Wasko and Garnham have already observed, this accommodation and recognition is a means of economic dominance. Wasko notes that 'The studios cooperate to determine industry polices and to protect and promote the industry.'[11]

The immediate implication of the term 'independent cinema' is that it is subordinate to the giants of the industry, which in the case of feature film production, are represented by the Hollywood studios, corporation such as Time Warner, Paramount, 20th Century- Fox, and Sony. All of these 'giants' invest in cinematic product as part of their grand scheme to maximize profit from a number of vertically related markets in which they are economically engaged as part of a cycle of mass production. Their investment is supported by additional expenditure with regard to advertising, which enhances the public profile of their products in short spaces of time. As Garnham observes,

> Advertising expenditure has always played an important role in the oligopolistic control of markets. It stimulates demand and maintains market shares...it further serves to defend the market against new entrants by raising the price of entry.[12]

This is to say that it is actually the spending power of the majors in a promotional capacity that ensures their dominance, as it shuts out independents by raising the cost of advertising to a level that smaller companies cannot compete at. With their ownership of additional media outlets, studios maximize all marketing potential. If the intertwined strategies of publicity and distribution fall into place, their movies make money at the box office, whilst product spin-offs add to the long-term profit.

Garnham notes that, to observe the political economy of communication, one must analyse the modes of cultural production and consumption that have been developed within capitalist society at large. Films exist as commodities that have been produced, distributed, and exhibited within the perimeters of an overarching industrial structure. By studying feature film production in this manner, Garnham effectively eliminates the notion of independent production as the film industry becomes a key part of the overall culture of mass media and, therefore, society as a whole. Mattelart follows a similar line of thinking when he observes that

The apparatus of cultural production of the North American Empire has suffered profound mutations. No sector, be it press, radio, television, cinema or advertising, has escaped. In the course of the process of industrial concentration, the owners of high technology have increasingly become the ones who determine not only the manufacture of hardware and the installation of systems, but also the development of programmes.[13]

Time Inc. and Warner Communications merged in January 1990, and then merged with American Online (AOL). AOL – Time Warner is the largest entertainment conglomerate, although most media communications companies conform to this model, establishing divergent divisions which can produce a range of related products across a variety of markets.

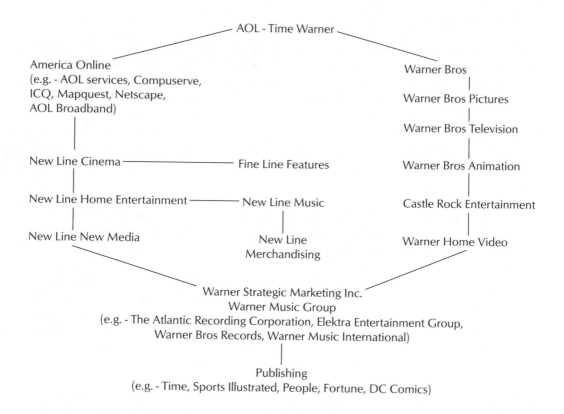

Operating in alignment with the cycle of production are the correlated cycles of publicity and distribution. If these intertwined strategies fall into place, the core product will make money at the box office and, whilst doing so, the stars of the movie appear on the covers of magazines and make appearances on television shows, boosting news-stand sales and television ratings, in turn generating healthy advertising revues. In addition, ancillary markets will flourish due to product spin-offs like soundtracks, posters, 'happy' meals, comic books and novelizations. There are also the seemingly non-related markets that are promoted via subtle, and sometimes not so subtle, product placements. This means that advertising is used to power the success of films, while films can then be used to further the success of other products. Film-related tie-ins with these other products can then be used to re-promote the feature film, creating a perfect circle of advertising activity. The 2002 film *Spiderman* featured a number of blatant product placements, most notably Rebok trainers, Carlsberg Lager and the singer Macy Gray. The third is particularly notable as she is signed to Sony Music, the audio division of the company which financed and distributed *Spiderman*. The film is used to promote a product which the corporation has a direct interest in, while the music artist can promote the film through her related pop video.

It would appear impossible for independent feature films to breakthrough and achieve sustained levels of success. However, while this study will show the economic limits that most independent film-makers and distributors have to accept, it will also discuss films that have managed to subvert the rules of the 'field of power' and the laws of the market, by achieving critical and commercial success in the face of Hollywood's monolithic corporate enterprises. In addition, it will show why this state of affairs has enhanced the critical appreciation of 'independent' cinema. As Mattelart states,

> 'Low profile' strategies, more subtle as forms of intervention against popular initiatives, have given the ideological level an importance of the first order within the international class struggle.[14]

This is to say that independent films represent a cinema of ideas and beliefs, both in terms of their individual context and the personal natures of their directors. Such films exist under the popular radar, publicly overshadowed by heavily promoted studio product, but are less concerned with commercial success and thereby open to formal experimentation and more capable of social-political critique. As Bourdieu claims,

> Freed from the censorship and auto-censorship consequent on direct confrontation with a public foreign to the profession, and encountering within the corps of producers itself a public at once of critics and accomplices, it tends to obey its own logic, that of the continual outbidding inherent to the dialect of cultural distinction.[15]

While independent films rarely threaten the economic prominence of their studio counterparts, they are more valued by the critical establishment as they address serious themes and issues, making them more intellectually prominent examples of America's cinematic output. It is now necessary to look at the technological changes, and market needs that have made some form of 'independent' production possible today, and enhanced Hollywood's interest in, and accommodation of, that cinema, while also observing how the strategies of the corporate giants make it possible for such 'subtle forms of intervention' to creep into the culture of mass consumption.

1.5 Supply and Demand – Why American Independent Cinema is Possible

For a period in the mid-1980s, the home entertainment boom was beneficial to the independent sector; providing film-makers with financing and distribution as projects were bankrolled as a means of supplying the market with fresh product. The year 1987 marked a precedent in that it was the first year that the amount of video cassettes rented in North America (1,040,000) eclipsed the amount of cinema tickets that were sold (1,030,000). The home video market and cable television created a need for product of a certain quality, so independent companies such as New Line, Island-Alive, Cannon, New World, Orion, and Vestron funded projects in the $3 million to $5 million range, while a studio production at the time would cost between $15 million and $50 million. With a number of independent features performing well at the box office, and winning enviable critical kudos, the studios realized that such films were courting a previously loyal audience that they had perhaps forgotten about. As Mattelart notes,

> The producers of so-called mass-culture are bringing their mode of operation up to date... this is a culture which is beginning to take into account the specific needs and interests of each age group, each social category.[16]

As a form of cinematic production, independent cinema shares similarities with its corporate counterpart, although there are distinct differences. As independent film-makers are largely working from self-originated material, their screenplays usually come first, while the concept-driven studio film-makers are likely to start with an idea for a project which, if the pitch proves to be successful, is developed into a screenplay. The casting process is occurs earlier in the studio system, with producers feeling the need for the commercially bankable assents of a name actor or/and actress and a director who has already enjoyed some success. With such a marketable commodity in place early in the process, it is also possible for the marketing team to develop a strategy without a finished feature, as much of the marketing will revolve around the image of the leading actor with his or her screen persona and public image dictating the audience that the film is aimed at, and how that audience is going to be reached.

However, the crucial difference between the two is that the development of independent features has a tendency to be much swifter than that of studio product. This is partly due to the lesser need for independent producers to fine-tune the commercially identifiable attributes of their product, in particular the attribute of star casting. The casting of actors in independent features can obviously be a factor in their success, but it is not the factor that the producer will be solely relying on. In an age when major stars such as Tom Cruise, Russell Crowe, Leonardo DiCaprio, and Jim Carey come with salaries of $20 million per picture, and sometimes a profit-participation stake in the box office gross, it is not possible for independent producers to attract such high-maintenance talent.

There are occasions when stars are willing to reduce their fees to work on independent projects that are of interest to them, but this is the exception rather than the rule. When independent features can cost as little as $750,000 and rarely cross the $10 million mark in terms of overall cost, it is not possible for producers to accommodate star names in their package when salaries are at their present premium. This, however, can speed up the process of independent film production, because producers can simply hire the most suitable actor available, without playing the bidding game, or waiting for a star to find a window in his or her schedule, or making adjustments to the screenplay which have been dictated by a star conscious of his or her screen persona and the alienation of their core audience. This is not to say that independent feature films are developed entirely outside of the creative culture of the studio system. Some are actually 'failed' studio projects, in that writers and directors have already 'shopped' the project around the majors, only to be turned down for finance for a variety of reasons, such as the lack of commercial viability of their project, the inability to attract a suitable star, or some similarity to another picture in development.

Comparatively low budgets also force film-makers to think on their feet, making them work intuitively, rather than theoretically. Shooting schedules are shorter, with location shooting often being utilized as sets and sound stages are rarely within budget, and last-minute changes are common. Reliance on film festivals, most notably the Sundance, for exposure means that production and post-production schedules are often arranged around festival submission dates, making the sequence of events that begins with the completion of a screenplay and ends with the completion of a feature film more compressed in the independent world than it is in its studio counterpart. Financing opportunities for independent features are presently at an all-time high, but directors and producers must rely on gut instinct and small windows of opportunity to take advantage of them, rather than submitting their projects for the comparatively long-winded process of studio development.

Ironically, many of these opportunities for American independent production come from foreign investors, such as the French-based companies Europa Corp and Lumiere, or the Japanese electronics giant JVC. While American independent films may generate much press attention in the United States through exposure at festivals, it is in Europe where they are most well received by the paying public. Tarantino's *Reservoir Dogs* struggled to gross $3 million during its domestic release, but was a massive success in Europe where some cinemas played the film for over one year, attracting a fervent cult audience. Some European producers have been swift to capitalize on this demand for American independent features in the overseas market, and have succeeded in putting together respectable budgets in the $3 million to $6 million range by pre-selling their films to European distributors. Film-makers who have not benefited from such funding have resorted to more desperate measures, such as financing their films from their credit cards and even mortgaging their houses, measures that distinguish 'independent production' (working with financial backing that has not come from corporate sponsorship) from 'guerrilla film-making' (doing it yourself, with no protection plan should your 'investment' run into trouble).

Independent production can be split into three tiers, each of which can be seen to represent an important step on the industry ladder for a director or a producer as, while they may remain categorically within the independent sector, they are gravitating towards the corporate majors and a potential crossover into the studio system. The three tiers are as follows:

(1) Independently financed feature film production with no prior arrangement for distribution upon completion.
(2) Independently financed feature film production with a distribution deal with an independent distributor.
(3) Independently financed feature film production with a distribution deal with a Hollywood studio or mini-major.

Although the content of independent cinema is often resistant of the direction of cultural consumption, it is in the interest of the Hollywood majors to allow, and even encourage, a cinematic movement that goes against the corporate grain. With their low production budgets and comparatively inexpensive marketing costs, independent films have always been a useful means of discovering the shifts in popular sentiment that will shape the next direction, or at least the next trend, in modern film. They have also been a way to discover young talent, mainly behind the camera, as the fast-moving world of independent film is more likely to take a chance on a young writer-director with 'vision', whereas a studio would usually prefer a director with a 'track record', a criteria which would exclude most film-makers under the age of thirty.

This is not to say that independent film is exclusively a game for the young. Robert Altman, Abel Ferrara, John Sayles, Alan Rudolph, Jim Jarmusch, and Jon Jost are still regularly working in the independent arena, but the perception of such 'older' independent directors is that their time has passed in terms of being in touch with popular culture. Young directors, meaning those in their twenties and thirties, working in the independent field are perceived to be more aligned with their generational sensibilities, and as the core cinema-going demographic in the United States is people in their late teens to mid-twenties, this makes them a potentially valuable tool for reaching a wide audience, if only in the short term.

When Miramax chairman Harvey Weinstein found out that Tri-Star, a division of Sony, had put production of Quentin Tarantino's *Pulp Fiction* on hold indefinitely due to fear of the explicit violence within the screenplay, he brought the project to Miramax. Weinstein has been remarkably prescient in targeting the twenty-something demographic, recognizing and supplying its need for generational heroes and satisfying its appetite for visual, as opposed to print, media. Speaking in 1992, when independent film was gaining popular momentum but yet to secure financial validity and longevity, he speculated that 'American independents may be more appealing to a generation that listens to the radio and watches TV, where reading may be eighth on the list.'[17]

If Quentin Tarantino became the 'face' of independent cinema in the 1990s, *Pulp Fiction* was the cultural behemoth that enabled him to do so. While he garnered critical kudos for his debut feature, *Reservoir Dogs*, it was *Pulp Fiction* that truly established him as not only a major film-maker, but a force of popular culture. While critics have claimed that *Pulp Fiction* was the film that put American independent cinema into the mainstream, it could also be argued that *Pulp Fiction* was the film that found the mainstream acknowledging the commercial possibilities of alternative film-making and adopting the sector for its own economic needs. While *Pulp Fiction* is very much a 'Quentin Tarantino film', it is also a film that was possible because of the $8 million budget provided by Miramax through the Walt Disney Corporation. It benefited greatly from the contributions of its 'star' cast, with Hollywood names such as John Travolta, Bruce Willis, Uma Thurman, Samuel L. Jackson, Harvey Keitel, and Christopher Walken adding glamour to Tarantino's criminal universe. With a worldwide box office gross of over $200 million, *Pulp Fiction* created the 'independent blockbuster', seemingly a contradiction in terms, but now a cultural and economic possibility providing that the 'vision' of the film-maker, the economic needs of the studio, and the demands of the audience are in aligned with one another.

Although the major studios dabbled in independent fare in the early-1970s by financing a number of low-budget, personal pictures in the wake of the success of *Easy Rider*, and again in the mid-1980s, picking up such pictures as *A Room with a View* and *The Kiss of the Spider Woman* for distribution, it was not until the mid-1990s that they started to invest in 'independent' production and created speciality divisions to develop, produce, and distribute the types of films that would previously have been made without corporate sponsorship. Universal Pictures partnered with Polygram to establish the now-defunct Gramercy Pictures, as well as buying the already-established October Films, while Paramount Pictures set up Paramount Pictures Classics and Twentieth Century Fox ventured forward with Fox Searchlight.

The most notable development, however, was the Walt Disney Corporation's acquisition of Miramax Films. Reports of the Miramax acquisition claim that Disney paid anything from $60 million, to $80 million to effectively buy their way into the 'independent' arena. Already a successful company, and arguably the leader of the pack in the independent field in terms of the commercial and critical success of its product, Miramax found itself operating as a 'mini-major', struggling balance the cultural credibility that it gradually cultivated, with the hard bottom-line economic principles of the Disney corporation. Biskind has documented this saga at length, but his text is the antithesis of this study is that he adopts an 'insider' perspective, rather than working from an analytical framework. On a superficial level, he offers some salacious stories and juicy gossip, but its author is too enamoured with his celebrity 'players', most notably Miramax Films president Harvey Weinstein, directors Quentin Tarantino and Steven Soderbergh, and Sundance figurehead Robert Redord, to step outside the cycle of production and offer a definition of 'American independent cinema', or any indication of its social and political significance, although Biskind is keen to note the economic rewards that have been enjoyed by some of its contributors.

Ultimately, Biskind succumbs to the temptations of the Hollywood narrative, portraying Weinstein as a charismatic, self-contradictory 'anti-hero', alternatively celebrating and burying the independent film movement with a combination of altruistic intent and hard-nosed business sense, attracting, exploiting, and spurning a number of talented contributors, whilst seeking to position himself as both a patron of the arts and an old-fashioned Hollywood mogul. Drawing crude comparisons to the events of *The Godfather* and other gangster pictures, Biskind claims that

> If Hollywood is like the mafia, indies are like the Russian mob. In both cases, the bad guys will cap the good guys, but in Hollywood they will do it with a certain degree of finesse – they send a basket of fruit over for your wife and kids for good measure. In the studio world, you're imprisoned in a gilded cage. In the indie world, you're in the hole, which is darker, dirtier and a lot smaller.[18]

Closer in intention to this study in that it approaches American 'independent' cinema as an aspect of the film industry rather than as a form of thinking, Levy seeks to emphasize the commercial, as well as the artistic, value of low-budget features, but crucially differs in its conception of the independent sector. Levy's views American 'independent' cinema as revolving around a loosely linked collection of individuals with the common goal of making films outside the 'system'. The needs addressed within his text are those of the film-makers, as opposed to the escapist appetites of their audience, or the economic prosperity of their patrons. He not only places their production methods outside those of the Hollywood system, but also asserts that these film-makers are also socially, politically, and, therefore, culturally removed from the machinery of the major studios, making them entirely autonomous of corporate influence or sponsorship. Levy suggests that there are actually two film industries operating in the United States – Hollywood and the independents. He maintains that both have their own organizational structure and means and methods of capturing an audience. According to Levy, independent cinema is, '...supported by an institutional network that runs parallel to, rather than against, the Hollywood industry.'[19]

By making such a distinction between Hollywood and the independent sector, Levy also suggests that there are two separate audiences, one that is attracted to studio productions, and one that prefers independent features. An assertion of this study will be that the independent sector is more integrated into the overall scheme of Hollywood's dominance. Therefore, Levy's two audiences are, in fact, one in the same, with the industry appealing not to different escapist facets of one carefully cultivated audience that can be broadly divided into a number of demographic groups.

If the involvement of studio money in production has made it less clear which films are independent and which films are not, a viewing of recent American independent features only adds to the confusion. When trying to define 'American independent cinema' based upon the culture of the films themselves, it is perhaps easier to state what modern American independent cinema is not – by no means is this radical, avant-garde cinema, made by cultural outsiders. It is not overtly politicized, aside from when such subject matter appears to be in vogue, and is often so polite in its social critique that it flirts with the anonymity of being 'middlebrow'. This is certainly indicative of the current audience that is being courted by modern American independent cinema through films such as *In the Bedroom*, *Chocolate*, *The Spitfire Grill*, *The Deep End*, *My Big Fat Greek Wedding*, and *The Virgin Suicides*. There is certainly conservatism at work, one that strives for the novelty value that will distinguish an independent film from a studio film, but at the same time does not wish to alienate or offend any potential ticket-buying demographic.

The past decade has found America's independent cinema assuming the place of foreign films in the theatrical marketplace. In the 1960s, distributors found that they could market foreign films to the American public through the novelty of the sexual content on display. More risqué than the American movies of the period, foreign films such as *Belle De Jour* and *La Dolce Vita* were able to play successfully in the United States after being promoted for their comparatively kinky content, and after being dubbed into English to appease an audience reluctant to succumb to reading subtitles as a means of following the on-screen action. With the American audience reluctant to read subtitles and infuriated with distracting dubbing, foreign cinema has struggled to maintain 'niche' status in the United States, only achieving a 2 per cent market share for much of the 1990s, and the industry's main interest in foreign films has been to use them as re-make fodder for more slick studio product.

In this sense, modern American 'independent' cinema, or at least the cultural conception of it, has taken up the mantle of being the 'cinema of discussion' from foreign cinema, and the films of Quentin Tarantino, Paul Thomas Anderson, and Steven Soderbergh have acquired the audience that four decades ago would have flocked to see the new offering from Truffaut or Fellini. It is the almost obsessive interest of this audience in the innovative films from the independent sector which makes them perhaps the most vital part of the cinema-going audience in that their cinematic preferences have ensured that there is a built-in audience for the offbeat cinema that is often more artistically influential in the long term than it is commercially successful in the short term.

It is, however, debatable as to how culturally 'independent' this cinema is from the Hollywood mainstream, and how 'alternative' the audience is. The reason for this debate has much to do with the superficial 'slickness' of the films that are coming from the 'independent' sector, especially when they are contrasted with the films of the 1970s. It is almost as if some of the concerns that distributors have about importing foreign films into North America, such as the variable production values, comparably lengthy running times, and meandering plot lines, seem to have been inherited by independent community. The promotional material for the 'no-budget' success stories

El Mariachi and *Pi* hyped the fact that these films had been made for the cinematic equivalent of pocket change, a marketing hook that could also have been a disguised warning to audiences to state that these films were rough and ready.

To see where modern American 'independent' cinema fits in to the grand scheme of popular culture, it is necessary to explore how it appears to exist between two tent poles of studio product. It is increasingly obvious that Hollywood is operating at two extremes of the cinematic spectrum in terms of its annual product. Firstly, there is the 'popcorn picture', usually expensive genre films featuring stars and marketed and released in such a manner that the target fan base is captured within the first three days of release. It says as much about Hollywood's shameless recycling of its more successful properties as it does about the escapist needs of the mass audience that many of these popcorn pictures are follow-ups to earlier popcorn pictures, or blatant re-makes, or thinly disguised re-workings of older examples of their genre.

The summer season of 2003 offered no less than ten sequels within a three-month period, with titles to cover every broad genre base from action-adventure (*Bad Boys 2*, *Terminator 3*), to horror (*Freddy Vs. Jason*, *Jeepers Creepers 2*), and comedy (*Legally Blonde 2*, *Charlie's Angels: Full Throttle*). Add to this already deeply derivative mix a questionable re-make of a much-loved classic (*The Italian Job*), two comic book adaptations (*League Of Extraordinary Gentlemen*, *The Hulk*) and a third comic book adaptation that was also a sequel (*X2: X-Men United*) and you have a slate of films which have as much intellectual substance as a bucket of popcorn has nutritional value.

Secondly, the studios of Hollywood offer the 'prestige picture', a form of cinematic entertainment that shares many of the attributes as the 'popcorn picture' in that it showcases big stars, expensive production values, and a large amount of hype, but at least appears to be a more noble filmic venture in terms of subject matter. Prestige pictures also rely on existing source material, but the basic ingredient for the average prestige picture is of a higher level of perceived quality. Instead of pillaging such examples of popular culture as comic books, television series, and old movies, the prestige picture usually finds its source in 'quality' literature, often with a historical slant. *A Beautiful Mind*, *The Hours*, and *Master And Commander – The Far Side Of The World* are relatively recent 'prestige pictures' which have neglected the superficial kinetic excitement of studio summer fare in favour of a comparatively reserved approach suited to a more adult audience, and yet these films have mostly found their roots in the previously existing source material of true stories and literary works, material which has been made palatable to a wide audience by the presence of major star names and the packaging of the material into classic Hollywood structure.

With such repetition, modern Hollywood has become the cinema of the 'routine'. The pattern goes from the low-profile releases of January to Easter when the 'popcorn pictures' start to come out, to June, July, and August when the studio's most expensive investments engage in a clash of the Titans at the global box office, and into the winter when more serious fare is released. Such a rigid schedule has forced the independent sector to mirror the corporate giants, if only to ensure being able to reach a novelty-seeking audience at the right time of year. February finds media attention firmly fixed on the Sundance Film Festival, as the major studios do not usually release their biggest films at this time of year, allowing the independent sector several weeks of high-profile coverage. Independent films are released throughout the year, but are mirroring Hollywood's release strategy, coming out in the summer to provide a more subtle cinematic distraction for those audiences not enamoured with the blockbusters, and towards the end of the year, in order to attract attention from industry and critics awards groups, thereby generating prestige and free publicity.

It is perhaps the 'independent' films that are released towards the end of the year that have come to define the sector's cultural position. Located somewhere between the 'popcorn picture' and the 'prestige picture', the modern American independent film has found its market niche as a middlebrow entertainment, thankfully devoid of the bombast of the 'popcorn picture', and not as self-consciously 'important' as the 'prestige picture'. These films tell the stories that Hollywood is not interested in telling, but do so with such commercially identifiable attributes as name actors and classy production values. Often offering the subtle qualities of good literary fiction without actually being adapted from a novel, although literary transfers are quite common, this product is reasonably intelligent, with recognizable, if not necessarily bankable, stars and a level of production value that is comparable to mid-range studio product. Sponsoring independent cinema through distribution eliminates an element of risk for all parties. The original producers have a guarantee of distribution, the studio gets to see a finished product before making a final decision, and the adult audience is treated to a film that has production value and the presence of recognizable stars, but also some novelty value and the cachet of being 'independent'. These films often take on the genres that have proven popular within the studio system, such as police procedurals, horror stories, and romances, but thanks to the independent 'spirit' of their writers and directors, they have a more personal perspective, investing as much screen time in the exploration of character and environment as they do in knee-jerk plot development and visceral action.

Notes

1. *Collins new English Dictionary*, p. 381, Glasgow, Harper Collins, 1997.
2. *Collins new English Dictionary*, p. 130, 1997.
3. Bourdieu, P, *The Field of Cultural Production*, p. 43, Cambridge, Polity, 1993.
4. Caves, R, 'Contracts Between Art and Commerce', *Journals of Economic Perspectives*, 17:1 (2003), p. 73
5. Garnham, N, *Capitalism and Communication – Global Culture and the Economics of Information*, p. 182, London, Sage, 1990.
6. Garnham, p. 182, 1990.
7. Wasko, J, *How Hollywood Works*, 1st edn, p. 223, London, Sage, 2003.
8. Belazs, B, *Spirit of Film Volume II*, p. 56, 1931.

9. Benjamin, W, *Illuminations*, 1st edn, p234, New York, Schocken, 1969.
10. Bourdieu, p. 39, 1993.
11. Wasko, p. 223, 2003.
12. Garnham, N, *Capitalism and Communication – Global Culture and the Economics of Information*, 1st edn, p. 201, London, Sage 1990.
13. Mattelart, A, *Multinational Corporations and the Control of Culture*, 1st edn, p2, New Jersey, Harvester Press, 1979.
14. Mattelart, p. 3, 1979.
15. Bourdieu, p. 115, 1993.
16. Mattelart, p. 3, 1979
17. Weinstein, H, quoted in *The New York Times*, 13/12/1992.
18. Biskind, P, *Down and Dirty Pictures – Miramax, Sundance & the Rise of Independent Film* p1, London, Bloomsbury, 2004.
19. Levy, E, *Cinema of Outsiders* – The Rise of American Independent Film, 1st edn, New York, New York University Press p. 53, 1999.

2

ANCESTRY OF INDEPENDENCE: *EASY RIDER* AND THE DECLARATION OF A NEW AMERICAN CINEMA

The cultural and commercial trajectories of most films are intertwined, in a manner that is both predictable and necessary. For a motion picture to prove financially successful, it should, through a variety of means of cultural inception, generate sufficient and immediate public interest that it attracts the paying audience. Yet it does not linger too long in the public consciousness, thereby opening the market for a steady flow of product from the competing, yet collectively supportive, producers of mass entertainment that are the major Hollywood studios. This process is the standard pattern for the majority of films, whether they be studio or independent productions, and it is now a pattern that is repeated through the ancillary markets of DVD, television, and movies-on-demand, where additional viewing materials and the convenience of home consumption makes the same product appealing to the same audience in a different environment, that is before another batch of recent theatrical favourites, or box office failures, require re-promotion. The majority of films enjoy a certain 'shelf life', generally conforming to industrial expectations when released for public consumption, rarely giving Hollywood reason to question its system of mass production, or its perceptions and assumptions regarding its consumer base.

There are, of course, the enduring crowd-pleasers that the Hollywood mainstream terms classics, in that they are films that find favour with audiences of different generations whether they are screened in the theatrical or home environment. Often technically innovative, rarely intellectually challenging or socially relevant, such films achieve the label of 'classics' due to their broad entertainment value, with the industrial seal of approval that is the Academy Awards forever fixing these entertainments as the standard that film-makers should aspire to reach, should they wish their work to meet the highest level of approval. In industrial terms, the success of these 'classics' and 'crowd-pleasers' re-affirms Hollywood's status as America's dream factory, the premier producer of populist entertainment that finds validation through the economic rewards bestowed on its studios by the public and their consumption of the product.

Every year, the studio system produces a number of failures, films that receive scathing critical notices and perform below commercial expectations. However, with Hollywood working on an economic principal that can be crudely characterized as a 'law of averages', meaning that one success recoups the losses of several failures, the industry is regularly able to reassure itself that it is quite right to adhere to its formula for cultural production and rely on commercially identifiable attributes like genre, stars, special effects, and spectacle.

Despite Hollywood's grip on the viewing sensibilities of the mass audience, and fiscal supremacy over film-makers with social-economic leanings of an 'independent' nature, there are rare occasions when unprecedented and unpredicted success can bring about a 'changing of the guard', seemingly revolutionizing the system of cultural production and bringing about a new 'era' of commercial film-making. Such 'watersheds' occur infrequently, and are based primarily on financial return, although economic achievement is a by-product of subtle yet significant cultural shifts, reflected in the repositioning of industrial practices and hierarchical change. Recent examples are Steven Soderbergh's *Sex, Lies, and Videotape* and Quentin Tarantino's *Pulp Fiction*, but this chapter will deal with Dennis Hopper's seminal 1969 'biker movie' *Easy Rider*, the first popularly celebrated 'independent film', and the film that is widely, if not correctly, credited with ushering in a more experimental form of American film-making. This was also a film that, albeit temporarily, affected the industrial structure and creative process of the 'dream factory' itself, prompting a brief move towards producing films that were reflective of society's often grim realities as opposed to projecting its overly simplified fantasies. Peter Guber, now a senior Hollywood executive, but then at the lower level of the corporate ladder, recalls how his career prospects brightened following the success of Hopper's film:

> Everything seemed different after *Easy Rider*. The executives were anxious, frightened because they didn't have the answers any longer. You couldn't imitate or mimic quite as easily, churn them out like eggs from a chicken. Every day there was a new person being fired...Because of my youth and inexperience, people asked, 'Well what do you think?'[1]

Although *Easy Rider* often serves as a cultural reference point for those looking to document the newfound freedom and experimental 'investments' that Guber and his contemporaries sought to endorse and exploit for their own industrial standing, this chapter will also examine other films and film-makers that brought about cultural change within the industry. As Bourdieu contends, artists have constantly struggled to free themselves from the requirements of their sponsors, a process that runs parallel to the development of the audience and the range of social positions that the audience encompasses. However, as the audience grows and diversifies, so do the sponsors, who are happy to recognize *any* social group or social-political leaning should it prove financially lucrative. Therefore, opportunities arise for artists to express themselves, providing they can do so within certain boundaries. Bourdieu claims that

> The autonomization of intellectual and artistic production is thus correlative with the constitution of a socially distinguishable category of professional artists or intellectuals who are less inclined to recognise rules other than the specifically intellectual or artistic traditions handed down by their predecessors, which serve as a point of departure or rupture. They are also increasingly in a position to liberate their products from all external constraints.[2]

Cinema, when it is produced with such autonomy, finds directors, writers, producers, and actors working intuitively, exploring the popular consciousness to communicate their own ideas to a mass audience. Hoberman asserts that

> One definition of a movie would be an idea successfully transformed into an industrially produced collective experience. Each movie is the result of a particular process by which an individual fantasy has been realized, first as a scenario and then again as a motion picture. This enterprise is further modified in the social world by the impersonal forces of money, marketing, and bureaucratic inertia – along with less rational factors of corporate power struggles, personal rivalries, aesthetic arguments, political disputes, and on-set love affairs.[3]

By chronicling the production of *Easy Rider*, this chapter will explore how such an idea comes to fruition, and how that idea is communicated to a mass audience as it becomes a part of the social world. American independent cinema was not brought into existence by *Easy Rider*, but it was brought to public prominence and gained economic significance within a system that did not then understand how to parlay this one successful experiment into the niche industry that has evolved today. As such, the film will be analysed as an industrial and cultural product, with respect to its formation and consumption, both of which reveal much about the cultural and industrial politics of the period in which it was made. As Jameson observes,

> There is of course no reason why specialized and elite phenomena, cannot reveal historical trends and tendencies as vividly as 'real life' – or perhaps even more visibly, in their isolation and semi- autonomy which approximates a laboratory situation.[4]

Through an account of the conception, production, marketing, and distribution of *Easy Rider*, this chapter will document such a 'laboratory situation', a rare instance when the needs of an industry and the ambitions of two film-makers were so precisely aligned that the end result effectively ushered in a change in the cultural landscape and a new mode of film-making practice.

2.1 Suspended Animation – Hollywood Culture in the 1960s

If the 1950s was the age of post-war adult conservatism, then the 1960s was the age of youthful rebellion, a decade in which the fabric of American life was so irreversibly ruptured, that the aftershock is still being felt in the popular culture of today. It was the first decade in which the youth of the country, as opposed to its elder statesman, dictated the direction that society was heading in, as young people all over America began to evolve towards a future ideal of rather than the established future represented by their elders. While the 1960s found cinema's cultural cousins, music and literature, changing radically to accommodate the scope of their contributors and the open-mindedness of their audiences, the decade found Hollywood to be largely frozen in a time capsule, offering 'safe' entertainments for a mass audience that was gradually slipping away. The top five grossing films of 1968 were:

(1) Funny Girl – $26,325,000
(2) 2001: A Space Odyssey – $25,533,00 (3)   The Odd Couple – $20,000,000
(4) Bullit – $19,000,000
(5) Romeo & Juliet – $17,000,000

The box office top five of 1968 shows that Hollywood studios of the period were more than adept at making dramas and genre pieces with mass appeal, whilst also providing room within the system for *auteur* projects from the likes of Stanley Kubrick (*2001*) and Franco Zefferelli (*Romeo & Juliet*). Crucially, however, what is missing is any sense of youth, any indication of the increasing awareness of American teenagers and college students with regard to social and political issues. While the underground music scene had grown in popularity to the extent that what was considered 'alternative' at the start of the decade had actually become 'mainstream' in terms of its commercial success, and the literary heavyweights, such as Norman Mailer and Hunter S. Thompson, were reflecting a growing disenchantment with the political system, Hollywood was existing in a state of suspended animation, drifting too high above the cultural radar for any of the radical thoughts or social impulses of the counterculture movement to seep into its often anachronistic output and 'corrupt' the values of 'good old-fashioned entertainment'.

Towards the end of the 1960s, the studio system could not fail to acknowledge a need for change in terms of both personnel and product. The long-serving studio heads and producers who had seemed to lose touch with the movie-going public were forced to concede their positions to younger executives, whose tastes were considered to be more in line with the audience that was slowly but surely deserting mainstream American cinema. As Jameson notes,

> The period in question is understood not a some omnipresent and uniform shared style or way of thinking and acting, but rather as the sharing of a common objective situation, to which a whole range of varied responses and creative innovations is then possible, but always within that situation's structural limits.[5]

This is to say that while the social uprisings of the period were not mirrored by shifts within the Hollywood system, the industry was taking note of these changes and how they were affecting its economy, leading to a number of methods to solve the serious issue of the gradual desertion of a once-faithful public. While this allowed for a certain level of formal experimentation on the part of producers and directors, it only did so within the industrial framework of Hollywood, with the core product expected to retain its key elements whilst establishing a 'daring' new aesthetic. With Hollywood becoming a key part of the entertainment industry as a whole, rather than a single-serving business entity, diversification and the economic power that was brought about by corporate takeovers guaranteed steady revenues and promotional opportunities through such markets as television, music, publishing, travel, and tourism. No longer dependent on the audience that had been carefully nurtured throughout the 1940s and 1950s, Hollywood was now pursuing a younger generation of cinemagoers. This courting of the liberal youth audience by the Hollywood majors risked the alienation of more conservative, older audiences, but still reaped economic rewards.

The Graduate, produced by the semi-independent Avaco-Embassy, was a movie about the erosion of upper-middle-class values, an insider's look into a closeted community. While it had much to satirise, about that community during the post-Kennedy era, it was a largely inward-looking picture that only considered the implications of the actions of young Americans behind the doors of their suburban homes. The film's soundtrack may have been written and performed by Paul Simon and Art Garfunkel, a singer-songwriter duo who had grown in popularity throughout the 'free love' movement, but they were relatively 'clean-cut', and their songs were questioning without ever being threatening, endearing them as much to middle-class housewives as to their teenage daughters, who were supposedly being corrupted by the suggestive lyrics of The Doors, The Rolling Stones, and The Velvet Underground.

Midnight Cowboy went out on to the streets of New York to follow the fortunes of male prostitute Joe Buck and his deadbeat, sickly friend Ratso who uses Joe as a partner to swindle others out of enough money to keep them in food. *Midnight Cowboy* appears to be quite radical for a 1960s studio film, featuring scenes of sex, drugs, and Andy Warhol groupies. Underneath this, however, is a relatively simple 'buddy movie', one of the oldest staples in the Hollywood catalogue, and a sentimental one at that. For much of its duration, *Midnight Cowboy* exhibits a certain edginess, mostly achieved by shooting on location in downtown New York. However, by the conclusion, director John Schlesinger is tugging at the heart-strings as the mismatched duo board a bus for Florida, only for Ratso to pass away upon arrival to the sound of Harry Nillsson's Oscar-winning song *Everybody's Talking at Me*. *The Graduate* and *Midnight Cowboy* may have been more socially aware than other Hollywood productions of the period, but it was a movie about a man who went looking for America, but could not find it anywhere, which would usher in a new wave of American film-making, and bring a younger audience back into the cinema.

2.2 The Road to Reinvention – The Making of Easy Rider

Dennis Hopper, the director, writer, and co-star of *Easy Rider*, described his 1969 biker odyssey as 'the first real independent movie that was ever distributed by a major company.'[6] If *Easy Rider* started American independent film, then it also started the movement's central contradiction – this is a cinematic movement that exists independently of the major studios, yet is reliant on their resources for distribution and exposure. However, while the eventual distribution of the film, and its then unprecedented commercial success, may have owed something to the promotional muscle of studio Columbia, *Easy Rider* was unlike anything that was being produced within the system. The creative origins of *Easy Rider* reveal that this film was conceived as a response to the direction in which producer and co-star Peter Fonda felt the industry was being pushed by the Motion Picture Association of America, whose president at the time was acting as the 'moral guardian' of the film community by trying to dictate to Hollywood the types of pictures that the industry should be making.

In the mid-1960s, Fonda was a handsome young actor who had found fame in a variety of B-movies, most of which featured motorcycles or drugs, and sometimes both. The son of the legendary Hollywood actor Henry Fonda, Peter was finding his acting career refusing to gravitate away from the exploitation ghetto. In 1968, Fonda found himself in Toronto, Canada to promote a Roger Corman production entitled *The Trip*, in which he had appeared and for which his future *Easy Rider* co-star Jack Nicholson had written the screenplay. Whilst there, he attended an exhibition for the Motion Picture Association Of America, an organization which had been formed to advocate the American industries of movies and television, and any future delivery systems for cinematic media. In the late 1960s, the MPAA was also trying to restore a favourable public image for the film business, which had often been accused of being rowdy and rambunctious, not to mention explicit in terms of its depiction of anti-social behaviour such as the indulgence in drugs, alcohol, and casual violence.

The chairman and CEO of the organization was Jack Vallenti. He took to the stage and spoke about how the film industry had to stop making films about anti-social behaviour in favour of more family orientated fare. After the exhibition, Fonda returned to the Lakeshore Hotel and proceeded to indulge in recreational pot and booze whilst signing some promotional photos. Whilst doing so, he came across a still of himself in the biker drama *The Wild Angels*. Fonda recalls that at this moment, 'The dubees and the Heineken kicked in, and I thought, "That's it! I know what I'm going to do for my next sex, motorcycles, and drugs movie!"'[7]

He immediately contacted his close friend Dennis Hopper, an actor who had made a striking appearance as a teenage thug opposite James Dean in *Rebel without a Cause*, but had since become more famous for his off-camera activities, most of which involved the consumption of alcohol and narcotics. Hopper was regarded as a loose cannon in Hollywood, meaning that although he was considered to be an exciting actor, he was difficult to work with, and a potential insurance risk. Fonda's idea was that he would produce the movie and Hopper would direct it, while they would both write the screenplay and take the leading roles. That way, they would both save money and maintain complete control over the project.

After Fonda had assured Hopper that he would be able to find financing for *Easy Rider*, Hopper started thinking about what his first film as a director would really be 'about'. Always ambitious, Hopper did not want to make an exploitation biker flick in the mould of the Corman offerings, but instead visualized a film about the era which he had been living through. Having immersed himself in the counterculture existence of 1960s America, Hopper was frustrated that people like himself had not been represented on screen. He remembers that

> Nobody had ever seen themselves portrayed in a movie. At every love-in across the country, people were smoking grass and dropping LSD, while audiences were still watching Doris Day and Rock Hudson.[8]

However, it was embarking on the project towards the end of the era that it was documenting that made the financing of *Easy Rider* possible. Had such a film been developed earlier in the decade, its social-political content and unorthodox aesthetic would have struggled to get through the Hollywood system. As Kracauer notes,

> Films are the mirror of the prevailing society. They are financed by corporations, which must pinpoint the tastes of the audience at all costs in order to make a profit. Since this audience is composed largely of workers and ordinary people who groups about the condition in the upper circles, business considerations require the producer to satisfy the need for social critique among the consumers. A producer, however, will never allow himself to be driven to present material that in any way attacks the foundations of society, for to do so would destroy his own existence as a capitalist entrepreneur.[9]

Although the 1960s were not yet over, it was evident that the counterculture revolution was winding down, with related industries such as music, literature, and television incorporating the more commercial elements of the decade's underground culture into its products and marketing mix. Without the risk of glorifying the hippie ideal, *Easy Rider* was ultimately not a socially threatening proposition, although it was likely to provide enough commentary to attract an audience looking to reflect on social change at the end of a turbulent decade. *Easy Rider* does question the values of capitalist society, but it also does enough to question the actions and lifestyles of hippies to make the film accessible to audiences of diverse social positions.

Fonda and Hopper knew how they wanted *Easy Rider* to look and sound, but were lacking one element necessary to generate solid financing – a script. Both men were too impatient and distracted by the alternative culture they wanted to document to sit down and put their project into screenplay form, which meant that Fonda was fortunate to meet Terry Southern. A hot screenwriter at the time, Southern was in Rome in the summer of 1967, working on re-writes for Roger Vadim's science-fiction folly *Barbarella* which starred Fonda's sister Jane in the title role. Fonda spent time with Southern and told him about his idea for *Easy Rider*, which was then titled *The Loners*. Southern loved the project and felt that he was the man to get it on the page. Although his fee at that time was higher than Fonda's projected budget of $360,000 could accommodate, Southern agreed to waive the cost of his services in exchange for points on the box office gross. After locking themselves away for five days, Fonda and Southern emerged with a twenty-one page treatment that Fonda could shop around Hollywood, and from which Southern could work to write the actual screenplay. The writing credit on *Easy Rider*, would later become a subject of fierce personal and legal debate between Southern and Dennis Hopper, with the former claiming that Hopper had filmed his script, and the latter insisting that Southern had provided an outline, which he had fleshed out into a full screenplay, often improvising scenes almost from scratch when the day came to shoot them.

The eventual screenplay for *Easy Rider* took the form of an episodic travelogue, told from the point of view of two motorcycle riding hippies, Wyatt (Hopper) and Billy (Fonda), named after the legendary Wild West figures Wyatt Earp and Billy the Kid. To emphasize the fact that these hippies are true outlaws, they begin their journey by selling Mexican cocaine to a dealer (played by legendary music producer Phil Spector), and then purchase their dream motorcycles and embark on a road trip to New Orleans. Their frequent stop-offs bring them into contact with other hippies who are living peacefully on a commune, and with a disillusioned, alcoholic lawyer (Jack Nicholson), who they induct into their free-spirited lifestyle, only for him to be beaten to death by a gang of rednecks that they had encountered earlier in a small-town café. Upon arrival in New Orleans, Wyatt and Billy meet a pair of prostitutes, with whom they drop acid in a cemetery. Billy seems to be disappointed by his lapse in idealism, for buying into the idea of the American dream by getting rich on drug money, but before he can change the direction of his life, both he and Wyatt are killed on an anonymous country road by two rednecks in a pickup truck.

For financing, Fonda initially approached Roger Corman's company American International Pictures, the leading distributor of independently produced 'exploitation' pictures at the time. Corman was not sure if there was much potential in *Easy Rider*, leading Fonda into contact with BBS Productions, who had the foresight to see *Easy Rider* in a broader context than AIP. BBS Productions was originally named Raybert Productions, and was formed by Bert Schneider and Bob Rafelson in 1965. Schneider had moved to independent production after a period of working for Screen Gems, the television arm of Columbia Pictures, which was controlled by his father. Schneider had been in the unusual position of having his father actually block his progress within Columbia, as he had been moved around the company without actually moving up, giving him an insight into, and a disrespect of, the corporate politics within a major studio, and how they can dilute the imagination of the company's output. Rafelson was also bouncing from job to job in television, without finding a position that suited him, and was frustrated that a move into features was eluding him. What both men had realized was that there was a number of directors and screenwriters with bold ideas but a lack of daring producers who would back them.

Schneider and Rafelson were culturally prescient enough to see that music was the scene of the era, not film, and tried to conceive of projects that would give visual media a fresh sensibility by incorporating musical trends. They succeeded with the TV series *The Monkees* and the feature film *Head*, which Rafelson directed. Despite success with their Monkees vehicles, BBS was still a small production company, reliant on major studios for distribution, meaning that each project had to be 'pitched' individually in the hope that one of the majors would be interested. When Schneider and Rafelson were brought the *Easy Rider* project, Schneider decided to pay for the $360,000 production out of his own finances so that BBS could retain ownership of what he was certain would be a hot cinematic prospect.

Although he was going out on a limb financially, Schneider knew that the major studios would not see the potential in the project, and would probably be put off at the idea of giving complete control to a producer (Fonda) and a director (Hopper) with patchy track records and even patchier reputations, but he felt confident that they would buy the finished product. Jacob Brackman worked with BBS as a screenwriter during the late 1960s and observed how Schneider managed the company by supplying the studios with movies they could market, but could not develop, and by keeping everyone within BBS creatively happy and financially comfortable in order to maintain an in-house team of forward-thinking collaborators.

The making of *Easy Rider* has been chronicled in many books and documentaries, with accounts of events differing depending on the individual. Associate producer William Hayward refers to an Akira Kurosawa classic concerning a murder story told from multiple points of view when summarizing the *Easy Rider* production: 'The whole thing has been like a *Rashomon* experience, the whole movie, the entire production, everybody's got an entirely different story on it.'[10]

Regardless of whose stories one prefers to believe, it cannot be denied that the production process of *Easy Rider* has been enormously influential on the way independent films are shot today. To save money, the scenes set during the Mardi Gras celebrations in New Orleans were shot during the actual festivities, with 'real' people, as opposed to extras. As an inexperienced producer operating more on gut instinct than hard economics, Fonda had not really bothered to establish exactly how much money it would take to bring the film to the screen. Instead, he had settled on the budget of $360,000 because that was the amount for which Roger Corman had shot his biker movie *The Wild Angels,* and therefore, Fonda concluded that his biker movie would cost the same amount of money. Although the 'official' budget for *Easy Rider* is usually reported to be around $360,000, with some accounts placing it slightly higher at $400,000, that figure does not include the amount of money that came from Fonda's own pocket to, quite literally, keep the show on the road. As Fonda recalls, 'Everybody was taking my credit cards and would pay for all the hotels, the food, the gas, everything with Diner's Club'.[11]

As much as *Easy Rider* was a film about the culture of the time, it was also a film that was shaped by the culture of the time whilst in production, or at least one important aspect of it – drugs. Aside from the presence of marijuana in the film, it was also ever present on set, to the point where the use of the drug by the leading actors actually ended up on the screen. The 'realism' of the campfire scenes in particular owed much to the influence of the drug, as the actors would smoke it, become so stoned that they would forget they were being filmed, and then talk about whatever subjects came naturally to them. Grass was so important to *Easy Rider*, both thematically and creatively, that the purchasing of a large stash was actually accommodated in the film's production report.

The production of *Easy Rider* was, by all accounts, a troubled shoot, with Hopper not so much directing the movie as enjoying an extended ego trip behind the camera. Relations between him and Fonda became strained, and rifts between them have not healed to this day. Much of Mardi Gras footage sequence was shot ahead of the rest of the film to capitalize on filming during the festival itself and to not have to pay to stage the sequence. Hopper went to New Orleans with a hastily assembled crew and appointed positions simply by saying that he needed certain types of personnel and seeing who would put their hand in the air to take the job. Even Fonda, who had always made it clear that Hopper was his first choice to direct the film, began to have doubts regarding his friend's ability to deliver a coherent motion picture.

Less personal, but more commercial, problems occurred when *Easy Rider* entered the post-production stage. Hopper initially delivered a five-hour cut, which he reluctantly cut down to three. BBS considered the film to be unreleasable, as Hopper's cut contained almost every frame that he had shot, every sunset, every line of semi-improvised 'stoner' dialogue. His ambition was for *Easy Rider* to be released on giant drive-in movie screens, where people could camp out and watch his 'masterpiece', an idealized synthesis of social experience and artistic expression. BBS Productions, however, had other ideas, such as selling the film to Columbia Pictures for distribution, and they knew that the studio would not lavish such expense on what they would perceive to be simply a 'biker film', or indulge a director with no track record and a widely noted dislike of corporate authority. Eventually, Bert Schneider stepped in, having become frustrated with Hopper who had spent almost one year in the editing suite, and told the film's director to take an extended 'holiday'. While Hopper was on enforced sabbatical, Schneider swiftly made sure that the film was cut down to a manageable length and cut into such a narrative form that it would be accessible for as wide an audience as possible. Kracauer claims that

Cinematic productions...are the homogeneous expression of one and the same society. The attempts by some directors and authors to distance themselves from this homogeneity are doomed from the start. Either such rebels are simply tools of society, unwittingly manipulated yet all the while believing they are the voices of protest, or they are forced to make compromises in the drive to survive.[12]

By re-editing *Easy Rider*, BBS Productions had made the film more palatable, more accessible to the mass market, in that it had been cut in a relatively conventional fashion and paced in line with audience expectations of narrative form. Hopper had been led to believe that he would be allowed creative freedom, but his subversive personality and working methods had been used by BBS to capture footage and performances that only a director operating outside of the system of popular culture would be able to get on film. If Hopper was a voice of protest during the production and post-production of *Easy Rider*, shooting in an unconventional manner, often whilst under the influence, and then arguing with the BBS hierarchy over the length of 'his' film, he became altogether more manageable once the finished feature was released to brisk box office business and intense media interest, happily playing along, or acting up, to his growing reputation as a 'visionary' film-maker of the New Hollywood, and taking whatever credit was offered for the final cut of *Easy Rider*.

Easy Rider ran just over ninety minutes and opened on 14 July 1969 at the Beekman cinema on Third Avenue and 58th Street in New York. Within its first week on release, the film grossed enough money to cover its costs, and by the end of its run had taken in $19 million. Adjusted for today's dollars, that would still make the film one of the most successful independent productions of all time, alongside the 1970s horror hit *Halloween* and the more recent *The Blair Witch Project*, *My Big Fat Greek Wedding* and *The Passion of the Christ*. Although this could be seen as the first success story of independent cinema, it was a success that was created by producers who took an experimental work into the editing room and cut away at it until Hopper's vision of late 1960s America had become a marketable product. While it would be convenient to chart the rise of independent film from the release of *Easy Rider*, it would be wrong to do so, as Hopper's hippie road movie represents not the start of a wave of independent productions, but the commercial peak of a movement that had been operating under the popular radar for several years due to Hollywood's dominance of the domestic market with big-star box office blockbusters, prestige epics, and wholesome family fare. *Easy Rider* may have brought an alienated audience back to the cinema with its cinematic representation of their alternative lifestyle, but niche movies that were expressing discontent with American society and experimenting with film form had been in circulation for some time.

2.3 Before The Bikers – Other Instances of Independence in 1960s Cinema

George A. Romero's *Night of the Living Dead* was so low-budget that there *was* no official budget. The film was shot on black-and-white film stock over weekends, taking almost one year to complete principal photography. The cast and crew were made up of friends of the director, some of whom became involved as means of obtaining production experience that could lead to paid work within the industry, with others helping out as an escape from their daily jobs. The cast contained only two professional actors, and the film was shot in Romero's home town of Pittsburgh, far away from Hollywood sponsorship or influence. Loosely derived from the gruesome EC comics series, *Night of the Living Dead* was the story of a group of people who find themselves holed up in a creaky old house when a strange epidemic breaks out and the dead return to walk the earth in the form of flesh-craving zombies.

As with *Easy Rider*, Romero's film took place within the context of an established genre, albeit one that had been relegated to 'B' status. Although widely credited with 'inventing' the zombie sub-genre, *Night of the Living Dead* was not the first film to feature members of the undead as a source of social threat. The director Victor Halperin had found his niche with the sub-genre, contributing both *White Zombie* and *Revolt of the Zombies* in 1932 and 1936 respectively, while *King of the Zombies* and *I Walked with a Zombie* appeared in the early 1940s. However, Romero's film appropriated the genre as a means of social commentary, and aesthetically rejected studio trappings, such as sound-stage shooting, happy endings, and the survival of principal players, which even the most surreal of the earlier horror films had been forced to conform to. As Hoberman notes,

> Produced outside the movie industry, *Night of the Living Dead* was not bound by Hollywood decorum. The rough-hewn style was closer to the raw immediacy of underground movies and cinema verite than to any studio production.... What's more, the movie asserted its marginal status by casting a black actor as the smartest, most sympathetic character. Nothing prior to *Night of the Living Dead* encouraged the audience to cheer when a black character shot and killed an unarmed white man.[13]

Night of the Living Dead was pioneering in its use of the genre film as social critique. With its rough visual style, necessitated by the circumstances of its production, but all the more effective for it, the film placed the horrors that it was depicting into a 'real life' context. Narrative digressions into the psychological exploration of its characters and their reactions to the horrific predicament they have found themselves in added a sense of naturalism, a documentary quality that was emphasized by still photographs of dead soldiers in Vietnam interspersed with the end credits. As Williams observes,

> Although ostensibly a horror film, *Night of the Living Dead* symbolically captures the mood of its era by allegorically representing an America divided against itself...As the film shows, the attitudes of the old society affect everyone – white, black, young and old. They also lead to chaos, disunity and destruction.[14]

Independent productions today still borrow from the aesthetic sensibility of *Night of the Living Dead*. The directors of *The Blair Witch Project* took Romero's naturalistic approach one step further by presenting their film as an actual 'documentary', also communicating a sense of fear through the psychological disintegration of their protagonists. Darren Aaronovsky's *Pi* was located within the science-fiction genre, but sidestepped the budgetary issues of making a genre film on an almost non-existent budget by placing the action in contemporary New York, lending its story a contemporary urgency. However, neither film has the prescient social commentary of *Night of the Living Dead* as the film features scenes that present a vision of government-endorsed carnage in Vietnam, and reflect the class and racial tensions in America at the time through the heated dialogue between the characters that are trying to survive the night, a 'night' that is symbolic of what Romero and his collaborators perceived as America's darkest hour in terms of both domestic and foreign politics.

While *Easy Rider* can be seen to pre-date such faux-independent feature films as *Pulp Fiction* in that it was aggressively promoted and immediately popular, with its 'independent' status being used as part of its marketing campaign, *Night of the Living Dead* set the distribution pattern for genuinely independent work. Released initially in 1968, the film played off and on for almost a year before it attracted serious attention, at first attracting only horror fans and being relegated to drive-in double bills and late-night showings, before eventually 'crossing over', thanks to reverent support from cultural critics, who did not review the picture until 1969.

If Romero and his associates represented the entrepreneurial aspect of alternative cinema, perhaps the true pioneer of the American independent movement was John Cassavetes. Although employed as an actor, the film-making process was his real passion, and he used his acting career in films such as *Rosemary's Baby* and the television series *Johnnie Staccato* to finance fiercely personal cinematic works which he was able to complete in his own time because they were being made from his own resources and not those of a private company. The working methods of Cassavetes were later adopted by other actor-directors such as Sean Penn, Tim Robbins, and Steve Buscemi, who have all appeared in studio productions to raise money for their projects. However, the difference between Cassavetes and the actor-directors of today is that his 'disciples' are still working largely within the constraints of the Hollywood system, with the most obvious constraint being time. Whilst making his 1968 drama *Faces*, Cassavetes could only afford to shoot in black and white and in 16mm, with the film being blown up to 35mm for its theatrical release, but he was able to shoot in sequence over eight months, and then edit for almost two years, allowing him the time to complete the film that he had envisioned, rather than being made to meet a deadline for a studio that had fixed a release date before even a single frame had been shot.

Another bold step that Cassavetes was willing to take was to distribute one of his films himself. When all the major companies passed on distributing his 1974 drama *A Woman under the Influence*, Cassavetes, set up his own distribution company, Faces International, and started booking it into cinemas, with stars Peter Falk and Gena Rowlands embarking on a self-financed publicity tour of the United States in the company of the writer-director to promote their labour of love. The film eventually grossed $6,000,000 in North America, making the project a successful gamble for Cassavetes who had mortgaged his house to keep it in production when his personal savings had run out. The works of Cassavetes were critically applauded, but they were reaching either an older audience interested in seeing mature drama, or the cinephile set, who considered Cassavetes to be the American 'answer' to the French New Wave, the films of Francois Truffaut and Jean-Luc Godard that were re-defining audience's perceptions of the film-making form across Europe.

Like *Faces* and *A Woman under the Influence*, the 1968 docu-drama *Medium Cool* was less easy to categorize than *Easy Rider* as it was a movie that criticized America not from the point of view of two hippie 'outsiders', but by showing the gradual change in personality of a Chicago television reporter (Robert Forster) who has been a passive observer in the stories that he has covered until the political and social ramifications of his work begins to sink in, eventually leading him to quit his job when he discovers that the tapes he has been filming for his reports have been seized and handed over to the F.B.I. by his network. Technically, *Medium Cool* was a departure in style from films at the time. While *Easy Rider* had gone on location by shooting during the actual New Orleans Mardi Gras celebrations, and dealt with the problems of filming the opening scenes at Los Angeles airport whilst planes were taking off overhead and ruining the audio track, the intrepid cast and crew of *Medium Cool* had gone one step further by placing themselves in genuine danger by shooting in a Chicago amphitheatre during the 1968 Democratic Convention. Vietnam War protestors had gathered outside for a demonstration, only to be beaten by the local police force. *Medium Cool* director Haskell Wexler was a former cinematographer who had previously worked on political documentaries, and his journalist instincts told him that the real 'action' was outside the theatre. Wexler captured some of the senseless violence that occurred that day, with leading man Forster placed in the thick of it, not so much acting as re-acting to the chaos that was occurring around him.

Ironically, for a film that was completed before *Easy Rider* and contained more anti-establishment feeling, *Medium Cool* was shelved by distributor Paramount and not released until 1971, when the company was looking for product that could emulate the success of the biker movie which had proved such a box office smash in 1969. Like *Easy Rider*, the climax to the film finds its central protagonist, along with his lover, meeting a fiery end as their car explodes in a park. Unlike *Easy Rider*, in which the camera pans away from the road and over to the river to suggest the calmer, more peaceful 'road' that society could travel down, director Wexler has his crew pan around to show him filming the scene with his camera, then pans to the audience watching him. By doing this, Wexler's ending becomes more confrontational; he is making his audience a voyeur, suggesting that they are perhaps as passive as Forster's reporter is at the start of the film and that they too need to become more aware and involved in the future of their country, regardless of the potential perils of doing so.

Despite support from leftist critics, *Medium Cool* was a commercial failure. Perhaps the younger crowd that had flocked to *Easy Rider* could not get past the fact that the figure at the centre of *Medium Cool* was an employee of a corporation, and not a motorcycle riding 'free spirit', or perhaps they were not interested in seeing how events of the time were also impacting on the lives of middle-class 'suits'. The other reason for the lack of box office revenue for *Medium Cool*, and the fact that Casavettes garnered critical kudos and audience interest from an older crowd as opposed to the younger audience who should have been enamoured of his experimental methods, could simply have been the fact that *Easy Rider* did not so much speak to a generation, as it was aggressively marketed towards them.

2.4 The Popular Phenomenon of Easy Rider and its Impact on the Industry of Mass Production

As noted, *Easy Rider* was almost a nostalgia piece when it was released in 1969, and it is tempting to view the film in that context. Taking its romantic notion of travel from Jack Kerouac's seminal novel *On the Road*, the film is a spectacular cross-country trip, with two characters from society's underbelly coming up for air and rejoicing in the freedoms afforded them by the open highways. Throughout the film, Hopper and Fonda drive across the country on their glorious machines, their journey scored by a soundtrack of radio-friendly hits, their visage of America somehow entirely free of gigantic advertising billboards, property developments or retail parks. As much as *Easy Rider* seeks to criticize the state of the nation, it also celebrates its awe-inspiring landscape, revelling in the romantic notion of travel as an escape from the drudgery of daily routine. As the reality of the failure of the counterculture movement was already setting in, *Easy Rider* was both a glimpse of what could have been and an insight into why it went wrong. Jameson asserts that

> One sometimes feels – especially in the area of culture and cultural histories and critiques – that an infinite number of narrative interpretations of history are possible, limited only by the ingenuity of the practitioners whose claim to originality depends on the novelty of the new theory of history they bring to market.[15]

The view that *Easy Rider* presents of the 1960s is an interpretation of the time in which it is located. The makers of the film were involved enough in the counterculture of the era to capture it with sufficient authenticity but, crucially, they were also detached enough from it by their position as actors and film-makers to theorize it and incorporate that theory into their narrative. Although Hopper and Fonda may have been portrayed as 'outsiders', they were really anything but. Both were employed within the Hollywood system and were fully aware of the commercial possibilities of their venture. The film they made portrayed hippie life within the context of the American narrative tradition, a series of anecdotes that occur on the road from idealism to disenchantment and, ultimately, destruction.

If one can bypass the cliché that *Easy Rider* 'spoke' to a generation, then it becomes clear that *Easy Rider* was successful because *Easy Rider* was marketable. Everything about the way in which the film was presented to the public was carefully calculated, from it's iconic poster design to the soundtrack album, featured the Steppenwolf hits

Born to be Wild and *The Pusher*, as well as tracks by The Band and Jimi Hendrix, and the Roger McGuin song *The Ballad of Easy Rider*, written by Bob Dylan. The film was not so much a hot new release as a cultural event, a phenomenon that everyone simply had to see, just to say that they had seen it. At the time, the pressure for the popular media to feel 'in' on the growing 'cult' of *Easy Rider* was so powerful that the cultural critics who had disliked the film found that their services were no longer required. Paul Schrader, later to be the writer of *Taxi Driver*, was working for the Free Press when *Easy Rider* was released and submitted a review in which he expressed a dislike of the picture. A few months later, with the phenomenon of *Easy Rider* in full swing, Schrader was fired from his position with the Free Press, probably for not being 'in' on the perceived counterculture, which was actually winding down at the time and, therefore, out of synch with the publications readership.

The film's promotional tag-line, 'a man went looking for America and couldn't find it anywhere', suggested that this was a film for a wider demographic than the initially intended hippie crowd, that it was a film that would have a resonance for anyone who was struggling to comprehend the shifts in American society over the past ten years. The motorcycles in *Easy Rider* serve as narrative vehicles, a means of transporting the audience across a changing landscape to encounter communal hippies, violent rednecks, and an alcoholic lawyer, all of whom are either reacting to the spirit of the times or seeking sanctuary from it.

Although the characters in the film were hippies, *Easy Rider* was a movie that had something for everyone. The visual landscape of the film, beautifully shot by Vilos Stigmond, and its soundtrack of instant rock classics made it an aesthetically pleasing experience, as easy on the eye as it was on the ear. Hopper's Wyatt may have been unsympathetic, and drug crazed, but Fonda's Billy was more laid-back and enigmatic, an easy-going dreamer with whom everyone could identify. The scenes at the hippie commune, an environment in which Billy fits in with ease and Wyatt noticeably does not, and the later New Orleans sequence in which Billy cries for his mother, suggest that he is something of a 'lost child', constantly moving around America simply because he is unable to find a place which would offer him true peace.

As much as the film seemed to be celebrating all things 'hippie', from the mind-expanding drugs to the protest marches, to the freedom of life on the road, it was also, perhaps unintentionally, critical of the alternative lifestyle. Audiences who did not believe in the anarchy of the counterculture movement could gain satisfaction with the nasty end that the characters meet, although it meant that hippies could hold them up as martyrs for their generation. Fonda's use of the phrase 'we blew it' in the film's final campfire scene is the most enigmatic line of dialogue, perfectly in keeping with the mood of the character, and suggesting that he has seen the potential of the counterculture movement, but also seen its failings. Billy is possibly acknowledging his own role in this as he has been knowingly transporting cocaine for a dealer. Cocaine was the drug that would re-invent the narcotics market in the 1970s, transforming the use of drugs in the

United States from a recreational activity to a full-blown business empire. If grass and LSD were social drugs for 60s hippies, then cocaine was a 70s lifestyle, essential for everyone from addicts of low social standing to high-powered executives. It is possible to imagine audiences with suspicions concerning counterculture seeing *Easy Rider* as a warning, watching Hopper and Fonda ride across America without a care in the world with the future threat to the fabric of society in the tanks of their machines.

The mass appeal of *Easy Rider* could be attributed to the cultural awareness of BBS, who saw the potential in the project, and then 'rescued' it from Hopper's hands, transforming directorial indulgence into something more marketable. In many ways, BBS was the forerunner of Miramax Films, in that Schneider and Rafelson at their peak were much like Harvey Weinstein is today – able to select talent and assign it the appropriate material, allow it a certain creative leeway, but not at the expense of the finished product. Like Miramax, BBS was a company that wanted to make films that were more challenging than those that were coming out of the studio system, but it was also a company that wanted success, even if it did try to project a laid-back, free-spirited image. BBS continued to produce successful 'independent' films that were distributed by major studios. Once again pre-empting Miramax, the company had its 'house' stars, with Jack Nicholson headlining both *Five Easy Pieces* and *The King of Marvin Gardens* for the company, under the direction of Bob Rafelson. Schneider and Rafelson were aware that it would not be possible to re-produce the phenomenon of *Easy Rider*, so they instead concentrated on making thoughtful films for a discontented generation. The studios, however, wanted their own *Easy Rider* and began investing in projects by unknown film-makers, who seemed to be on the 'pulse' of popular culture, only for most of these projects to attract little interest upon release.

Perhaps the biggest loser in this rush to capitalize on the counterculture audience was Universal Pictures, who started a scheme entitled 'movies for a million dollars', meaning that they would finance any film that could be made for under $1 million and give complete control to its director. They swiftly signed Dennis Hopper, and allowed him to take a crew down to New Mexico to shoot *The Last Movie*, an eccentric oddity about a Hollywood stuntman who becomes mixed up with a strange community. Eventually completed over-budget and over-schedule, *The Last Movie* was deemed a failure when released in 1971, although it did win the top prize at the Venice Film Festival. Hopper's directorial career stalled, and his hippie audience deserted him, showing that the counterculture crowd was no less fickle than the more conservative audience that Hollywood regularly courts with its more mainstream fare.

However, the documentary realism and social critique of independent productions would be appropriated by Hollywood, as the studios found they could adapt the attributes of *Easy Rider* to their preferred forms of film-making, without having to allow for artistic indulgence. Stock genres such as the police thriller found a new lease of life in the early 1970s, as studio productions such as *The French Connection* and *Serpico* took their stories from the newspaper headlines, while directors were encouraged to shoot on real locations and experiment with hand-held camera techniques, allowing actors to improvise dialogue and explore 'naturalism'. The leading characters in such films as *Marathon Man*, *The Parallax View*, and *The Candidate* were often 'hippie' outsiders, left-wing idealist campaigning for trust and justice in the face of indifference, but their disenchantment in the system was filtered through the movie-star glamour and charisma of Dustin Hoffman, Warren Beatty, Jack Nicholson, and Robert Redford, actors who could make such subject matter marketable through their on-screen magnetism and off-screen grace. Such actors proved to be the more respectable collective face of the New Hollywood, more well-mannered and less socially psychotic than Dennis Hopper, and eager to follow through the commercial opportunities that Peter Fonda recognized, but did not capitalize on following his breakthrough success. By adopting the aesthetic approach of independent cinema and allowing a level of social commentary that both inspired creative personnel and attracted a politically minded audience that had been deserting its product, Hollywood was able to absorb alternative cinema, both eliminating economic competition, and adding much-needed cultural legitimacy to its enterprises.

Notes

1. Guber, P, quoted by Biskind, P, *Easy Riders Raging Bulls*, p. 75, London, Bloomsbury, 1998.
2. Bourdieu, p. 112, 1993.
3. Hoberman, J, *The Dream Life – Movies, Media, and the Mythology of the Sixties*, 1st edn, p. xi, New York, The New Press, 2003.
4. Jameson, F, 'Periodizing the 60s', *Social Text*, 1984.
5. Jameson, p. 178, 1984.
6. Hopper, D, quoted in *Shaking the Cage*, 1999.
7. Fonda, P, quoted in *Shaking the Cage*, 1999.
8. Hopper, quoted in *Shaking the Cage*, 1999.
9. Kracauer, S, *The Little Shopgirls Go to the Movies* in *The Mass Ornament – Weimar Essays*, 2nd edn, p. 291, Cambridge, Mass, Harvard University Press, 1995.
10. Hayward, W, quoted in *Shaking the Cage*, 1999.
11. Fonda, quoted in *Shaking the Cage*, 1999.
12. Kracauer, p. 291, 1995.
13. Hoberman, p. 260–261, 2003.
14. Williams, T, *The Cinema of George A. Romero – Knight of the Living Dead*, 1st edn, p. 26–27, London, Wallflower Press, 2003.
15. Jameson, p. 179, 1984.

3

THE ART OF THE POSSIBLE: HOLLYWOOD FEATURE FILM PRODUCTION SINCE 1970

In order to examine American independent cinema as a method of cultural production and political thinking, it is necessary to provide some analysis of Hollywood production and its social-economic framework. In discussing 'Hollywood filmmaking', this chapter will be referring to those films that have been exclusively developed, produced, and distributed by the major studios and are, in terms of both economic ownership and cultural positioning, products of the Hollywood system. Therefore, this chapter will largely ignore films that can be seen to exist on the fringes of Hollywood, having been partly financed by studios after being developed through independent resources or purchased by major companies for distribution, and instead focus on the corporate giants and their economic dominance of the industry.

The aim of this chapter, through reference to cultural and economic theory and analysis of the lineaments of mainstream movies, is to outline the economic structure of the American film industry since 1970. This will explain how the Hollywood studios have diversified across a variety of inter-related markets to ensure dominance of the entertainment industry, at once nurturing, encouraging, controlling, and marginalizing additional forms of production. It will then be necessary to discuss Hollywood's cultural appeal, its adherence to genre conventions and reliance on the allure of celebrity to provide product that can be mass-produced to satisfy a captive global audience. Only then will it be possible to show where and how independent cinema fits within Hollywood's rigid machinery, and how independent cinema has undergone subtle but notable change as a result of, a perhaps a reaction to, Hollywood's own social and economic re-positioning.

3.1 Hollywood Economics – The Studio System and the Need for Mass Appeal
When discussing Hollywood economics, it is crucial to view Hollywood as 'industry'. Like all industries, Hollywood is inherently and necessarily competitive, with competition

being represented by the Hollywood studios – Paramount, Universal, Twentieth Century Fox, Warner Brothers, Metro-Goldwyn-Mayer, and Columbia-Tristar. While these studios are separate economic entities in that they have their own financing sources and structures, and work independently from each other in terms of product development, they work cooperatively as an industry, protecting the interests of the industry through the constant production of feature films and related media, and through the careful and considered promotion of Hollywood as a creative, socially aware and politically democratic community, and economic power.

The film industry is regarded as a high-risk venture in that it requires a relatively high level of financial investment in product that can yield a slim profit margin. Every year, a large number of studio productions fail to recoup their production cost at the domestic box office, suggesting that studios will be severely damaged financially, especially when the additional cost of prints and advertising is taken into account. For a film to be considered a success, it must deliver a return that is double its initial outlay. A film that simply returns its investment is considered to have 'broken even', while anything less is a failure. Only one in five Hollywood feature films turns a profit at the domestic box office, indicating that success is rare in movie business. However, the major studios have not been in business for a number of decades by losing money. The filmic output of the Hollywood studios is but the tip of the iceberg in terms of their economic dominance. As Garnham explains,

> Thus control of the production and distribution of filmed entertainment is now closely integrated...not only within the media and leisure industries in general, but within the wider financial and industrial sectors of a world economy increasingly dominated by large, multinational enterprises.[1]

Warner was bought out in 1969, changing its name to Warner Communications Inc. in 1971, with the other business interests of the conglomerate reducing its feature film output to only 32 per cent of its annual turnover, while Paramount entered a merger with Gulf & Western in 1968. United Artists has been a part of numerous corporate models, firstly merging with the Transamerica Corporation in 1968, then joining Metro-Goldwyn-Mayer to become MGM/UA and more being bought out by Sony in 2004. In terms of feature film production, the majors do engage in relationships with independent producers and distributors. These relationships exist both as a means of sourcing talent and discovering and developing product at a low-risk level, maintaining an illusion of diversity and equality in terms of industry opportunity. While 'independent production' has been a part of the studio model since 1970, it is not Hollywood's core business, and investment in such lower budget fare increasingly appears to be studio contingency planning in case their higher profile slate of films encounter scheduling problems or fail altogether at the box office.

The film-making that is practised by Hollywood is what Bourdieu refers to as the field of 'large-scale' cultural production, where profit comes from being seen by a wide audience. In pursuit of this 'mass audience', Hollywood produces a small number of films each year, small in relation to the number of films which are released to theatres, or available through the home entertainment market. In 2003, the average number of features produced by a Hollywood studio was 26, and in 2004 it was 29. These figures represent films for which the entire development, production, post-production, and distribution costs were paid for by Hollywood studios. This could be seen to represent a high-risk level of investment, and suggest that, if a studio experienced a number of costly failures over several years, it could be out of business. However, studios also invest in smaller films at different levels of risk, stepping in to provide distribution but not covering the initial development or production cost.

3.2 An Analysis of the 'Blockbuster' – Deconstructing Hollywood's Favourite Weapon of Mass Consumption

The 'blockbuster' is a motion picture that grosses a box office revenue of, or exceeding, $100 million. The blockbuster is commonly huge in terms of financial investment and production scale, with budgets now regularly exceeding the $100 million mark, meaning that it is necessary for such a film to recoup that amount just to break even, and to gross twice that amount to be considered successful. The very term 'blockbuster' has come to be synonymous with the use of the word 'Hollywood' as a summation of the American film industry. As Hall points out,

> 'Blockbuster' has entered common parlance as a term to describe the kind of cinema most readily associated with the dominant commercial forms of modern, mainstream, 'postclassical' or 'post-studio' Hollywood.[2]

The fact that many films are designed to be "blockbusters", and referred to as such before they have been released, is a prime example of Hollywood's system of production and the precision-planning that goes into the designing, manufacturing, marketing, and releasing of their product. Aside from being granted the largest possible production budgets, 'blockbusters' are also allocated the most extravagant advertising campaigns and the widest possible releases. A comparatively smaller studio product, with a production budget of $50 million, will be allocated less for prints and advertising and open in around 2,100 – 2,800 screens in North America. A film that is receiving the blockbuster treatment, however, will receive a prints and advertising budget that is equal to, or even higher than, its already excessive production cost and be released on 3,000 – 4,000 screens depending on how many have already been secured by rival studios to exhibit their own 'blockbuster' product.

As with many aspects of modern Hollywood, the 'blockbuster' has become an economic category of film, with such aesthetic elements as name actors, expensive special effects, taking prominence over any social or thematic concerns. The marketing and release strategy of such 'blockbusters' is a key indication that the one aim of this category of film is to make the largest amount of money by reaching the widest audience in a relatively short space of time, allowing another window of opportunity to open for the next film of its type. Given the cyclical nature of all cultural enterprises, it is not surprising that much of Hollywood's current 'blockbuster' product is reminiscent of such films from previous eras. At the peak of the 'roadshow' era, which lasted from approximately 1952 to 1965, Hollywood's 'blockbuster' product consisted of biblical epics, war movies, and musicals, pictures such as *The Ten Commandments*, *Ben-Hur*, *Cleopatra*, *My Fair Lady*, and *West Side Story*. Notoriously expensive to produce, as they relied on massive sets, exotic locations, major stars, and extensive promotion, these were pictures that did ultimately prove profitable for the studios, but only after extended periods of pre-multiplex distribution, which meant that corporate expenditure was not swiftly recouped and the studios were often operating at a deficit.

This explains the rush to cash in on the youth market following the success of *Easy Rider*, which was produced quickly and economically, but technological innovation and changes in exhibition since 1970 have enabled Hollywood to return to traditional narrative forms. Developments in special effects and the ability to release a feature film on thousands of international screens, has given the industry a renewed confidence in genres that were perceived to be no longer economically viable. While Stanley Kubrick once needed hundreds of extras and grand sets to achieve a cinematic vision of the Roman world in *Spartacus*, Ridley Scott can now commission a visual effects team for *Gladiator*, creating lavish detail on a budget and schedule that causes the studio no concern, yet still satisfies the audience in terms of spectacle. The revival of the historical adventure genre through films like *Troy* and *Kingdom of Heaven* and the resurrection of the musical with *Moulin Rouge* and *Chicago* are both indicative of the cyclical nature of the industry and its reliance on the familiar.

3.3 Dominance of the Mass – Necessary Changes in Distribution, Exhibition, and Marketing of Hollywood Product since 1970

Prior to the early 1970s, Hollywood released films in what has been termed 'roadshows'. This pattern of distribution would allow a certain number of prints and advertising materials to be available to a particular city or state within North America for a certain period. The prints and advertising would then be withdrawn from that territory and sent to another market. This meant that many films would be on release for anything from six months to two years depending on how successful they were, often returning to key cities or states where they had previously proved popular. Although the studios were handling the distribution of their product, they were crucially not in control of exhibition. Therefore, exhibitors would bid against one another to secure available prints for their theatres, providing the studios with considerable bargaining leverage when they were negotiating over the exhibition of a successful product, but undermining them when trying to secure further bookings for a feature film which had not performed as well as expected in its earlier engagements.

The end of the 'roadshow' era stems from the beginning of Hollywood's takeover by multi-business conglomerates around the end of 1960s, and it was this change in the economic structure of the film industry which not only led to new avenues of distribution and exhibition, but new methods of generating audience awareness. Firstly, conglomerate interests and money were able to secure theatres and lead to the construction of the first multiplex cinemas, meaning that multiple films could be screened at the same time at the same site, and the necessity for the studios to negotiate with exhibitors over booking fees was largely eliminated. The wide availability of cinema screens led to increasingly bullish release policies for the most expensive studio product, with the 'blanket' release, the opening of a film in the widest possible number of venues, becoming commonplace, starting with Universal's *Jaws* in 1975, opening on a then-record 464 screens, heavily promoted by a national print and television campaign. Secondly, studios were now no longer separate entities but units within conglomerates. The involvement of conglomerates led to vertical marketing strategies, allowing feature film to be widely promoted across a variety of mediums, at no additional cost. The necessity for the product to be immediately recognizable regardless of which medium it was being promoted in, led to Hollywood's reliance on established properties that had already achieved success in one commercial form, hence such 70s feature films as *Airport*, *The Exorcist*, *Jaws*, and *The Godfather*, which were already popular in their original form as novels, *King Kong*, which was a re-make of one of the earliest examples of the Hollywood 'blockbuster', and *Star Trek – The Motion Picture*, a film that was tied to a popular television series.

Hollywood's need for the immediate recognition of a product in any medium accelerated in the 1980s and 1990s with an increasing number of films being based on existing source material such as novels, computer games, television series, or comic books, and then continuing the recycling process by being transferred back to their original mediums in an updated form, or spinning off into new commercial avenues in the form of soundtrack albums, posters, and other merchandising. Such regurgitation of its most successful output is now characteristic of the entertainment industry's pursuit of the mass audience, as if a small degree of novelty multiplied by large quantities of familiarity is a prime selling attribute. The transparency of formula, such a negative attribute in the critical evaluation of an individual work, is often an overwhelmingly positive attribute in terms of consumer economics, as it provides an immediate conceptual and cultural touchstone to which its target audience can connect.

This 'safe bet' policy towards established properties also represented a significant cultural change in a Hollywood which had lost large amounts of capital by trying to emulate the success of *Easy Rider*. With the college-based audience proving too unpredictable in taste and relatively insignificant in terms of spending power, Hollywood sought to recapture its flagging core demographic by proving both the product that would excite its imagination, and the environment to consume it. With a 1973 report by the American Film Institute showing that 73 per cent of cinema tickets sold in North America were purchased by individuals aged between twelve and twenty-nine, Hollywood aligned its new distribution strategy with the improved state of cinema exhibition. Aside from the development of multiplex cinemas, theatres were built in already established consumer environments, most notably America's never-ending stream of shopping centres, or 'malls'. An open acknowledgment of the feature film as cultural 'product', this development physically positioned cinema, or at least Hollywood's conception of it, at the heart of consumer culture, ensuring audience awareness and greater financial stability. As Acheson and Maule observe,

> Vertical integration from production through distribution reduced the risk of films not having adequate screenings, and allowed producers to plan more effectively the timing of new releases and promotional campaigns...At the same time, theatres and the associated real estate represented tangible assets which could be used as security for loans from financial institutions unwilling to lend against the risky prospects of a film in development.[3]

While the ownership of theatre chains enabled Hollywood to consolidate its interests in distribution and exhibition, the changes made to the theatres themselves ensured a renewal of interest in cinema attendance by the younger audience, who found an appropriately modern and socially convenient environment in which to view Hollywood's product. This has expanded into ancillary markets, mainly as a result of advances in home technology, the video cassette recorder which has been succeeded by the DVD player, and the rise in popularity of video games and interactive technology. These developments have ensured Hollywood's dominance by enabling studios to guarantee a full return on their investment. From the late 1970s to the late 1980s, only 40 per cent of Hollywood productions were able to recoup negative costs from domestic releases, with the then-limited ancillary markets and foreign revenues rarely providing financial salvation for those productions that had flopped altogether in North America. As early as 1992, however, the economic structure of feature film production, distribution, and exhibition had been so altered by accelerated potential of ancillary markets that the domestic gross of a Hollywood feature film was estimated to account for only 16.9 per cent of its total revenue. This accessibility of Hollywood product in an appropriate environment is, therefore, the end result of a cycle of production, promotion, and distribution, a point of consumption by the consumer. Hollywood product can be seen as a flexible mass of content which can be re-formed to adapt to other mediums, whilst maintaining the same conceptual and cultural appeal that made it successful in cinematic form. This is what the industry describes, in its favourite corporate cliché, as 'synergy', a group of interrelated units working in unison, or as Wasko defines it, 'the cooperative action of different parts for greater effect.'[4]

3.4 Building the 'Blockbuster' – Hollywood's System of Mass Production
The system of production within the Hollywood studio system follows a fairly rigid formula, which can best be flow-charted as follows:

Concept – Manager/Agent – Producer – Studio Executive –

Development Deal – Studio President/Chairman – Casting –

Green Light – Pre-Production – Production – Post-Production.

Within the Hollywood system, feature film production begins with a 'concept', or a central idea. Unlike the independent sector, where a complete screenplay with talent attached is necessary to encourage interest from financiers, Hollywood is a 'system of ideas', where a concept that is perceived to have high commercial value can become a hot property in itself and initiate the development process. Post-1970, Hollywood has largely focussed on the production of the 'high concept' film, not so much a film as a pop-cultural event that can be condensed into one simple sentence, thereby inspiring a marketing campaign, luring audiences, and separating box office success from box office failure. Hollywood studios invest heavily in concept, with many writers being paid to develop ideas that will never be filmed, or even drafted into a full screenplay. After a concept has been successfully 'pitched' to a studio executive or producer, the project is still not yet in production, but instead in development, meaning that the studio covers the expenses of the producer, writer, and possibly a director, while they transform the concept into a 'treatment', or blueprint for a film covering the key sequence of narrative events, and then into a fully-fledged screenplay. With a completed script and creative personnel in place, the studio producer will now decide whether they wish to move forward with the project and enter the production phase.

However, the interest of the producer is not enough to guarantee the necessary funds from the studio, as the project must be approved by a more senior member of personnel, such as the studio president or chairman. In the case of particularly expensive productions, studio board members will also contribute to the decision-making process. If they decide to move ahead with the project, it receives the often elusive 'green light', meaning that it is now a 'go' picture. Alternatively, the project could be placed 'on hold' if there is some uncertainty about budget, marketability, or social-political climate, or even be put into 'turnaround' with the studio going back on its initial interest and possibly cancelling a project altogether or selling the property to a rival studio as a means of recouping its development costs. With a 'green light' secured, casting can commence. In fact, casting is a factor which can also determine whether or not a project receives the 'green light', as scripts will be sent out to actors to determine interest and to see if the project is sufficiently enticing for a star name to sign on. The casting process usually starts with the hiring of actors for the principal roles, while the supporting cast is gradually filled out with whichever professionals are available or affordable once the cost of star salaries has been established.

The film can now enter into the pre-production phase, usually taking several months. Crew members are assembled, sets and locations are prepared, special effects are designed, and the marketing department begins work on deciding how best to promote a film which has yet to be shot, although some of their decisions are dictated by the genre that the film is going to be in, and by the stars who have been cast in the leading roles. Production on a Hollywood studio film can last for anything from three months for a logistically simple comedy, romance, or drama that utilizes studio soundstages or North American locations, to six to eight months for a more technically complex action-adventure, historical, or science-fiction film, which requires special effects and international locations. Throughout the production process, the marketing department is at work preparing promotional materials, such as the ubiquitous 'making of' documentaries that are later used for electronic press kits. However, recent years have seen cultural change which has demanded higher levels of ingenuity from marketing departments, resulting in more creative campaigns, often conducted via the Internet.

Once physical production is complete, the film enters the post-production phase where it is edited, scored, digitally corrected, and prepared for public consumption. Post-production times can vary depending on when the studio may require the product, such as the summer season or end-of-year Oscar consideration. It is also during this period that films are test-screened both to industry members and movie-going patrons to assess its commercial prospects and to decide if any changes need to be made. These changes can be as simple as cuts to the running time or changes to the score, or the order of certain sequences within the film, or they can necessitate a last-minute return to the production process, with cast and crew returning to re-shoot existing scenes or even brand new material, that is then incorporated with the already existing footage to complete the final product to the studio's satisfaction.

3.5 Essential Ingredients – The Lineaments of Mainstream Movies
Hollywood feature films are constructed around three essential attributes – The narrative or genre, star casting, and marketing. Although each of these attributes can be analysed separately, they are inexorably intertwined as each one informs the other two, and all three must work in unison if the 'blockbuster effect', the acceptance of the film by a mass-paying audience, is to be achieved. The three attributes that this section focuses on are somewhat broad, with themes, psychology, social-economic perspective, aesthetic form, and other artistic attributes being largely ignored. This is because Hollywood product consists of broad films for a mass audience.

3.6 Three-Act Structure – Genre and Narrative Form in Hollywood Cinema
As in Bourdieu's field of cultural production, the artist, who in the case of Hollywood studio feature film production could be said to be the director, is most certainly in a dominated position. He or she finds themselves working in accordance with the demands of both the field of power, in this case the studio that owns the project, and to a lesser extent, the demands of the market, meaning the audience and its expectations. A negative audience reaction could damage relations between the artistic field and the field of power. This state of affairs necessitates a reliance on generic formula, within which the artistic players can only distinguish themselves through their skilled practice of such conventions.

The assignment of films to particular categories of genre is crucial to an industry that prides itself on being able to reach large numbers of particular 'demographics, that is to say particular groups of consumers with broad popular taste that is a reflection of the key facets of their social identity, such as age, gender, race, income, education, and location. Action-adventure films are a staple of the Hollywood production line as they target a key demographic – males aged approximately from twelve to twenty-five, with a keen interest in leisure activities and relative amounts of disposable capital. This demographic is economically vital, as it will consume the product in other forms through ancillary markets such as DVD and video games, providing that the cinematic experience is adaptable to other formats that can maintain brand recognition. Romantic films are generally popular with female audiences and although they offer less obvious ancillary opportunities, they can be an excellent opportunity for vertical promotion, by integrating promotions for products and services for this high-spending consumer into the film itself and its marketing machinery.

This is not a reductive form of analysis as a cursory glance at the last decade of Hollywood production shows a number of accomplished films across a variety of genres by a range of gifted directors, writers, and actors. The Shawshank Redemption, Unforgiven, Schindler's List, and Fight Club are just four examples of the exceptional work that can be produced by Hollywood cinema, and in some cases, only by Hollywood cinema, as the budgets that are allocated for independent films would be insufficient to bring some films to the screen. However, it must be acknowledged that these films have been the exception rather than rule, with most mainstream cinema conforming to the least discerning audience expectations rather than challenging them.

Aside from a golden production period in the 1970s, when Hollywood studios responded to the American public's dissatisfaction with the state of post-Watergate government with such paranoid classics as All the President's Men, The Parallax View and Three Days of the Condor, Hollywood films are neutral in their political position. Any topicality that they may have is now more of a concept than a serious debate. If in the 1970s, the popular sentiment of the American public was manifest in the film-making practises of Hollywood, it has now been distilled into the conceptualization and marketing of its product. The only Hollywood movie to approach the 1990s hot topic of sexual harassment was the 1995 thriller Disclosure which gave the issue a sensationalist twist by making the man the victim, and then sidelined the issue in favour of a mundane corporate conspiracy story. In the same year, the killer virus drama Outbreak opened with the suggestion that the US government is involved in potentially apocalyptic germ testing before degenerating into the usual thriller mechanics, with the hero racing to save the country from extinction. This stems from the need of the system to make films that exist within the parameters of genre rather than expanding them, thereby diluting any radical social impulses through the application of formula and marketable attributes.

Therefore, it is possible to regard 'mainstream movies' as films that deal with events, rather than themes, as they are consciously driven by their plots, many of which become interchangeable when compared to other examples from the same genre. What follows is a broad synopsis for three of the most enduringly popular forms of filmic entertainment offered by the Hollywood mainstream – the action-adventure, the romantic-comedy, and the thriller – which will serve to show that a key characteristic of mainstream movies is the reliance on narrative formula.

Action-Adventure – The audience is introduced to their hero in an explosive opening, which establishes his abilities to defy death and overcome any obstacle, whilst maintaining a sly sense of humour and ignoring the rule book. Usually a cop, secret agent, or criminal with a Robin Hood complex, he will then be assigned a mission which will entail a variety of locations, a feisty love interest, or mismatched partnership, and an adversary in the form of a colourful villain with a difficult-to-place European accent, before the 'story' is wrapped up with an extended climax.

This synopsis is obviously relevant to the James Bond franchise, and the 007 adventures have set the tone for many of today's action-adventure movies. However, it is also applicable to everything from *Raiders of the Lost Ark* to *Lethal Weapon* and *Mission: Impossible*. The three acts of action-adventure movies are generally structured around three key set pieces, or locations, which form convenient junctures for the narrative to hang itself from. *Speed* begins in a lift shaft, then moves to a bus and concludes on a subway train. While the stunt sequences themselves often display individual inventiveness, the narrative of action-adventure cinema is reliant on a rigid structuring of key events, although the tone and social perspective of the piece is usually in alignment with the cultural iconography of the film's star.

Romantic-Comedy – A genre that could be alternatively dubbed 'Opposites Attract', as that phrase encompasses the formula of the 'rom-com'. The film begins by establishing two central characters, each of whom is settled in their life/relationship/career and not looking for a new relationship. These characters are smart, funny, good-looking, and upwardly mobile, and they also come equipped with a 'best friend', usually a quirky/overweight/homosexual individual, present for comic relief or to make the co-lead look more glamorous by comparison. By a circumstantial contrivance, the leads meet and instantly dislike each other, but keep coming into contact with one another until they realize that there is an attraction between them and embark on a relationship. At the end of the second act, a 'crisis point' is reached and the relationship abruptly ends, until one of them comes to his/her senses and makes a final reel race against the clock to win the other back before it is too late.

This synopsis can be applied to everything from pre-1970s Hollywood comedies such as *Bringing up Baby* and *It Happened One Night* to modern productions like *Runaway Bride* and *How to Lose a Guy in Ten Days*. When the comedy element outweighs the romance, the narrative serves to connect a chain of events which will yield a number of comedic highpoints, as in *There's Something About Mary* where Ben Stiller's romantic infatuation with Cameron Diaz finds him trapping his penis in his fly zipper, being arrested by overzealous undercover cops, and being 'attacked' by his sweetheart's dog. If the romantic element prevails over the humour, the narrative is structured around several will-they/won't-they moments, many of which can be found in *Serendipity*, wherein soul mates John Cusack and Kate Beckinsale meet in the first ten minutes, then spend the rest of the film narrowly missing each other before being romantically reunited in the final scene.

Thriller – If the romantic-comedy can be alternatively titled the 'opposites attract' genre, then the thriller genre could be re-named 'cat and mouse', or 'the spider and the fly' because it usually follows two protagonists who play games with each other on route to a climactic face-off. The self-consciously dark mood of the thriller genre suggests that it is a more intellectual affair, but the narrative once again follows the battle between good and evil. The hero is a professional, often a police detective, or psychologist, or an Everyman figure, dealing with a menace that comes almost out of nowhere. Although usually expert in his/her field, the hero will be initially thwarted at every turn by the villain, but will gradually learn about the antagonist by studying his modus operandi and eventually use it to beat the villain at his 'game' of choice.

Although this synopsis applies to most mainstream thrillers, it is important to make a social distinction between two forms that the genre explicitly takes – the 'urban' and the 'domestic'. The 'urban thriller' deals with professional conflict between individual parties, such as the detectives and the serial killer in *Seven*. Drama takes place in public, as the events of the story are often re-capped as television news reports, putting the battle of good and evil in the public eye. The distinction between the two types is perhaps best exemplified by a pair of 1992 releases, *Cape Fear* and *Ricochet*. In both, a dark figure from the early part of the hero's life resurfaces, threatening his comfortable existence. The difference being that, in *Cape Fear*, the war between Nick Nolte's lawyer and Robert De Niro's ex-convict is played out in private, with De Niro's vengeful actions threatening the stability of Nolte's domestic life, while in *Ricochet*, Denzel Washington's district attorney is publicly humiliated by John Lithgow's sociopath, and finds his career taking a downward spiral as a result.

The generalization of plot outlines can be applied to less consistently popular genres such as the 'disaster movie' or the 'super-hero' movie. Locations and choice of disaster aside, there is little to distinguish *Earthquake* from *The Towering Inferno* or *Airport*, all of which focus on a group of people trapped in a dangerous situation and trying to deal with it as the lesser names are bumped off by the real star of the genre, the special effects department. The 'super-hero movie' usually takes the form of an origin story. *Batman Begins*, *Spiderman*, and *Daredevil* all focus on how their titular hero has acquired his superpowers, and why he chooses to use them to fight for the cause of good. This makes the 'super-hero' film an offshoot of the action genre in that it establishes the ingredients for a 'franchise' – a recognizable brand, a name actor, and a property that can be marketed across a wide variety of ancillary markets.

What this analysis shows is that mainstream narratives are largely interchangeable. What the analysis does not show is why audiences keep paying to see new versions of films that they have already seen. Narrative is obviously an important aspect of any feature film, and a film with a strong story and a solid three-act structure will always be more accessible than one that is bereft of both, but there are other factors which serve to distinguish one film from another. It has been argued by Benjamin that there are only seven plots from which fictional stories can be derived, such as the 'lone hero', 'Romeo

& Juliet', or 'the spider and the fly', and it is these basic plots that have been elevated to the higher status of 'genre' by critics and writers. What distinguishes one cinematic work from another is that the *details* change from film to film. The familiarity of genre makes the mainstream audience comfortable, but the details are changed in order to maintain interest in the annual offerings of major studios. These details can be anything from the type of protagonist, to the location, to the camera work and editing style, to the soundtrack, and the actors in the cast.

A classic example is the 1988 action movie *Die Hard*. Bruce Willis is a New York cop, trapped in a Los Angeles skyscraper, fighting against a team of terrorists lead by Alan Rickman. The combination of brash stunts and sardonic wisecracks was standard for the 1980s action movie, but what distinguished *Die Hard* was its emphasis on its location, and the fact that the hero was trapped within it, a marked contrast to the globetrotting adventures that Hollywood was offering at the time. The success of *Die Hard* led to numerous re-workings, all of which retained the central plot of the hero single-handedly dealing with a threat in a confined space, but which remodelled the concept by changing the key detail of the location from an office building to a plane (*Passenger 57*), a military gunship (*Under Siege*), a bus (*Speed*), or an ice hockey arena (*Sudden Death*). Even *Die Hard* itself was derived from elsewhere, with the film's format being a more restrained update of the 1970s disaster cycle, replacing forces of nature with a gang of European terrorists, and scaling down the cast of heroes to a lone cop with survival skills.

Such changes in detail are relevant to a discussion of mainstream Hollywood narrative because studio product is usually concept-driven. The term 'high concept' was coined in the mid-1980s and was applied to a project which was so attention grabbing in its state of conception that it could be described in a single sentence or with one image. The production team of Jerry Bruckheimer and the late Don Simpson have been credited with bringing the term into the cultural lexicon. Screenwriter Danilo Bach recalls of meeting with Simpson regarding a project, 'There was no story. There was just this vague idea of a black cop who turns Beverly Hills upside down.'[5]

This 'high concept' would develop into the 1984 film *Beverly Hills Cop*, which became one of the biggest grossing comedies of all time. Two years later, the dynamic duo delivered *Top Gun*, a glossy account of the US Air Force's training programme. Simpson secured a 'green light' from Paramount with the aid of fighter plane footage and a photograph of a handsome military pilot wearing a bomber jacket and a pair of Ray-Bans, then hired a series of writers *after* the deal was done.

3.7 Cultural Constants – The Star as Genre

> Movies are complex products and the cascade of information among film-goers during the course of a film's run can evolve along so many paths that is impossible to attribute the success of a movie to individual causal factors. The audience makes a movie a hit and no amount of 'star power' or marketing can alter that. The real star is the movie.[6]

They {studio executives} were congratulating me on the great success of *Twelve Monkeys* and I started to say, 'Yes, isn't it wonderful that an intelligent –', but they said it was all down to two words: Brad Pitt. It doesn't matter how many times you do a film with Harrison Ford or Brad Pitt that falls on its face, they still want to believe in those two words, whether it's Brad or Harrison or Bruce.[7]

It is appropriate that a discussion of the importance of star names to the American film industry should follow an analysis of Hollywood's reliance on genre because some stars have become genres in themselves, their presence guaranteeing the cinematic experience that the audience will enjoy. Star names are believed to be so essential for success that actors are often cast in roles for which they are entirely inappropriate. The robustly healthy, all-American Tom Cruise as an impoverished Irish peasant in *Far and Away*, or the wholesome Michael J. Fox as a yuppie coke fiend in *Bright Lights, Big City*, and the decidedly non-threatening Leonardo DiCaprio as a turn-of-the-century gang leader in *Gangs of New York* are just three examples of Hollywood's willingness to ignore unsuitability when a career is at its commercial peak.

The characters that inhabit Hollywood films are more generic archetypes than they are individual psychological constructs. As such they behave in accordance with the rules of genre they occupy, rather than in any idiosyncratic manner. If psychology is largely absent, characterization is present in the screen persona of the lead actor, who brings his or her own cinematic identity to the role, with the audience inferring knowledge of the character based on their prior experience of the actor's earlier performances in similar roles in films of the same type. Qualities or characteristics which the audience has come to associate with a star from their earlier roles can be used to the advantage of the commercial movie, which is driven more by concept, incident, and action, than it is by character. The casting of certain stars carries connotations that eliminate the need to explain the actions of a principal character. As the titular lawman in *Dirty Harry*, Clint Eastwood brought the 'outlaw' image that had been cultivated through the westerns that he had made in the 1960s. As soon as he appeared on screen, regardless of the fact that he was wearing a suit and patrolling a city, rather than dressed in poncho and wandering the Wild West, audiences knew that his character was an individual who will use any means necessary. The moral ambiguity of Eastwood's western persona is here suggested by Harry Callahan's grey suit, as he exists between two social extremes, maintaining the values of law and order, but dispensing them through extreme force, with scant regard for proper procedure.

Such iconography has made Hollywood's biggest stars genres in themselves. On promotional material, the names of Tom Cruise, Harrison Ford, and Julia Roberts are more prominently displayed than the title of the actual film, an indication that the Star has become the identifiable product. If films can be re-formed to adapt to other commercially viable mediums, stars as products can be utilized in other industry areas, such as television and magazines, promoting their films and other products to which they are associated as a commercial sponsor. In this context, the star is another example of the synergy which the industry as a whole seeks to achieve, and through the star's cultural iconography, the star becomes a genre or brand. Dyer notes that

> By image...I do not understand an exclusively visual sign, but rather a complex configuration of visual, verbal, and aural signs. This configuration may constitute the general image of stardom or of a particular star. It is manifest not only in films but in all kinds of media texts.[8]

Therefore, stars are also another means for the industry to promote itself, as they provide the business with a public face, or façade, an image of success and a suggestion of the diversity. In this sense, stars act as ambassadors for the entertainment world, and it is rare to find an actor who is prepared to discuss any negative industrial experience. Each 'star' is not so much a person as a social role that is being inhabited by a human being, with the popular media manipulating their image to project a variety of attributes and values that the industry wishes the mass audience to associate with its business culture.

The star is both extraordinary and ordinary. Extraordinary in that stars are bestowed the highest level of global celebrity for their perceived 'individuality', but ordinary in that their stardom is constructed, presented, and communicated in an industry-sanctioned manner that is common to all popularly recognized performers. The manner in which the media and the public fawn over movie stars also serves to distract from their professional position within the industry and their role in the sequences of production. Stars are not usually involved in the conception of a feature film, but become involved at the pre-production stage, reading scripts, providing notes, and selecting roles. They then work to a strict schedule in their capacity as a performer. Contributions can also be made in post-production, as the star may be required to re-dub lines, add a voice-over, or even re-shoot scenes if footage is deemed to be unsatisfactory. It is in the promotional stage, however, that stars do their most valuable work and, in some cases, their best 'acting'. Essentially the public face of the studio, the star participates in press junkets, making the most of each opportunity as a means of increasing public awareness of their latest picture. As Kerr notes,

> A star is a screen name that is its own trademark. Like a trademark, the star cannot be duplicated nor can she be reduced to a commodity for exchange although, paradoxically, a performer becomes a star by packaging her identity for continuous duplication and exchange.[9]

It is the public prominence of the star that has made the casting process the most important part of Hollywood feature film production. The relationship between stars and audiences is so strong that it has become the attribute of the product which influences, or entails, the other lineaments which are required to produce a feature film within the studio system. When trying to finance a film version of *A Tale of Two Cities*, director Terry Gilliam attracted the interest of Mel Gibson, at which point the studio who owned the project agreed to budget the film at $60 million should Gibson commit to play the lead. Unfortunately, Gibson decided to take a different film, meaning that Gilliam had to look for alternatives, settling on Liam Neeson. Although an established actor and an Oscar nominee for *Schindler's List*, Neeson, either through lack of indefinable star quality or industry promotion, is not the box office force that Gibson is. Therefore, the studio informed Gilliam that he could only make the film with his second choice of leading man if he could bring the budget down to $23 million. Even with the money saved from casting the mid-range Neeson as opposed to the 'A'-list Gibson, this was a significant cut in funding, and Gilliam left a project that the studio was enthusiastic about but unwilling to 'green light' without the box office guarantee of a proven star name. As Gilliam explained,

> It's their project, they want the same production values, but they won't give us a realistic budget. They took the view that Liam was fine in a Holocaust movie, backed up by six million dead Jews, but was he a true star?[10]

Star names are the most important component of mainstream movie-making because the entire process rests on their availability and willingness to commit to a project. In the case of the aborted adaptation of *A Tale of Two Cities*, the studio was sitting on a classic literary property in the Charles Dickens novel and had a visionary director attached in Gilliam. However, this was not enough to secure a 'green light'. When the box office record of the film's star dictates the production value that the film will have, and the effort that the studio will spend on marketing the finished feature, it becomes apparent that they are the most important component of Hollywood movies.

It is, however, debatable as to how reliable star names are with regard to ensuring box office success. Harrison Ford has been successful as an action hero in the *Indiana Jones* trilogy and other pictures, such as *The Fugitive* and *Air Force One*, but his failure to dominate the box office in comedies and dramas like *Sabrina* and *Regarding Henry* has been put down to the fact that the audiences does not accept him in less physical roles. However, this does not explain the failures of *Firewall* and *K-19*, both of which found Ford in 'action-man' mode. Adam Sandler and Jim Carey have made numerous successful comedies, but failed to generate the expected revenue with *Little Nicky* and *The Cable Guy* respectively, although both films were targeted at their presumed audience. While the presence of a star name may reduce the level of risk by providing the film with a cultural anchor and media exposure, it does not eliminate that risk altogether. The following case studies show the box office track records of three Hollywood stars over the course of their last ten films, with analysis of their appeal and assessment of their value as commercial attributes and cultural constants.

Case Study 1: Tom Cruise

Salary: The Last Samurai (2003) – $25 million + profit participation.
Minority Report (2002) – $25 million + profit participation.
Vanilla Sky (2001) – $20 million + 30% of profits.

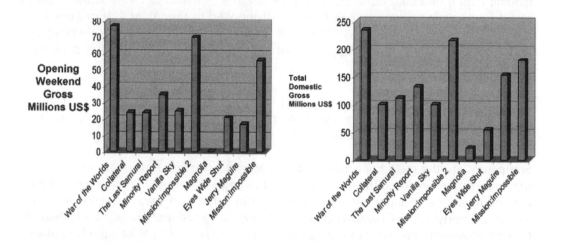

The chart for Tom Cruise is almost consistent, with the actor having an unprecedented streak of box office hits, his only relative commercial failures being *Eyes Wide Shut* and *Magnolia*. It should be noted that neither film was a commercial venture. *Eyes Wide Shut* was a Stanley Kubrick project which opened at number one at the box office thanks to Cruise's pulling power, while *Magnolia* was an 'independent' picture by the critically adored Paul Thomas Anderson, in which Cruise played amongst an ensemble cast, enhancing his cultural credibility. All of his starring roles in studio productions since the early 1990s have opened at number one, with the exception of *Jerry Maguire*, which was marketed as a 'sleeper', and each has grossed over $100 million domestically. His choice of roles has been consistent, with the actor portraying military men and government agents in six of his most successful films, *Top Gun*, *Minority Report*, *The Last Samurai*, and the *Mission: Impossible* series, while he played a lawyer in both *A Few Good Men* and *The Firm*, and enterprising businessmen in *Magnolia*, *Rain Man*, *Jerry Maguire*, *Risky Business*, and *Vanilla Sky*. Beyond the professional nature of his characters, his enduring screen persona of being cocky, charming, yet ultimately dedicated, has also served him well in *Cocktail* and *Days of Thunder*, while these facets have also been in evidence whilst supposedly playing 'against type' as a villain in *Interview with a Vampire* and *Collateral*.

With the exception of *War of the Worlds* in 2005, every poster for a Tom Cruise film has focussed on the actor's face, and his name has been as prominently displayed as the title. The trailers for his movies also follow a similar pattern, often presenting him as a wholesome all-American, a hero, or someone who is enjoying great personal success, before showing him in situations of distress, and then suggesting that he will triumph against the odds. Essentially a swift montage of the key emotions of delight, desperation, and determination, they act as a succinct summary of the identifiable characteristics of the 'Tom Cruise movie', and studios have always adhered to this formula when promoting a Cruise vehicle. While most of his films have featured some action content, his 1994 offering *Jerry Maguire* was a comedy-drama that revolved around characters and relationships. However, Tri-Star managed to emulate earlier Cruise campaigns by taking a short piece of footage of Cruise running through an airport and cutting it into the trailer at a particularly dramatic moment.

Case Study 2: Sandra Bullock
Salary: Murder by Numbers (2002) – $15 million.
28 Days (2000) – $12.5 million.
Hope Floats (1998) – $11 million.

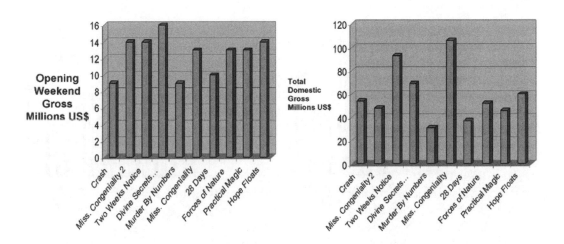

At first glance, Bullock's box office track record is acceptable rather than astounding, with only one $100 million hit in her last ten films in *Miss Congeniality*. However, her status as a 'star' is ensured through her ability to attract a female demographic that is notoriously hard to sustain in an era of male-centred action-adventure pictures. Most of her starring roles have been profitable in relation to their cost, with the average budget of her pictures coming in at $40 million, as opposed to $80 million for Tom Cruise. Her most successful roles have been in light comedies with a romantic flavour, usually opposite a leading man of lower stature in the Hollywood pecking order, such as Ben Affleck in *Forces of Nature* and Aidan Quinn in *Practical Magic*. When paired with a male co-star who has enjoyed similar success in the same genre, such as Hugh Grant in *Two Weeks Notice*, her grosses have almost doubled, indicating that she may have more star value in appropriate partnerships than in solo vehicles.

Although not complete failures in that Bullock's star power opened the films in the higher reaches of the box office chart, and helped to turn profit in ancillary markets, more dramatic films like *28 Days* and *Murder by Numbers* failed to connect with the public. However, her early success with the thriller *The Net* suggests that the stock excuse that the star has been ill-suited to a genre is not always applicable. The most successful of her films have found her playing quirky, but upwardly mobile, romantics who have to balance entanglements of the heart with other pressing matters, either professional or familial, while marketing campaigns have tried balancing the comic and dramatic elements as a means of attracting her core female audience.

Case Study 3: Nicolas Cage
Salary: National Treasure (2004) – $20 million.
Windtalkers (2002) – $20 million.
Snake Eyes (1998) – $16 million.

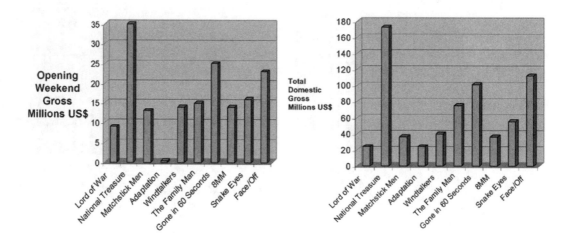

Although Cage has enjoyed his biggest commercial success within the action-adventure genre, represented in his filmography by *Gone in 60 Seconds* and *Con Air*, he has not portrayed the typical invincible hero, bringing his offbeat persona to *The Rock* and *National Treasure*. His status as a dramatic actor who won an Academy Award for playing an alcoholic in *Leaving Las Vegas* has lent cultural currency to his more commercial endeavours, legitimizing the action pictures in which he has appeared to an audience that would usually prefer more serious fare. Unlike Cruise and Bullock, Cage has been less consistent in his choice of roles and genres, making his chart more difficult to analyse in terms of positioning the star as genre.

This would seem to make him a less bankable star prospect, although his lower grossing films, such as *Adaptation* and *Bringing out the Dead*, on which he was directed by Spike Jonze and Martin Scorsese, have enhanced his reputation as an actor willing to take risks, adding to his artistic stature and longevity. Thrillers such as *8MM* and *Snake Eyes* have underperformed commercially, most likely a result of poor reviews and indifferent word of mouth, but like Sandra Bullock, his stardom has contributed to their decent opening weekend grosses, while more formally experimental and politically challenging films like *Adaptation* and *Lord of War* have enjoyed exposure, if not great commercial success, because of his name value. The marketing of his films has been as varied as their subject matter, although most campaigns are consistent in reminding audiences of Cage's calibre as an Oscar-winning actor.

An early prospectus on bond financing for the film industry stated that

> The 'star' of great box-office pulling power must possess a successful combination of (1) personality, (2) acting technique, (3) photographic ability, and (4) that unnameable capacity to grip the public imagination.[11]

Cruise, Bullock, and Cage all possess personality, and acting technique, and certainly look, or are at least made to look, appealing on screen, and have at some stage gripped the public imagination as a result of their work, although only one has maintained that grip. Of the three case studies, Tom Cruise is the only one who epitomizes the idea of the all-conquering movie star, the reliable commercial attribute who can always attract a large audience when cast in an appropriate role. Cruise has delivered hits with lightweight, critically derided popcorn fodder such as *Days of Thunder*, *Cocktail*, and *Mission: Impossible 2*, all of which seem to exist as extended advertisements for the commercial potential of their star, rather than as actual films with a coherent storyline and social-political perspective. However, it should be noted that with an average cost of $80 million, and budgets often in excess of $100 million for his action-adventure pictures, not to mention a heavy marketing cost, Cruise's stardom and bankability is expensive to maintain.

By comparison, Bullock's box office track record is solid but unspectacular, while Cage has can be seen as a commercially erratic performer. If Hollywood makes its money not on individual films, but a catalogue of films, then both can be considered stars in that their overall box office receipts are impressive. Taking their films as catalogues, the average gross per picture would be $59.6 million for Bullock and $67 million for Cage, making them relatively 'safe' investments once overseas revenues and ancillary markets are taken into account, while both have starred in projects that have cost much less to produce than the average Cruise picture, enhancing their profitability. However, it is debatable as to whether the box office performance of their biggest hits can really be attributed to them. De Vany and Walls argue that

By making strategic choices in booking screens, budgeting, and hiring producers, directors and actors with marquee value, a studio can position a movie to improve its chance of success. But, after a movie opens, the audience decides its fate. The exchange of information among a large number of individuals interacting personally unleashes a dynamic that is complex and unpredictable.[12]

What De Vany and Walls term the 'information cascade' is what the industry refers to as 'word of mouth', meaning how an audience responds to a motion picture socially, by discussing it with others. This is particularly important today, as through the Internet, viewers can comment on films not just through personal e-mail contact, but through sites such as the imdb.com (internet-movie-database) which provide the opportunity to write reviews, discuss actors and directors, and potentially assist or hinder the box office performance of a film through a positive or negative response. *Jerry Maguire* had one of the lowest openings for a Tom Cruise film, taking $17 million, but excellent word of mouth led to a $153 million total, with the first few days representing just 11 per cent of the eventual gross. By contrast, the heavily promoted Disney release *The Village* opened with $50 million and eventually grossed $114 million, meaning that 44 per cent of its total was achieved in its first weekend, an indication of poor word of mouth which led to sharp declines in business throughout its theatrical run.

3.8 Re-Packaging the Product – Marketing and Distribution
As the major studios spend at least as much, or more, on marketing as they do on script development and production, it is clear that marketing is regarded as being an integral part of the 'creative' process, and more important than good writing, acting, or direction when determining the success or failure of a feature film. A look at how studio productions are promoted shows that there are two distinct styles of marketing for increasing public awareness of forthcoming attractions.

The Hard Sell – This method has traditionally been reserved for blockbusters, usually released during the lucrative seasons of summer and Christmas, but as studios have become more reliant on such extravaganzas, the marketing of big-budget features is becoming a monthly fixture. In 1997, Fox and Universal bankrolled rival volcano movies. The Fox feature, *Volcano*, had a firm summer release date, and the studio was building up audience awareness by any means possible with promotional materials ranging from the teaser trailer to the car bumper stickers proclaiming, 'This summer, the coast is toast.' To avoid a summer showdown, Universal moved the release date of their rival lava spectacular, *Dante's Peak*, to the month of April, meaning that a hype machine emerged to promote the $120 million adventure. The battle between the two studios was not one of quality but of awareness and accessibility, with both aiming to have their product available to the public at the right time with the maximum amount of publicity. *Dante's Peak* benefited from the novelty value of being the first of the two films to hit cinemas and achieved a marginally higher domestic gross.

Such marketing usually takes the form of blanket promotion, with as many mediums as possible being exploited to ensure that the film is firmly ingrained in the minds of the cinema going public by the time of the opening weekend. Advertising the film through trailers on both the big and small screen is essential, but press exposure is also crucial. In October 2002, the extreme sports adventure *XxX* was released in the UK on a wave of hype, which found star Vin Diesel appearing on the cover of almost every magazine in the country, from established film publications such as *Empire* and *Total Film* to glossy magazines with a broader focus, like *Esquire* and *GQ*. The trick of such marketing campaigns is to make films familiar and yet fresh. In the case of *XxX*, the Sony marketing machine film made deliberate references to the popular James Bond franchise, along with the explosions and cheap jokes that are expected from the action genre. Yet it also aggressively promoted Diesel as a 'new breed' of action hero in that he is multi-ethnic and emphasized the 'extreme sports' angle which became the backdrop for the stunt sequences.

This promotional strategy usually leads to a 'big opening' and a 'sharp drop-off', meaning that media saturation creates awareness of the product that results in attendance at multiplexes on the first weekend, followed by steep declines in revenue in the month that follows. Below is a graph based upon the domestic box office performance of *The Hulk*, a heavily promoted Universal release from summer 2003.

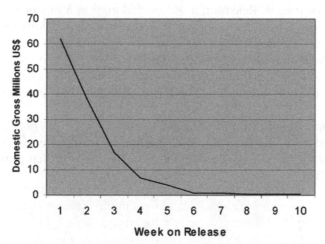

Based on an established Marvel comic book that had also enjoyed life as a successful 1970s television series, *The Hulk* was released on over 3000 screens, making it one of the widest releases in history. It was advertised through not only trailers and posters, but via related tie-ins, such as comic books, children's toys, and fast-food promotions. The status of the property as a widely recognized cultural product, coupled with Universal's aggressive advertising strategy, and saturation release, led to an opening weekend haul of $62 million, followed by a swift tumble from the top of the box office tree. The film grossed 45 per cent of its overall take in its first three days on general release, and most 'blockbuster' films conform to this pattern.

The 'Sleeper' Hit – It could be argued that there is no such thing as a 'sleeper' hit. It is industry terminology for a film which becomes a big success, despite having seemingly little promotion, and which plays successfully for a long period, without having a record-breaking opening, or a run at the top of the box office chart. *Sleepless in Seattle, My Best Friend's Wedding, The Sixth Sense, Forrest Gump,* and *There's Something about Mary* are all examples of the 'sleeper' hit, surprising when you consider that those six features feature the collective 'name' value of Tom Hanks, Meg Ryan, Julia Roberts, Cameron Diaz, and Bruce Willis. They are films which are strategically marketed so that audience can 'discover' them, as opposed to feeling obliged to catch the latest 'must-see' event movie. Such infiltration of the conscious of cinemagoers is achieved by 'sneak' previews of the film a few weeks prior to release. This therefore qualifies the 'sleeper' as an alternative marketing strategy.

Screenings are usually held in an area chosen to capture the right demographic, which in the case of a romantic-comedy such as *Sleepless in Seattle* would mean suburban malls where couples in their mid-twenties and early-thirties will spend much of a Saturday afternoon before checking out a new movie. If the screening proves successful, the couple will then go into their work places on Monday and talk to their co-workers about the unexpectedly great little movie that they saw at the weekend, generating interest through word of mouth. Releasing a 'sleeper' alongside a bigger picture can prove to be a lucrative move, in that cinemagoers unable to obtain tickets for the more overtly publicized picture due to demand, will instead see the 'sleeper' and boost its box office. In 1999, the Hugh Grant-Julia Roberts romance *Notting Hill* opened alongside *Star Wars: The Phantom Menace* and attracted an audience that was either unable to see the George Lucas juggernaut on its opening weekend or had little interest in galaxies far, far away.

Below is a graph based upon the box office performance of *There's Something about Mary*. Released in the summer of 1998, the film was promoted by Twentieth Century Fox, but not to the same extent as the 'blockbuster' films of that period.

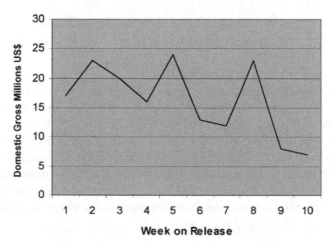

Week on Release

As the graph shows, *There's Something about Mary* opened solidly, but not spectacularly, with $17 million, failing to capture the number one spot for its first weekend, but benefiting from good word of mouth and an ongoing advertising campaign by the studio. The film eventually grossed $177, which meant that its opening weekend accounted for only 9 per cent of its final take at the domestic box office take. As a 'sleeper', the audience for *There's Something about Mary* was gradually courted and expanded over several months of general release. This is actually similar to the box office pattern of many independent films, but at a greater scale of revenue. Although *There's Something about Mary* had an opening weekend that would be considered modest for a studio picture during the summer season, it still opened on 2186 screens and grossed more money in its first three days than most independent features manage in their entire theatrical release.

3.9 Faith in the Formula – A Summary of Modern Hollywood Cinema
As in all capitalist enterprise, Hollywood cinema is driven by a desire for profit and an awareness of a market that can yield such profit should it be properly exploited. Hollywood's enduring success has come about by solidifying the base of its enterprises through the combined dominance of real estate and technology, achieving ownership of sites of exhibition that correlate with other consumerist activities, and actively supporting new advances in software and hardware. Hollywood cinema, as a business, strives to eliminate uncertainty, and therefore novelty. As Bourdieu states,

> The field of large scale production, whose submission to external demand is characterized by the subordinate position of cultural producers in relation to the controllers of production and diffusion of media, principally obeys the imperatives of competition for the conquest of the market. The structure of its socially neautralized product is the result of the economic and social conditions of its production.[13]

This is to say that visionary film-makers have little room to manoeuvre in the Hollywood system, where the money men, and their advisors, ultimately dictate the types of films that will be produced. By seeking to appeal to a mass audience, the films that are developed, produced, and distributed by modern Hollywood are free from socially radical impulse, and rarely possess much intellectual stimulation, even when they exhibit a pervading air of conservatism. Potentially controversial elements, notably sex and violence, are included as a means of attracting adult audiences, but the overriding moral scheme is one that condemns social practises of a destructive nature. The manipulative nature of Hollywood's product is reflected in the social manner in which it is consumed. Big 'event' films such as *The Day After Tomorrow* and *The Hulk* open loudly, their marketing fanfare and global releases encouraging a stampede to the box office as consumers line around the block for their weekend popcorn fix. 'Sleeper' successes like *Sleepless in Seattle* and *There's Something about Mary* are marketed as such, their word-of-mouth success a result of more gradual release and patterns of promotion. However, both breeds of Hollywood features are amenable to existing popular sentiment.

How an audience is 'sold' a Hollywood picture, or how many screens it opens on, or how much money it makes in its third weekend as opposed to its first, is unimportant, providing that the picture itself performs the social need of satisfying an audience, and the economic function of turning a profit for its investors. Audiences have any insatiable appetite for escapism, and Hollywood has the product that they desire. However, what is important is the increasingly corporate nature of the films themselves, the reliance on the star as brand or genre, the perceived need to impress the audience with expensive pyrotechnics, rather than to inspire and educate through sustained storytelling and political perspective.

Within the current Hollywood system, original ideas are largely rendered stillborn, or are watered down throughout endless development meetings, re-writes, casting sessions, re-shoots, test-screenings, and marketing campaigns. If the best films from the independent sector reveal something about the world today, and the views of their creators on society at large, the most commercially successful films from the Hollywood system are more telling of their industrial origins and reflective of American popular sentiment.

Notes

1. Garnham, p. 176, 1990.
2. Hall, S, 'Tall Revenue Features: The Genealogy of the Modern Blockbuster', *Genre and Contemporary Hollywood* (editor Neale, S), 1st edn, p. 11, London, BFI, 2002.
3. Acheson, K, Maule, J, 'Understanding Hollywood's Organization and Continuing Success', *Journal of Cultural Economics*, 18 (1994), p. 282.
4. Wasko, p. 170, 2003.
5. Bach, D, quoted by Fleming, C, *High Concept – Don Simpson and the Hollywood Culture of Excess*, 2nd edn, p. 53, London, Bloomsbury, 1998.
6. De Vany, A, Walls, DW, 'Uncertainty in the Movie Industry: Does Star Power Reduce the Terror of the Box Office?', *Journal of Cultural Economics*, 23 (1999), p. 285.
7. Gilliam, T, interviewed by Christie, I (editor), *Gilliam on Gilliam*, 1st edn, p. 234, London, Faber & Faber, 1999.
8. Dyer, R, *Stars (Second Edition)*, 2nd edn, p. 34, London, BFI, 1998.
9. Kerr, CE, 'Incorporating the Star: The Intersection of Business and Aesthetic Strategies in Early American Film', *The Business History Review*, 64:3 (autumn 1990), p. 409.
10. Gilliam, T, interviewed by Christie, p. 221, 1999.
11. Haley, Stuart, & Co, *The Motion Picture Industry as a Basic for Bond Financing*, 27th May 1927.
12. De Vany, & Walls, p. 286, 1999.
13. Bourdieu, p. 125, 1993.

4

OPPOSITIONAL FANTASIES: THE ECONOMIC STRUCTURE OF AMERICAN INDEPENDENT CINEMA AND ITS ESSENTIAL LINEAMENTS

Existing somewhere between a method of physical production and a form of popular thinking, American independent cinema is a term that is open to interpretation and discussion. Critics, cinephiles, industry-affiliates and even film-makers themselves rarely agree, with some favouring a definition-based financial background and others basing their assessment on the more elusive 'independent spirit', the notion that work undertaken within the system of mass production can be recognized as 'independent' through its social-political leanings and aesthetic approach. This chapter will seek to provide some means of categorizing American independent cinema, at least in relation to its Hollywood studio counterpart, by analysing its output in terms of narrative and aesthetic approach, and its emphasis on character psychology. In addition, to support the argument that independent cinema is as much a reference to a form of production as it is a description of a certain conceptual type of film, it will be necessary to outline the process by which such films are developed, filmed, and distributed, emphasizing their logistical similarities and differences to their Hollywood equivalents.

4.1 Alternative Hollywood – American Independent Cinema as an Industry of Cultural Production

Within Bourdieu's cultural construct, American independent cinema is the field of restricted production, an artistically heightened, if economically subservient, means of artistic expression which finds limited consumption when made available to the mass public. Bourdieu regards the field of restricted production as being in direct opposite to the field of large-scale production, to such an extent that the field defines itself through a rejection of the audience that is catered for by its more economically powerful rival. As Bourdieu claims,

> The field of restricted production can only become a system objectively producing for producers by breaking with the public of non-producers, that is, with the non-intellectual fraction of the dominant class.[1]

This would be to say that American independent cinema can only claim autonomous status by alienating a large portion of the cinema-going public and producing work for an audience of intellectuals, cinephiles, academics, and individuals who are themselves engaged in artistic endeavours. However, such a definition of American independent cinema would avoid any discussion of the ambiguities of its social-economic practices, and the economic necessities of sustaining any form of production. While many independent productions are completed on budgets which may appear limited in comparison to those of Hollywood films, they still require additional distribution and marketing expenses, costs that can only be recouped by appealing to the mass public. Hollywood has an interest in independent cinema, both economically and creatively, and this existence of this interest is enough to show that independent cinema is not that far removed from the cultural mainstream.

If Hollywood, as the field of large-scale production, is as far removed from the sensibilities of the field of restricted production as Bourdieu claims, then it would be unlikely that the corporate mainstream would have any interest in its more esoteric counterpart. This, however, is not the case. As Garnham observes,

> As is the case in other sectors of the culture industry, the leading firms maintain a dominating, but necessary and valuable relationship with a large number of fragmented so-called 'independents' in both production and distribution. Not only do these myriad 'pilot fish' give the industry an appearance of diversity and competition, thus helping at least to mitigate public concern and pressure against oligopolistic control, but they also fulfil a valuable economic function by attracting risk capital and creative talent which the majors can then exploit through their control of distribution. The independent but junior section fulfils the vital function of research and development, the overheads of which the majors thus do not have to bear.[2]

Some directors, writers, actors, and producers have used the independent sector as a means of demonstrating their talents to secure more lucrative employment within Hollywood. This can be achieved through the successful navigation of the network of the independent sector, an area of production which, in spite of its supposed rejection of the Hollywood system, comes with its own hierarchy of producers, financiers, distributors, actors, directors, agents, and festivals. While some of the creative talent involved in American independent cinema, such as directors Jim Jarmusch and Abel Ferrara, may shrug off the corporate structure of the sector with studied nonchalance, the economic benefactors of their work are more than aware of the necessity of industrial structure, hence the adoption of a Hollywood methodology. Without some semblance of business plan, and an awareness of markets both established and untapped, the independent sector at large would be unable to sustain itself economically, either from its own profits, or the subsidies which are afforded it by major corporations. However, the reliance on genuine talent as opposed to massive budgets, allows film-maker operating within the sector more leeway than their studio counterparts, and this can produce original, and sometimes commercially successful, films that the studios attempt to emulate. As Merritt notes,

> The off-Hollywood arena is American cinema's laboratory, proving ground, and launching pad. It's also its sideshow, filled with burlesque queens and bloodthirsty geeks. Over and over again non-studio motion pictures have blazed a successful path that Hollywood has then followed, sometimes paving it over with a superhighway. Other times, the major studios decide, perhaps wisely, not to venture down that trail at all. In all but big-budget scenarios, independent movies lead the way.[3]

This ties in with Garnham's notion of independent cinema as an unofficial extension of Hollywood's research and development division as the sector is free to experiment since its audience is so interested in novelty. Merritt sees independent cinema as an area of cultural production for the development of new ideas and talent that can later be employed by the studio system, but also as a sector that exists parallel to Hollywood, daring to make films that the studios would never consider to be economically viable, or in alignment with its own social-political ethos.

In economic terms, the description 'independent cinema' implies a film that is made outside the studio system, or at least on its industrial margins. Budgets within the sector are much like those within the Hollywood in that they are as large as the subject matter is commercial. Therefore, the romantic-comedy *My Big Fat Greek Wedding*, a broad send-up of Greek family rituals, was budgeted at $5 million, whereas the drama *Slingblade*, which concerned a mentally retarded man re-entering society, was completed for $1.2 million. In contrast to Bourdieu's view, the field of restricted production does *not* break with the field of large-scale production, and even uses a similar economic theory when allocating funding. Subject matter is important, as is the presence of 'name' actors and a director with a track record of films. Many films made within the independent sector are commercial films and could be regarded as 'Hollywood' films were it not for the economic circumstances of their production. Independent cinema is not opposed to genre films, with such categories as action, horror, romantic-comedy, and science fiction being covered, albeit on a different scale, often with an emphasis on character and drama to offset the absence of visual spectacle. While independent film-makers often take inspiration for financing their first and second features from earlier non-studio success stories, it is often the Hollywood cinema that provides them with their storytelling models, although these models are usually adopted in order to work with more limited economic means.

It is at this juncture that serious debate arises about what constitutes an independent feature film, as the economic background of a motion picture and its cultural content and commercial aspirations can be wildly divergent. It can be argued that the term 'independent cinema' is used too broadly, as its economic reality encompasses more than feature films that are regarded as 'independent' because of their cultural content. In the late 1980s and early 1990s the production company Carolco was operating on the same budgetary level as the Hollywood majors, pre-selling the domestic and foreign distribution rights to its future productions as a means of securing financing. Carolco produced *Rambo III* in 1988 for $65 million, *Total Recall* in 1990 for $75 million, and *Terminator 2: Judgement Day* in 1991 for $100 million. A look at these titles makes it difficult to regard Carolco as an independent in terms of content, as it produced big-budget genre films, often sequels to earlier hits and featuring expensive stars like Arnold Schwarzenegger and Sylvester Stallone, particularly beneficial in lucrative foreign markets where a lack of understanding of the English language is not a cultural barrier to enjoying mindless spectacle.

The sector is also responsible for producing hundreds of similar films every year on what the industry terms a 'B' scale, meaning genre pictures that are as low in budget as they are in cultural value. Budgeted between $1 and $5 million, the 'B' film industry is the modern equivalent of the 'poverty row' productions of the 1940s, and like that era, the modern 'B' films come with their own network of stars, producers, and directors. From an economic point of view, 'B' movies are independent films in that they are made outside of the major Hollywood studios. Most are shot with the small screen in mind, devoid of any cinematic flair, and edited to tight 90-minute lengths which will make them ideal 'fillers' for late-night cable television. In terms of discovering new audiences, 'B' movies have little use because they court the same market as the Hollywood studios, the difference being that their efforts do not challenge the studios for theatre space, instead carving out a portion of the ancillary market. Therefore, the content of most 'B' cinema is not independent in that it is mostly imitative of expensive Hollywood features – cops track serial killers, teenagers are stalked by maniacs, houses are haunted, and everything is wrapped up before the end credits, although there is often the vague promise, or threat, of a sequel. In this sense, 'B' films are dependent on the popular market that is cultivated by the studios. This market has an insatiable appetite for 'more of the same' and is ably exploited by 'B' movie producers, who offer their own inexpensive imitations, although their concessions to character, motivation, and cultural context are often on a par with their big-budget models.

Independent cinema could then be considered to be a form of production which is free of both the economic and cultural practices of the Hollywood studios. It could be said to be self-defining, imposing its own set of rules and values. Bourdieu insists that

> The autonomy of a field of restricted production can be measured by its power to define its own criteria for the production and evaluation of its products...Thus, the more cultural producers form a closed field of competition for cultural legitimacy, the more the internal demarcations appear irreducible to any external factors of economic, political or social differentiation.[4]

If Bourdieu's analysis of the field of restricted production indicates anything, it is that American independent cinema is not restricted at all, and that it is not autonomous from the industry of mass production. Within industry sectors, and in certain environments such as film festivals, there may be criteria for evaluating the output of American independent cinema, but as film is a popular art form, it is ultimately consumed by the mass audience and, therefore, evaluated in the same way as Hollywood product. This is one of the great challenges of the independent film-maker, to make a movie with limited resources that exhibits great artistry and can play alongside Hollywood features without attracting criticism for its budgetary shortcomings, instead succeeding because of its characters, storytelling, and overall cultural impact, the same attributes which are required of studio offerings.

This leads to the matter of competition. In commercial terms, cinema is extremely competitive, as film-makers vie for the attentions of audiences. However, preferences are fragmented due to the diversity of subject matter covered. With their eccentric approach to the action genre, Quentin Tarantino and Robert Rodriguez could be considered to be independent film-makers competing for the same audience. However, Greg Araki and Todd Haynes are also independent film-makers, but their studies of gender issues and social alienation are far removed from the comic book escapades of Tarantino and Rodriguez, and likely to appeal to a different segment of the crowd. As Tarantino and Rodriguez make films that offer visceral thrills, their work is more likely to achieve a 'crossover' effect and play to an audience that also enjoys studio productions, while Araki and Haynes are unlikely to breakthrough, leaving them with a small but loyal and appreciative group of art house patrons and individuals with a specific interest in the issues that their films discuss.

However, this is not always the view of financiers and distributors, whose level of expectation for commercial success has been adjusted following the box office performance of *Sex, Lies, and Videotape* and *Pulp Fiction*. Independent features that turn a profit of a few million dollars are no longer appealing to distributors, certainly not those that are affiliated with the Hollywood studios, and this has given rise to the 'independent blockbuster', low-budget movies that function in the art house in a similar manner to how big-budget movies function in the multiplex in that one or two titles prove extremely popular, monopolizing screens and driving out the competition.

In the early 1980s, there appeared to be a commercial 'ceiling' on the independent sector, a 'ceiling' that was high enough for certain distributors and exhibitors to take risks on the sector's output, but too low for the Hollywood majors to show much enthusiasm. Eventually, however, there were breakthrough successes. Oliver Stone's 1986 Vietnam drama *Platoon* was turned down by all the Hollywood studios and produced by Hemdale, an independent company based in London, with a complicated foreign financing structure. Budgeted at $6.5 million, a low amount considering that the film was to be shot in a jungle overseas, the film won five Oscars including Best Picture and Best Director, making it one of the most celebrated pictures of the year.

More importantly, it grossed $100 million domestically, and also proved successful in foreign markets. Other independent productions, such as *Kiss of the Spider Woman* and *The Trip to Bountiful* also proved popular choices at the box office, providing the independent sector with 'crossover' success. These films had appealed to audiences outside of the cinephile set who would usually view studio productions.

As more non-studio features enjoyed box office success, as well as critical acclaim, it became apparent that a 'new' independent cinema was emerging, one that was not in opposition to the Hollywood mainstream, but one that was catering towards an audience that the majors had cultivated, and then neglected. In pursuit of $100 million hits with product tie-ins, Hollywood had largely forgotten about the middle-aged, adult audience that had been the prime consumer of serious dramas and prestige pieces, films that could not be developed in a studio system that was fixated on brand recognition. It was at this stage that the studios began looking to the independent sector to purchase the kind of films that they were no longer developing themselves.

Today's independent cinema is able to explore characters and themes that the studio system shies away from through fear of alienating a mass audience. Social outsiders and people dealing with economic deprivation are recurrent characters and violence and sexual deviance that was implied in the 'B' movies of the 1940s has been allowed to run riot in a modern independent cinema which can operate free of the censorship code. This applies not only to films that conform to genres such as thriller, or horror, or the crime film, but also to domestic dramas wherein topics such as infidelity, homosexuality, and abuse can be discussed. It is also a continuation of the alternative cinema of the late 1960s and early 1970s, in that it is more freewheeling in terms of its visual sensibility, often employing non-linear visual language to guide viewers through sub-cultures that the Hollywood mainstream is reluctant to explore.

The classification of a film as 'independent' based on its 'independence of spirit' is much like the 'auteur' theory, which was devised by French film critics in the 1950s to refer to films made by a directors of singular vision, thereby implying that the director is the sole 'author' of the feature. It is an appropriate way of describing American independent features from directors of unique visual sensibility, especially when thematic concerns can also be traced through their bodies of work. However, such a definition is blind to the economic structure of the industry, which requires directors seeking finance for projects of a certain scale and scope to work within the studio system. As this definition is culturally based, it allows films to be classed as 'independent' even when they have been bankrolled by Hollywood studios.

There are directors, such as Hal Hartley, Jim Jarmusch, Abel Ferrara, and John Sayles who have worked constantly in the independent sector, rarely making films that rely on Hollywood studios for financing or distribution. However, there are also directors of singular vision who have alternated between studio and independent projects, releasing films that show little or no sign of compromise. This particular category of film-makers would include Oliver Stone, Martin Scorsese, Spike Lee, Steven Soderbergh, and Paul Thomas Anderson. Their films are independent of spirit because their personal imprint is so distinct, yet these film-makers have worked within the Hollywood mainstream by finding finance and distribution from the studio system.

From an economic perspective, a truly independent film-maker would be one who finances his or her own work, retaining complete control of the project, even through to the marketing and distribution of the film. Modern cinema has thrown up a number of examples of films that have been truly independent in terms of financing, but the financial demands placed upon any individual who tries to promote and distribute their finished feature are so great that, at this stage, it is often necessary for a larger film company to step in. This makes it difficult to classify a film as 'independent' based solely on its financial history, especially when the deals that take place to ensure distribution and promotion of a feature film entail that the larger company will be taking a substantial cut of any profits generated from the film's cinema release and such markets as video, pay-per-view, and network television.

In 1991, the then 22-year-old Mexican director Robert Rodriguez embarked on a project entitled *El Mariachi*, an action-adventure film about a wandering musician who finds himself mistaken for an assassin and targeted by a local gangster. Originally intended for the Spanish-language video market, *El Mariachi* was bought by Columbia Pictures and released to critical acclaim in 1992. To promote Rodriguez's first feature, the marketing department decided to focus on his 'rags to riches' story by making sure that everyone from critics to ticket buyers knew that this movie had been made for 'just' $7,000, with Rodriguez making appearances at film festivals and on television talk shows to cheerfully explain how he had financed his movie by taking part in shady medical experiments at a Mexican drug clinic.

While *El Mariachi* may be lacking the production value or star power of a studio action film, it is still a vibrant, amusing, occasionally exciting yarn, which manages to pack such ingredients for mainstream success as action, romance, music, and humour into its trim 73-minute running time. As this was produced for $7,000 in an era when the average Hollywood action movie was costing $50 million, it has to be asked why Rodriguez could not have been completely independent and promoted and distributed the movie himself, putting all of the profits into his next venture. Although $7,000 was the cost of producing the film and editing it to the state in which Rodriguez submitted it to Columbia, the version of *El Mariachi* that became a favourite on the festival circuit almost a year later cost around $5 million, as costly work was required to transfer the movie from the video format on which it was shot, to the film format required for theatres, not to mention a new sound mix and, perhaps most importantly, the cost of marketing a theatrical feature all around the world. This is not to say that *El Mariachi* cannot be classed as an 'independent' movie, but it is to say that the definition of independent cinema as being financed outside the studio system is only valid with regard to the production process.

Modern American independent cinema exists somewhere between the two definitions offered. It is independent of 'spirit' in that it deals with subject matter that the Hollywood mainstream ignores and accommodates films that are not conventionally structured or reliant on star power. However, much of its output is inherently generic and star casting and marketability can also play a crucial role. Hillier encompasses a number of views on the sector when he claims that

> Independent cinema today is doing what it always did – offering films made on modest budgets with potential for considerable success reinvigorating narrative and generic conventions and providing a source of new filmmakers, some of whom are only to ready to graduate to dependency.[5]

Hillier's description serves to underscore some of the contradictions of the American independent sector. Budgets are modest but not minimal. Films that are labelled 'independent' regularly cost $5 to $15 million. In addition, their potential for success is also indicative of commercial considerations concerning subject matter, genre, and casting. The conventions that such films serve to reinvigorate are often those of the studio system, with Hollywood popularizing techniques that have been developed in the independent sector. However, for all the 'independent' films that are actually produced by speciality divisions of Hollywood studios, there are still a large number of features that are made free of influence from the corporate giants, and it is necessary to look at the production process of such films.

4.2 Ten Stages of Independence – Making American Independent Feature Films

The process of making and releasing an independent feature can be broken down into the following ten stages:

1. A screenwriter, also potentially a director, identifies and conceptualizes a movement of popular feeling, or a genre that has been neglected by the Hollywood mainstream, and completes their screenplay.
2. Finance/Casting is arranged.
3. Shooting commences.
4. Film enters post-production.
5. Festival engagements.
6. Film acquires a distributor.
7. Further festival engagements and screenings for key critics who are known to favour independent features, and whose reviews carry influence.
8. Platform release – Theatrical run on a limited number of screens.
9. Wide release – Theatrical expansion, if platform release has proved successful and critics have been supportive.
10. Ancillary markets – DVD, cable television, pay-per-view, video-on-demand.

The process within the independent sector is often more organic in that the screenplay will be written without any input from a corporate representative. In the studio world, projects are usually 'pitched' by writers to studio executives based on a treatment, with the screenplay yet to be written. Therefore, corporate response to an artistic idea has already taken effect. The independent screenwriter, however, works more freely, following his ideas, thoughts, and themes intuitively, without external interference. Certain factors are often taken into account, however. Most screenwriters are aware of the workings of the industry, and whether their project is likely to be an 'independent' or 'studio' production. Therefore, a screenwriter who believes that his project will be set up as an 'independent' may acknowledge that it will have to be produced on a low budget and consider matters of production value whilst developing his screenplay. This means that such elements of action, special effects, and famous locations will be downplayed or omitted. The screenplay will probably rely more on strong characterization and dialogue than action, although some screenwriters know that such factors are crucial in attracting 'name' actors to an independent project, where they may earn considerably less money than on a studio assignment, but be given the opportunity to play a role with greater depth and complexity.

The developments that follow from the completion of a screenplay to the securing of financing are less finely tuned in the independent sector than in the studio system. While the Hollywood studios have a network that can be traced by job titles and box office statistics, the independent community is comparatively ramshackle in its construction, with a number of sources of economic and cultural power, such as established production and distribution companies and 'name' actors and directors, being shadowed and intercepted by fringe players, such as actors and directors with several notable credits but no commercial guarantees, or private financiers who have a business interest in film production that can be at odds with the sector's rhetoric.

Within the independent sector the studio system is still a dominant force and is acknowledged as such by producers who will initially approach the majors with material as such an economic arrangement would take care of marketing and distribution. However, it is rare for the studios to take on independently generated projects at an early stage, preferring to purchase films when they are in production or fully completed. Therefore, most producers have to turn to independent sources of finance. Projects that are considered to be 'difficult' will often be sent to actors before financiers, as the attachment of a 'star' will ease the commercial concerns of the money men. For instance, Nick Nolte was attached to star in Paul Schrader's *Affliction* six years before the film began principal photography, with the actor's commitment to the project being used to 'sell' the film to potential backers.

After financing and casting have been secured, shooting commences. Production on independent features is more ad hoc by nature, with directors having to adapt to changes in their environment and incorporate them into the film. In some cases, production takes a lot longer than on a Hollywood film, as many of the cast and crew will be working on the picture as a 'labour of love', taking little pay and fitting the project around their other commitments. Most independent features are shot on location, as sets and soundstages are out of budgetary grasp. As a means of controlling the environment, many are designed at script stage to be logistically manageable. *Reservoir Dogs*, *Clerks*, *Go Fish*, and *Cube* all take place in a few locations, usually indoors so that shooting is not affected by weather or light changes.

Post-production can also be a lengthy process. While studio features have to meet a 'locked-in' release date and tie in with marketing materials that have already been made available to the general public, independent features are not working to such a strict schedule, although directors are now pressured to have their work ready for festivals. Many privately financed films only have sufficient funds for production, meaning that additional funds have to be sought before the film can be completed, as securing post-production facilities can be extremely costly, although the communal nature of the independent sector means that equipment can be 'borrowed' or rented at a deferred payment. It is around this stage that the most enterprising producers will submit for festivals or show 'rough cuts' directly to distributors. Festival screenings will come before general release, as most independent features require such exposure to secure a distribution deal. This does not necessarily mean that all independent features play at the most prestigious festivals. Due to the level of competition, many are reduced to playing smaller festivals or 'film markets'. After acquiring a distributor, some independent films will play at more festivals, picking up media coverage and critical kudos that can be incorporated into their marketing strategies.

The majority of independent features that secure a theatrical run are initially granted a 'platform release'. This means that they play limited engagements in select cinemas in particular cities. This small-scale release secures the film some media attention and reviews from critics without the distributor having the expense of a nationwide opening. If results are encouraging, the distributor will expand the film into other urban areas and more suburban venues. How 'wide' the film goes from there is a result of how confident the distributor is in the film's ability to 'crossover' and attract a more mainstream crowd. Although many independent feature films have proved to be popular choices at 'art house' venues, distributors have been reluctant to expand their release because they have believed the film to have reached its audience already. Shortly after theatrical release, independent films follow their studio counterparts into the ancillary markets. Given their niche appeal, independent films rarely 'spin off' into related mediums in the way that studio features do, so they do not present many merchandising opportunities although soundtrack albums are often made available.

4.3 Alternative Perceptions – Narrative and Character

The narrative form of American independent cinema is not unlike that of Hollywood in terms of the types of stories that it tells, but it is distinctive in terms of the scale and structures that are employed to tell them and, most importantly, in their approach to character. Hollywood films conform to a linear narrative structure, taking the audience from the beginning to the end of the story in systematic fashion. Independent cinema is more flexible in terms of narrative form, sometimes because the character-driven stories that it tells are reliant on overlapping plot strands and attention to detail rather than extraordinary events. The following case studies exemplify the difference between independent and Hollywood cinema through narrative and thematic analysis, and reference to the moral economy of the non-studio sector.

Case Study 1: Drugstore Cowboy (1989)

Synopsis – Bob (Matt Dillon) and Diane (Kelly Lynch) are heroin-addicts who travel the Pacific Northwest with a crew of fellow junkies, preparing and conducting raids on pharmacies as a means of sustaining their habit. A well-known operator in his area, Bob has to avoid the attentions of the local police, a difficult matter when one of his group overdoses in a motel, and the body has to be disposed of. Taking the death as a 'sign', Bob decides to check into a rehabilitation programme and go 'cold turkey', before finding a regular job and becoming a law-abiding member of society, although the reappearance of his wife and former associates complicates matters.

Analysis – The title of *Drugstore Cowboy* has superficial similarities to *Easy Rider* in that it suggests romanticism, implying that the junkie is the last outlaw of modern society, but it also states that this outlaw is fuelled by chemicals, and that such a lifestyle is far removed from that of the travellers of the Old West. The episodic narrative focuses on a band of social outsiders and their travels across the American landscape, but to describe the film as a 'road' movie is somewhat contradictory as these characters travel within a restrictive area, unwilling to move far away from the terrain of Portland, Oregon that they know so well, while their narcotic dependencies prevent them straying too far from pharmacies and low-rent motels. Whereas Hollywood cinema focuses on individuals, people of great nobility or extreme evil, and how those individuals bring about environmental change, independent cinema works form the environment itself to show how individuals and social groups are products of the world they inhabit.

Gus Van Sant's film suggests the drug problem in the United States is not the pervading evil that it is portrayed as in Hollywood cinema. The director locates the problem within social structure and works from that to explore the workings of an urban underbelly with its own networks of supply and demand. This informs the narrative of the film, the first half of which revolves around a series of scores, as Bob and his gang alternate planning and committing robberies with getting high and functioning as a surrogate family. Sudden bursts of activity, either through criminal acts or narcotic consumption, are juxtaposed with periods of inactivity, as the gang kill time between robberies or recover from a drugs binge. The second half follows the attempt made by Bob to clean up as he takes a low-paying factory job, with Van Sant once again emphasizing the routine nature of human existence, but one that is without illicit thrills. While a Hollywood film would build gradually, Van Sant prefers to open the film with a daring robbery, and following a group of people who are already deeply addicted to both drugs and the lifestyle which comes with them. This enables the audience to better understand Bob's heroin withdrawal when he suddenly decides to quit, and to appreciate the comparative calm of his law-abiding new life.

Drugstore Cowboy concludes with its central character at a crossroads as a climactic robbery on Bob's apartment leaves him wounded and heading for the hospital. In the closing voice-over, Bob comments on all the 'free' substances which will be 'available' whilst he is receiving treatment, referencing an earlier sequence in which he steals morphine from a hospital whilst desperate for a fix. Van Sant's film does not show Bob returning to a life of drug abuse, nor does his character's voice overtly state that he intends to do so, but it does leave the audience with the possibility. Of course, it is also possible that his narration is only pointing out the irony of taking a reformed junkie to a medical facility that holds many of his former drugs of choice. Such ambiguity in the closing frames of an independent film is typical of a cinema which encourages, and thrives upon, audience discussion.

Case Study 2: Memento (2000)

Synopsis – Lenny (Guy Pearce) is an insurance investigator whose memory has been damaged following a head injury he sustained during a home break-in, a robbery which also resulted in the murder of his wife. He now lives in fifteen-minute periods, incapable of forming new memories, and he tattoos notes on his body, takes photos, and writes notes as a means of sustaining knowledge of himself and his environment. Seeking revenge, Lenny travels the country, assisted by a suspicious ex-cop (Joe Pantaliano), following leads that may not be reliable. Living out of a low-rent motel, Lenny believes he may have found the killer, but his condition makes him susceptible to those around him, such as a waitress (Carrie Anne Moss) who may be manipulating him for her own ends. The film alternates between Lenny's quest and an extended telephone conversation in which he refers to an old insurance case as a means of explaining his condition and his methods for recording information.

Analysis – *Memento* offers the same 'revenge' scenario as a number of Hollywood thrillers. However, it is distinct in that the events of the story are played backwards, revealing the twists and turns of the plot through a reverse structure. Other revenge stories start with the hero suffering a loss, and then proceed to show how he tracks down the responsible party, but *Memento* instead opens with the hero taking revenge, and then runs backwards to show the investigation that brought him there. While the narratives of Hollywood cinema appear to be the primary concern, with the characters being secondary to the situations that they find themselves in, the narrative of independent cinema exists on the same level of importance as character, with one feeding the other. With the audience seeing the events of the *Memento* through Lenny's eyes, his internal narrative becomes the external narrative of the film, with the audience reliant on Lenny's instinctive responses and personal discoveries to take them to the next level of narrative experience.

Lenny is a character of independent cinema in that he is ultimately not a moral crusader, but instead revealed to be a social threat. He also has none of the 'special powers' that Hollywood cinema grants people with mental or physical disorders, such as the numeric abilities of Dustin Hoffman's autistic Raymond in *Rain Man* that will eventually rescue his brother's troubled business. *Memento* goes to great lengths to show Lenny's system for dealing with his inability to form new memories. While a Hollywood film would show how these ingenious methods ultimately enable Lenny to overcome his condition and catch the killer, *Memento* instead reveals them to be unreliable, mere notes, the meanings of which can change when taken in a different context. At the conclusion of the film, or its beginning if analysed in 'real time', Lenny is revealed to be the villain, as he is in fact inventing new 'killers' to be tracked down in order to deal with the fact that he no longer has any purpose in the world.

Lenny is cross-motivated, in that he is trying to find his wife's killer and also maintain a reason for his existence. This contrasts with the vengeance seekers in Hollywood features such as *Death Wish*, *Hard to Kill*, or *Collateral Damage*, all films that offer protagonists for whom revenge is the sole motivational factor. While *Death Wish* uses the revenge scenario as a vehicle for white male fantasy by showing how an ordinary civilian can take action against anti-social forces, *Memento* is more of a white male nightmare in that it presents a character whose actions cannot compensate for the loss of the person he cared for, and whose mental condition has forced him to the fringes of society. The vigilante portrayed by Charles Bronson in *Death Wish* takes control of every situation he finds himself in, but Lenny lacks such control because his condition leaves him open to manipulation at the hands of those around him, such as the motel clerk who is charging Lenny for renting three different rooms because he knows that Lenny cannot remember checking into any of them. While the characters in Hollywood films can put the world to rights and rebuild their shattered lives, Lenny is unable to move beyond the events that have abruptly altered his existence.

Case Study 3: Lord of War (2005)

Synopsis – In the early 1980s, Yuri Orlov (Nicolas Cage) is a Russian immigrant growing up in Little Odessa, working at his parent's café. Aspiring to lead a prosperous life, Yuri begins selling guns to the mobsters in his neighbourhood, and by the 1990s he has parlayed his connections into becoming an arms dealer. He solidifies his position when the cold war ends and factories full of abandoned weaponry become available to the highest bidder. An African warlord makes contact with Yuri and become his biggest client, but Yuri's frequent trips to lawless territory threaten to unearth a long-buried conscience. Whilst dealing with his inner turmoil Yuri must balance his family life, which involves a wife and son who believe he is a legitimate businessman, whilst also evading idealistic F.B.I. agent Jack Valentine (Ethan Hawke), who is determined to put him behind bars.

Analysis – Andrew Nicol's *Lord of War* is a rare case of an independent feature made on the same scale as a Hollywood production. With its $42 million budget, locations in South Africa, the Czech Republic, and New York, and a major leading man in Nicolas Cage, the film has many of the key attributes of a studio picture, and even adopts the 'rise-and-fall' narrative arch of every gangster drama from *White Heat* to *Carlito's Way*. However, inter-textual analysis of *Lord of War* reveals it to be a fiercely independent picture in stylish studio clothing. In order to bring *Lord of War* to the screen, Nicol buried himself in research for several years, to make sure that the film was authentic in its depiction of the arms trade.

While many Hollywood films are based on true stories, they are rarely made when a situation is at its most politically contentious point. It took a long time for Vietnam films to emerge from the system, and those that Hollywood chose to produce took a humanist approach, bemoaning the loss of life, yet avoiding direct criticism of the US government. *Lord of War* at times feels like a cinematic *Newsweek* article, plunging the audience into the world of gunrunning, with its industrial hierarchies and moral quagmires. Its 'insider' approach keeps didacticism at bay, even when the events depicted would seem to be ample fuel for the anti-gun lobby.

Rather than presenting a general overview of the subject and a one-note moral message, *Lord of War* adopts Yuri's point of view and engages the audience in an ethical debate. The opening credits sequence follows the 'life' of a bullet, as it is manufactured, transported, and inserted into a gun, then mercilessly fired into the skull of a child. The film then steps back from the battlefield to show the workings of the arms business, with Yuri arguing that the trade is like any other industry, with its products, suppliers, buyers, trends, and turnarounds. Having placed the audience at one side of the debate, with the unforgivable killing of a child, Yuri engages in a two-hour rebuttal, presenting his case for the arms trade in voice-overs that compare guns to other lethal products such as tobacco and alcohol, and claim that combat and death are a causal necessity. There are points in the narrative, such as when Yuri witnesses carnage in Africa, or objects to his son playing with a toy gun, and causes the death of his brother, that he threatens to have a change of heart, but he always rationalizes his 'purpose' in the world and adopts the stance that 'business is business'.

Lord of War has many of the commercially identifiable attributes, and narrative characteristics, of a Hollywood 'event' movie. Every scene advances character and plot, there is suspense and dark humour, action and drama, romance and tragedy, all played out within a globe-hopping narrative with a major star at its centre. However, *Lord of War* is an independent picture in that it subverts all of these Hollywood attributes to seduce its audience into an unpleasant environment, maintaining interest in a potentially repellent character and his morally bankrupt but economically rewarding enterprises. Its final scenes are also critical of the US government in that Yuri is apprehended by Valentine, but allowed to walk away free and resume his business, because his playing a crucial role in the country's biggest business.

Results of Case Studies – In Hollywood cinema, story is of primary importance, with characterization often appearing to have been added to deflect any criticism about a lack of 'depth'. This is why Hollywood cinema is so reliant on the stars, as the audience's familiarity with actors allows them to make assumptions about the characters they are watching based on their prior experiences of the star's work. Therefore, any character trajectory will be working in tandem with narrative trajectory. Within independent cinema, this is less common, with films being more concerned with character than narrative, or using narrative trajectory to highlight lack of character trajectory, while characters are more morally ambiguous. The romantic-comedy *My Big Fat Greek Wedding* finds its narrative in its central character, a frumpy woman from a Greek family who wants to find Mr Right and move away from her eccentric family. While this independent feature may feel like a studio picture, with its romantic pairing and a supporting cast of colourful characters who aid and impede in equal measure, it is different in that the story is driven by the desires of its characters rather than by events that are external to them. By contrast, the studio-financed romantic-comedies *Forces of Nature* and *Runaway Bride* feature characters that are brought together through freak events and professional interests respectively. The narratives then proceed because other events are inserted at key moments to keep the story moving, rather than by the character arcs of their protagonists.

The characters that populate independent cinema put its social perspective at odds with mainstream Hollywood. When an independent film explores the world of crime, it usually does so through the eyes of those who inhabit the criminal underworld, while a Hollywood film is more likely to tell its story from the perspective of those involved in law enforcement. This is not to say that independent cinema is morally flexible in its treatment of characters that break the law, as the protagonists of *Reservoir Dogs* and *Things to Do in Denver When You're Dead* mostly find their lives coming to an abrupt end as a result of their actions. Independent cinema provides an insight into the lives of people who exist on the social fringes, and in doing so suggests why such characters make choices that would be considered to be anti-social by most audience members.

4.4 Playing Against Expectation – Actors in American Independent Cinema

Within the studio system, casting is considered to be one of the keys to success. Independent cinema is similar in this respect, in that it also uses celebrity as a means of attracting interest in the movies that it produces. Casting is also of importance in that independent movies are often more character than plot driven, or at least more reliant on actors than on expensive special effects. Casting is the area in which it is perhaps most apparent as to how Hollywood cinema and independent cinema are dependent upon one another. As much as independent cinema is a breeding ground for new directors, writers, and producers, it is also very much a finishing school for actors talented enough to be cast in a feature film, but not well known enough to the general public to land a role in a major studio feature. While the production of a film is a collaborative effort, the public perception of a film is usually based on the principal players in the cast, and this is where the importance of casting comes into play.

As independent cinema is funded on budgets that range from the modest down to the shoestring, such productions cannot afford A-list acting talent, unless the talent is willing to work for scale or on a deferred salary. If such an arrangement cannot be made, independent productions are forced to take chances on either actors who are recognizable but are not enough of a box office draw to command a million dollar salary, or on an unknown actor who may well be perfect for the role, but is unfamiliar to audiences, leaving the film to get by on its own qualities without the benefit of exposure that celebrity brings. If an established star cannot be contracted, the alternative is to 'create' a star by casting someone relatively new and to use their fresh face to attract an audience looking for novelty. Once an actor from the independent sector has found a 'breakthrough' role, it is likely that he or she will be 'promoted' to Hollywood productions, at which point it will become the choice of themselves, or their agent, as to whether they continue to work in the independent field.

This is not to say that the casting relationship between Hollywood and independent cinema is one-track, with Hollywood taking the cream of the crop from the independent circuit. Established stars now take pay cuts to work on independent productions as it is now considered good business practise for actors to mix lucrative studio assignments with more artistically rewarding independent projects. Bruce Willis followed *Die Hard with a Vengeance* with a role in Tarantino's *Pulp Fiction*, while Tom Cruise and Julia Roberts stepped back from the limelight of leading roles to play as part of the ensemble casts of *Magnolia* and *Full Frontal* respectively The independent sector benefits from Hollywood star power when the actor in question finds that their career is flagging, or wants to re-position themselves with a riskier role which will change both the industry and public perception of their on-screen persona.

However, independent producers are just as ambitious as those within the studio system and will compete fiercely if there is even the slightest chance of signing a major star for a project. Lions Gate Films fired Christian Bale from the title role in *American Psycho* when a post-*Titanic* Leonardo DiCaprio expressed interest in the part, only to re-instate Bale when DiCaprio selected a different project. Therefore, the independent casting system operates much like that of the any major studio, as 'hot' actors head up every 'wish list', and those felt to have little box office pulling power are sidelined until bigger names have passed. As ever, the crucial difference between the independents and the majors is that of money. Independent producers have to deliver films on stringent budgets, meaning that they have to tempt acting talent with the quality of the material and its potential prestige. This lack of economic means also prevents independent producers from approaching actors, as they are represented by powerful agencies that will not accept offers of work unless the right figure is attached.

While independent producers revel in landing a major star, the presence of a big star in a small film does not always pay off at the box office. The cultural iconography of a star can be an asset to an independent picture, or a stumbling block for the audience, in that the public associate a particular star with a particular role. As many stars are genres in themselves, this can prove problematic, as was the case with Sylvester Stallone in *Copland*, who alienated an audience that expected an action picture, or Mel Gibson in *Million Dollar Hotel*, where the actor's presence was more prominent in the advertising campaign than it was in the film itself.

4.5 Selling the 'Spirit' – The Distribution and Marketing of Independent Cinema

Distribution deals are essentially licensing agreements, in which a completed film changes hands from its producers to its buyers, who now hold the rights to the project as a commercial property. The term for which they hold the rights can vary, with deals ranging from three to ten years or more. While producers may be able to maintain the rights to some merchandising and options to sequels or remakes, the distributor now owns the more immediately lucrative rights to theatrical, home video, and other ancillary markets. While independent distributors have often expertly marketed their products towards the art house audience, and beyond, there are many cases of low-budget features slipping through the cracks, being eclipsed by not only glossier Hollywood vehicles, but other independent feature films.

Distribution within the independent sector suffers because it is rarely the case that the creative and financial team that put together a film is actually involved in releasing it, leading to a gap between completion and distribution where momentum is lost and difficult material if often inappropriately marketed as an independent distributor tries to 'commercialize' their product through the advertising process. This partially explains the gradual shift of such film-makers as David O'Russell, Alexander Payne, and Steven Soderbergh to projects subsidized through the Hollywood majors courtesy of their 'speciality' divisions, such as Fox Searchlight, Warner Independent, and Focus. Corporate sponsorship ensures that their films will be released theatrically and later in ancillary markets and have a chance of reaching the intended audience.

The marketing of independent cinema is somewhat subtler than that of its studio counterparts, but no less calculated. It could be said that the trick of successfully marketing an independent film, is to disguise the fact that it is being marketed at all, so that the audience feels that it has 'discovered' the film and made it a success through their own good judgement. Part of this comes from what is known as 'word of mouth', with select screenings of certain films, to the right audiences in the right locations, allowing the film to be promoted through the recommendations of audience members rather than through expensive advertising campaigns.

As much as positive word of mouth is an important factor in the success of independently produced features, a strong marketing push is also essential. While audiences may have felt that they had 'discovered' *My Big Fat Greek Wedding* and *The Usual Suspects*, it must be noted that such films have benefited from sound marketing strategies. The positive word of mouth from that core audience has then spread into the mainstream, and the cultural value of the films is often enhanced by award nominations that coincide with expansions from limited release to nationwide distribution. The charts below chronicle the commercial fortunes of *Sideways* and *Lost in Translation* over the first twenty weeks of their theatrical releases.

Sideways (2004)

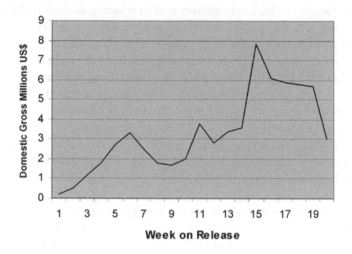

Lost in Translation (2003)

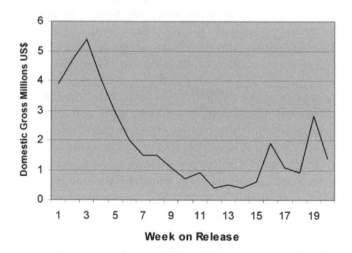

Both films opened on a small number of screens, maintaining strong attendance in carefully selected venues in major cities through critical support and low-level marketing. *Sideways* played in limited engagements for the longer period, gradually expanding its audience and maintaining a steady screen average, indicating that the film appealed to a broad spectrum of cinemagoers. After a small dip, the film experienced a second increase in attendance when it went into wide release, and a third when the Academy Award nominations were announced. It's most successful release period was actually its sixteenth week. *Lost in Translation* went into wide release earlier than *Sideways*, as distributor Focus tried to parlay its status as a critic's darling into a box office success. However, it peaked early, with its fourth week being the most successful of its run. Aside from positive word of mouth, both films benefited greatly from end-of-year release dates which tied in to the awards season.

These are textbook examples of the marketing and distribution strategy of films from the independent sector, or the 'speciality' divisions of the studios. However, there are occasions when such films stumble at the first hurdle, failing to generate audience interest, or succeed in limited engagements only to crumble when expanded into wide release. The 2000 independent feature *Girlfight* was awarded a prize at Sundance, and was purchased by Screen Gems, the art house division of Sony Pictures that has since been re-branded Sony Pictures Classics. For a film which dealt with the tough subject matter of a young Latino woman training to become a professional boxer, the marketing was surprisingly soft and shied away from the grittier aspects of the material, leaving a genuinely tough and uncompromising story stranded in the marketplace

Independent features that deal in difficult subject matter are reliant on critical goodwill to spearhead their marketing campaigns, hoping that critical praise will create a sense of social responsibility within the paying audience. The independent film *Dead Man Walking* had star names in Susan Sarandon and Sean Penn, but it was favourable reviews and related articles in the media about the death penalty issue that turned it into a worthy option for discerning cinemagoers. By marketing independent cinema in this manner, distributors are able to attract middlebrow ticket buyers, an audience that is concerned about the politics and social infrastructure of the modern world, even though the impact that the film will probably lead to nothing more than some topical discussion. In the case of *Dead Man Walking*, it is unlikely that many of the people that saw the film on its release in 1995 went out to campaign against the death penalty, but their sense of social responsibility was enough to help the film to a $40 million gross at the domestic box office. In this sense, American independent cinema is reliant on the adult audience that Hollywood has largely stopped catering to, an audience that is concerned, but conservative, intellectually active, but not socially activist.

4.6 Independence Today – The Current State of American Independent Cinema

Independent cinema today is a mirror image of the audience that it caters to, a crowd that is seeking novelty and quality, but not necessarily looking for the extreme provocation that would lead it to revaluate its social-political values. The relation between modern American independent cinema and its audience seems to be based upon a compromise of interests, the silent agreement that films can approach serious subject matter, providing that they do so within a relatively linear structure that adheres to the narrative codes that the audience is familiar with and does not embark on too many experimental tangents. As such, modern American independent cinema is not so much an opposition to the Hollywood mainstream, but an alternative version of it, telling similar stories but placing a different emphasis on key elements as a means of distinguishing itself. *The Blair Witch Project*, the directorial debut of Daniel Myrick and Eduardo Sanchez, is located firmly within the horror genre, yet is shot as a mock-documentary, with an improvised feel that belies the circumstances of its production. With three unknown actors in the principal roles, and appearances from non-actors who thought they were participating in a real documentary, *The Blair Witch Project* was shot in a few weeks with an outline serving in the place of an actual script, and the actors being given suggestive notes by the directors instead of more formal instruction.

The concept of the film was that a documentary crew making a film about a mysterious 'witch' would become lost in Maryland wilderness whilst gathering footage, only to fall victim to an unseen 'evil' within the woods. While the directors would film the actors as they became increasingly lost in the wilderness, the actors themselves were required to shoot their own footage with a 16mm camera and a black-and-white camcorder, essentially video diaries that would then be incorporated to add to the documentary aesthetic. Partly improvised and formally different to anything in the marketplace at the time, whilst also carefully conceived and targeted at a specific audience, *The Blair Witch Project* is very much a modern American independent feature film. It successful melds two forms of American independent cinema – the 'B'-movie that is designed to scare and shock, and the 'art' film that is more formally experimental and challenges its audience to adapt to a new narrative form.

Completed for just $35,000, although eventual distributor Artisan would spend much more on the ingenious advertising campaign that started life on the Internet, *The Blair Witch Project* grossed $140 million in the domestic market, eclipsing more expensive Hollywood competition to emerge as one of the most successful films of 1999. However, this was not a film that came about through the need of writer-directors to address a particular issue or impart a world-view. Located within a specific genre and dealing with human emotion only as a means of audience manipulation, it was as skilfully crafted a scare-machine as John Carpenter's *Halloween* or Tobe Hooper's *The Texas Chain Saw Massacre*, two horror hits of the 1970s which were also produced outside the studio system. Like those earlier films, *The Blair Witch Project* takes the trappings of a specific genre and then uses its pervading low-budget atmosphere to unsettling effect. As *The Blair Witch Project*'s co-director Eduardo Sanchez explains,

> *Blair* just happened to be the best low-budget idea we had at the time. It used all the weaknesses of independent film – used them in its favour – like shaky camera work, no lighting, no-name talent.[6]

This is to say that American independent cinema has reached a state of self-awareness, wherein film-makers acknowledge the audience's familiarity with the distinction between low- and high-budget movies, and can then use that familiarity in their favour, developing stories that can not only be told inexpensively, but also benefit creatively from being produced in such a manner. However, this is worrying in that it suggests that the term 'American independent cinema' is becoming indicative of a certain aesthetic approach, and an enterprising attitude towards film-making, but not a means of referencing a certain mode of cultural thinking or artistic expression, as the content of such cinema, or at least the examples of it that find favour with a relatively wide audience, is becoming increasingly conventional and mostly non-political.

Notes

1. Bourdieu, p. 115, 1993.
2. Garnham, p. 117–118, 1990.
3. Merritt, G, *Celluloid Mavericks – A History of American Independent Film*, 1st edn, p. xiv, New York, Thunder's Mouth Press, 2000.
4. Bourdieu, p. 115, 1993.
5. Hillier, J, *American Independent Cinema – A Sight and Sound Reader*, 1st edn, p. xvi, London, BFI, 2001.
6. Sanchez, E, quoted in article *Fresh Blood*, Timberg, S, *New Times Los Angeles*, 08/07/1999.

5

LOYALTY TO THE RHETORIC: FOUR AMERICAN FILM-MAKERS AND THEIR COMMITMENT TO AN AUTONOMOUS MODE OF CULTURAL PRODUCTION

To define what is meant by the term 'American independent cinema', and in order to exemplify it as a method of cultural production rather than a mode of expression or form of popular thinking, it is necessary to examine not only the form and content of the sector's cinematic output, but to provide some insight into the logistical methods that are employed by American independent film-makers in order to bring their visions to fruition. By understanding how these methods differ from those practised by Hollywood studios, the true extent of their autonomy, and how that autonomy is manifest in the work itself, will become apparent.

There are independent film-makers who aspire to a level of creative freedom, at which they are in complete control of their work, operating intuitively, without an external influence that is governed by the desire for profit. Such a method of production is necessary for independent film-makers, as their films do not exist simply as individual features, but as parts of a body of work, a collection of films that complement one another, revealing social-political through the recurrence of ideological theme and aesthetic sensibility. These bodies of work can only be achieved through an unflinching loyalty to the rhetoric, as even occasional excursions into more commercial territory can undermine the cultural value of the collective work and the reputation of its creator. However, this chapter will also highlight the fact that that these film-makers are still subject to the rules, trends, and economic fluctuations of the industry and the changing preferences of its audiences, even whilst seemingly operating outside of its cultural and economic restraints.

The four directors under examination here are John Sayles, Abel Ferrara, Jim Jarmusch, and Spike Lee. Each has amassed a substantial body of work over a long time and has acquired the label of 'American independent film-maker', either through the media or self-reference. Each has gone to great lengths to establish their independent credentials, although they have differed in their methods of certifying their autonomous status. In addition, they also disagree about whether 'independent' is a mode of cultural production or cultural thinking. Sayles, Ferrara, Jarmusch, and Lee are all examples of what could be termed the 'second wave' of American independent cinema, following the 'first wave' best exemplified by *Easy Rider*, BBS Productions, and the films of John Cassavettes, and preceding the 'third wave' spearheaded by such figures as Quentin Tarantino, Harvey Weinstein, and Robert Rodriguez. The 'second wave' of American independent cinema was spurred on by two distinct but interrelated factors – the audience's need for novelty in the wake of Hollywood's pursuit of the 'blockbuster', and the advancement of film technology, namely the video cassette recorder, or VCR, which opened up new avenues of distribution, exhibition, and return on investment.

As with many examples of cultural change, it is difficult to point to an exact starting point. Nonetheless, 1984 is often regarded as a banner year for American independent cinema, in that it saw the emergence of several films which succeeded critically and commercially, expanding the art house niche to find a wider audience. The independent feature films of 1984 also established the template for much of the 'second wave' of American independent cinema as they shared a distinctive aesthetic approach and were financed privately, with directors raising funds through their own financial ingenuity and completing films without a distributor in place. The year 1984 was the year that Jim Jarmusch's *Stranger than Paradise* parlayed its success at the New York film festival into national release, while Alex Cox's *Repo Man* appropriated punk culture to the framework of film noir, and the Coen Brothers debuted with the crime thriller *Blood Simple*. It should be noted that the latter two of these films are genre pieces, working from narrative frameworks familiar to the Hollywood mainstream, but subverting their cultural perspectives and moral economy. Locating such artistic activity within his field of restricted production, Bourdieu observes that

> The dominated producers, for their part, in order to gain a foothold in the market, have to resort to subversive strategies which will eventually bring them the disavowed profits only if they succeed in overturning the hierarchy of the field without disturbing the principles on which the field is based.[1]

This is to say that the 'second wave' of American independent cinema found directors carving out their own niche within a limited market from which they could build proper careers, as opposed to making films as a hobby or one a one-off, experimental basis. In order to solidify their position, they achieved cultural prominence, earning critical acclaim for their work, but not actively pursuing financial reward, thereby ensuring their 'independent' status in industrial context as the commercial performance of their films never challenged that of their studio rivals.

The emergence of home video as a competitor of the theatres meant that there was a greater need for product, a need that the Hollywood studios could not satisfy. Aside from the ever-present 'B-movies', which found a second home on the video market after the decline of the drive in market and the eradication of the second feature, independent films were now required to swell the coffers of the video retailers and meet the need for novelty that was growing within the market. The home entertainment revolution solved one of the main problems for independent films up until that time, namely distribution. Even in today's market, where independent film has proved to be a valid cultural and economic commodity, there are areas where the lack of suitable 'art house' venues, or the high cost of marketing, prevents many independent films from enjoying a cinematic life. However, with home video, and later DVD, it has become possible for independent films to be viewed by audiences outside major international cities, and for films to develop a word of mouth following. The potential revenue in the home video market also provided new financing avenues for independent film-makers in that they could raise production funds by 'pre-selling' their projects, generating capital by arranging the sale of home video rights in advance of production, ensuring both completion funds and future distribution based on a growing need for a variety of cinematic product for the home market.

However, the 'second wave' really began in the late 1970s, partially as a reaction by directors to Hollywood's move away from serious subjects or small-scale adult pictures. As Hollywood became besotted with the 'event movie', or the 'blockbuster', in the wake of the success of Star Wars, Jaws, and Superman, independent directors such as Sayles and Ferrara were shooting their early films with funds raised outside the system. While it is tempting to view independent cinema as being exempt from the trends of the Hollywood studio system, with its own social and political framework, it is actually more of a responsive, but not submissive, cousin to the Hollywood mainstream, making subtle shifts and adjustments in both its theoretic content and finance method. This can create windows of opportunity for film-makers, especially when the corporations that run Hollywood invest and diversify into new technologies, such as the VCR, or neglect a segment of their audience, allowing, or allocating, a niche to the independent sector.

Sayles, Ferrara, Jarmusch, and Lee have all been courted by the Hollywood studios, and have, in their individual ways, resisted its allure, even though the system has affected and informed their work to various degrees. Their swift rejection of work that would be considered to have more 'populist' appeal has led Sayles, Ferrara, and Jarmusch to be largely exiled to the industrial margins, while Lee has seemingly secured 'independent' status within the studio hierarchy. As with other independent film-makers, their refusal to compromise has had some effect on the Hollywood mainstream in that the product of the studio system often apes the independent sensibility that refuses to be co-opted into its mass production of popular culture. As Jarmusch observes,

> There came a point where Hollywood started imitating what they thought independent cinema was and they came up with American Beauty...it's pretty obvious that they were trying to cash in on something that appeared to be a marketing niche.[2]

Jarmusch is quick to distinguish between the output of Hollywood, which he regards as 'product', and the work of himself and his contemporaries in the independent sector, to which he assigns the comparatively artistic term of 'films'. He states that

> We are outlaws, because we don't do it for a studio, we're not there to make your product for you, we're there to make films for our soul. If people find them we're happy. But if they don't, that's not our problem. We're not salesmen.[3]

While it is unlikely that Jarmusch wants audiences and critics to be uninterested in his work, he would not mind too much if this were the case. He follows Bourdieu's line of thought that there is cultural legitimacy in disinterestedness, and that if his films were to stray into the territory of 'popular' because of commercial success, he would feel that he had not been true to his singular vision through the making of a film that could be widely accessible. Jarmusch is very much one of Bourdieu's 'intellectuals', an artist who possess much symbolic capital, in that he is formally educated and a cultural contributor, but who exists in the dominated position of Bourdieu's field of cultural production due to not only his lack of economic capital, but his unwillingness to pursue such capital he does not want to be seen to be seeking economic gain. Although a contemporary of Jarmusch, with a similar background and trajectory, Spike Lee is a polar opposite in terms of his views of economy, audience, and use of symbolic capital. As a serious film-maker, Lee has seen no profit in occupying a dominated position, and has instead used his cultural capital to generate economic capital to enable him to gravitate towards a more dominant position. As Bourdieu notes,

> The fact that the disavowal of the 'economy' is neither a simple ideological mask nor a complete repudiation of the economic interest explains why, on the one hand, new producers whose only capital is their conviction can establish themselves in the market by appealing to the values whereby the dominant figures accumulated their symbolic capital, and why, on the other hand, only those who can come to terms with the 'economic' constraints inscribed in this bad-faith economy can reap the full 'economic' profits of their symbolic capital.[4]

Each case study in this chapter is intended to show how, in their respective ways, Sayles, Jarmusch, Ferrara, and Lee can be considered to be 'independent film-makers' and how they have sustained their status through their own relations within the field of cultural production.

5.1 John Sayles

John Sayles exemplifies much of what is popularly associated with American independent cinema, both in terms of the films he makes and the way in which he makes them, often financing his work out of his own resources in order to retain control, or waiting patiently for the right creative and economic conditions to fall into place before embarking on a particular project. He regularly delivers engrossing stories about characters inadvertently trapped in situations of cultural change in order to offer informed social commentary without being as bombastic or as reductive as Oliver Stone, or as inflammatory as Spike Lee. As Andrew notes,

> Sayles is left-wing in the old tradition a fundamentally decent, humanist belief in the right of any individual or group to be accorded equality, freedom and justice.[5]

At odds with his reputation as a worthy, socially conscious film-maker is his alternative profession as a 'writer-for-hire'. As a director, *Baby It's You* in 1983 is the only time Sayles has worked with a Hollywood studio, although not intentionally as the film was bought by Paramount in mid-production. As a writer, however, he has penned monster movies like *Piranha* and *Alligator*, as well as the horror film *The Howling*, the revenge drama *The Lady In Red* and the martial arts adventure *The Challenge*, not to mention his 'script-doctoring' assignments on major Hollywood productions that require structural or dialogue changes prior to production. His understanding of narrative structure and audience expectations, gained through work on Hollywood genre films, has allowed him to frame his own stories in an accessible manner, although he adopts a more relaxed approach, relying on established structures as a crux for his own concerns. As he says,

> In the movies I've worked on that attempt to push beyond genre, it's important who does what and why, and the manner of the storytelling is important only in its effectiveness in bringing the audience to its basic questions...the movie has to make them willing not only to think beyond the boundaries of genre but also to revaluate what they know or think about the world.[6]

As a means of maintaining narrative focus, he has developed his own formula and 'set pieces' – his films will start by broadly establishing a community in a moment of cultural or economic change, before focussing on a particular protagonist who will serve as a guide through that community, often as a result of his investigation into a crime or involvement in a business venture. This element of plot is usually a method for Sayles to examine the moral fabric of the community, to see how it evolves at times of social duress and economic fluctuation. A supporting character will often be an elderly communal statesman, who will lecture a younger individual on the history of the community under scrutiny, as a means of filling the audience in on crucial back story and also providing social context. Sayles is pragmatic when approaching an independent production and acknowledges that working with a low budget places certain creative restrictions on the film-maker. However, he also refuses to allow his economic restrictions to dictate scale and scope, preferring instead to reverse Hollywood studio storytelling practices. Hollywood features often favour action in the sense of physical motion and the collision of characters and events, but only for the sake of the immediate escapist thrill, rather than the long-term implications of such behaviour or natural circumstance. They are also reliant on special effects, exaggerated humour, popular music, and fashion, pushing such elements as character, dialogue, and social comment into the background. Sayles instead brings these neglected elements into the foreground, maintaining some of the commercially identifiable attributes of Hollywood cinema, but in smaller, more logistically manageable quantities. As he explains, 'Rather than eliminate all these elements, I try to minimize and control them.'[7]

By working in this manner and cutting costs by deferring his own fee until the film is officially in profit, Sayles has been able to mount films such as *Matewan*, an ambitious period piece dealing with a West Virginian mining community in the 1920s and the efforts of a Union organizer to lead his fellow workers in a non-violent protest. In order to secure the $4 million budget, the lowest possible sum he felt he could make the film for given that it was a period film with a large cast, Sayles contacted potential investors. Knowing that the subject matter of the film was unlikely to make it a huge box office success, he raised the budget gradually, finding investment from those who were interested in contributing for more personal reasons, such as an interest in the subject matter, or the desire to see more feature film production brought to a certain state. Once in pre-production, he ensures that his screenplay is pared down with regard to any elements which could cause additional expense, and plans a shooting schedule which will allow him to capture the maximum amount of potentially expensive footage in the shortest possible time frame.

Lone Star is Sayles's most successful movie to date in terms of finding an audience for his more literary approach. Shot for $5 million, it eventually grossed $13.2 million and was partially financed by Sayles's script-doctoring job on the Universal production *Apollo 13*. The events of *Lone Star* centre on Buddy Deeds, the Sheriff of Frontera, a town precariously located between the USA and Mexico on the Texan side of the border. Buddy is still held up by the town as a symbol of all that is good and necessary about law enforcement, even though his ride from deputy to sheriff coincided with the sudden disappearance of Charlie Wade, a nasty piece of work who abused his position as sheriff to terrorize the community for his own economic gain. The present-day sheriff is Sam Deeds, the son of Buddy, who is frequently and unfairly compared to his father's legend. When evidence comes to light that Buddy may have been involved in the disappearance of Deeds, Sam finds himself trying to piece together a decades-old murder mystery, whose resolution may discredit his father and destroy the iconography that the town holds so dear. Although superficially a murder-mystery, *Lone Star* is an examination of how the events of the past can affect those of the present, and how much of that effect is determined by collective memory, while at the same time Sayles remains comfortably within familiar narrative territory. As Andrew observes,

> Sayles avoids the dissolves and cuts usually used to introduce and exit from flashbacks, and instead simply pans the camera from left to right or up or down, to show an event from the past in exactly the same spatial setting. The result not only suggests that the past is always with us, exerting an influence on the here and now, but even allows Sayles to show, by beginning with a 'flashback' with one character in the present and then ending on another character in the present, that what we are seeing is a shared memory.[8]

It is this approach to flashbacks that best exemplifies his approach to narrative and genre, and to questioning his audience. Although the elderly characters in *Lone Star* talk of the 1950s as the 'good old days', Sayles uses the flashbacks to show that they were anything but, presenting a community that is fragmented, full of racial hatred and police corruption. Although his politics obviously lean towards the democratic left, the films of John Sayles are 'independent' in the sense that he tries not to impose social-political judgements through his work, exploring characters and their circumstances in a manner that is intended to make their actions and reactions understandable, if not always entirely sympathetic.

Sayles's films usually feature a 'leading man', but he is often a cipher, acting as a link between groups who, due to social-economic and racial divides, may not interact. The Union organizer in *Matewan* who acts as a go-between for both the workers and their bosses, and the private detective in *Silver City* who is hired by the wealthy right-wing politicians, and comes into contact with illegal immigrants and activist journalists, serve this function and bring colourful supporting characters into the story. By taking an ensemble approach to his storytelling and focussing on characters from either side of the social-economic divide, Sayles is able to present the perspectives of characters who appear to be acting on capitalist instincts and those who may seem more idealistic, then to place these perspectives into a social-political context which reveals motivations that are occasionally surprising, and altogether more personal and humanist. Although the overarching schemes of major corporations are presented in the usual American way, as a faceless force that can deprive a community of its social identity, it is always emphasized that corporate investment is an economic necessity for communities that, for whatever reason, lack an industrial structure.

5.2 Abel Ferrara
The origins of Ferrara's career are as mysterious as those of his cinematic alter egos. A New Yorker with no formal training in feature film production, Ferrara is rumoured to have gained technical experience on various pornographic films, working under the alias of Jimmy Laine, under which he has sometimes credited his own acting appearances in his films. Ferrara is an independent film-maker in the sense that he has learnt to make films simply by making films, finding methods of self-expression by working intuitively through his key themes whilst also flirting with the narrative parameters of genre. His controversial body of work has dealt with the topics of violence, racism, emotional and physical abuse, alienation, and Catholicism, although Johnstone argues that these are all aspects of one overarching theme, that of 'absenteeism'. As he insists,

> Abel Ferrara's films are all about absenteeism; the absence of love, family, faith, justice, loyalty, respect, God, purity, feeling, law and order, security and safety, balance.[9]

Ferrara has been able to attract financing for his projects by locating his themes within marketable genres, particularly those beloved by 'B'-movie producers, such as horror and gangster drama. Absenteeism often becomes the psychological reasoning behind lapses in moral judgement, which enables Ferrara to deliver the shoot-outs, graphic sex scenes, and car chases which are required by producers looking to invest in a product that promises to have a high return through ancillary markets. For Ferrara, this financing method has become something of a double-edged sword in that he has made his work appear commercially viable to backers, but it also led to critical charges of being an exploitation film-maker, a director who includes the aforementioned themes to add a sense of importance and relevance that his films do not deserve.

This assessment serves to introduce the significance of the duality which is omnipresent in Ferrara's work, the balance which he continually strikes between art house meditation and 'B'-movie exploitation. In *King of New York*, Christopher Walken portrays Frank White, an inner-city drug lord determined to put something back into the community which has made him so wealthy. With his frequent use of mirrors, Ferrara makes visual references to the duality within White, and even his surname is an indication of his spiritual conflict – white is a colour which signifies purity, but it is also the colour of cocaine, the drug which White's henchmen are pushing on the crime-infested streets beneath his plush penthouse apartment. The theme of duality is also central to *Bad Lieutenant* in which the title character portrayed by Harvey Keitel is an officer of the law and a man of the Cross, an individual who is driven by professional and Catholic beliefs to apprehend the violent youths who have raped a nun. He is also an alcoholic and a drug abuser, heavily in debt to local bookies and incapable of communicating with his children. If Ferrara's films are indebted to the Hollywood system for their narrative framework, they are socially and politically independent, as Ferrara's moral perspective would be considered difficult in the context of the studio system.

While he may tackle subject matter and characters that mainstream Hollywood prefers to ignore, Ferrara has no qualms about using the most commercially identifiable attribute – the movie star. Although the actors in his films are not those that the Hollywood studios would consider capable of 'opening' a movie on the value of their name alone, they are recognizable, often with a certain amount of 'cult' cachet that plays well with critics and niche audiences. Dennis Hopper, Harvey Keitel, Christopher Walken, Matthew Modine, Anabella Sciorra, and Asia Argento are just some of the mid-range stars who have worked with Ferrara throughout his career, ensuring enough interest in his films that he can raise funds by pre-selling projects to distributors, guaranteeing that the film will be available on the home video market should it fail theatrically. Working with Abel Ferrara is not an opportunity for actors to swell their bank balance, but it does represent a chance to play a challenging role in a film that may bring them some cultural credit through an association with a particular director and his choice of material. After working with Ferrara on *The Blackout*, Matthew Modine was eager to express his gratitude to the director:

> I do feel like this is a re-birth. If the significance of baptism is to wash something away, this role has changed me. I have a different understanding of myself, I have a different kind of maturity, and I'm really glad that I met Abel Ferrara.[10]

Where full financing and distribution has not been in place, Ferrara has ploughed ahead with production anyway, operating much like Sayles in that he has bankrolled pre-production out of his own pocket through money gained by working on purely commercial assignments, such as *The Gladiator*, *Cat Chaser*, *Body Snatchers* and television series like *Crime Story* and *Miami Vice*. As with Jim Jarmusch, Ferrara has at times been fortunate to be a producer for other producers, in that his work has had enough of an effect on other industry professionals for his productions to receive donations. He received a cheque for $40,000 from Ed Pressman, the producer of such hit films as *Conan the Barbarian*, *Wall Street*, and *The Crow* with which he was able to begin production on *Bad Lieutenant*, gradually raising the remainder of the $1 million budget by pre-selling the distribution rights based on the cultural currency of his name, and that of his star, Harvey Keitel, who was enjoying a critical resurgence following his role in Quentin Tarantino's *Reservoir Dogs*.

Without any formal training, Ferrara has taken director-for-hire opportunities to finance his productions and learn the rules of genre film-making by working from scripts written by others. His commitment to his own projects has meant that he has accepted work to which he has exhibited a flippant attitude, such as the feature *Cat Chaser*, which he did not finish editing because the financing for his script *King Of New York* came into place, leaving the producers to complete post-production without his services. While Bourdieu observes that it is common for the field of large-scale production to borrow from the field of restricted production in order for it to renew itself at certain cyclical junctures, Ferrara has allowed a limited borrowing of his aesthetic sensibility, not fully committing himself to assignments, even though their production budgets and financial rewards may be more plentiful

5.3 Jim Jarmusch

In literary terms, the films of Jim Jarmusch are vignettes rather than novels, and to those unfamiliar with his oeuvre as a whole, appear almost 'throwaway' in their tone and execution. While nationality qualifies Jarmusch as an 'American independent' film-maker, his cinematic influences are altogether more Eastern, which is appropriate given that he receives funding from the Japanese corporate giant JVC. In a manner in keeping with the laid-back nature of his films, Jarmusch did not aggressively pursue the patronage of JVC, who contributed finance to *Mystery Train* and *Night on Earth*; he was simply contacted by a director of the company who had particularly enjoyed his work and wanted to help with future funding.

Jarmusch's enormously influential 1984 feature *Stranger than Paradise* is often cited as his debut film, but his first feature was actually *Permanent Vacation*, the story of a disillusioned drifter who wanders around New York city before deciding to make a break for Paris. *Permanent Vacation* was produced for just $12,000, with Jarmusch cutting corners by filming on New York locations without the proper filming permits, hiring non-union actors for most of the roles, and working with a crew comprised of friends and NYU students who were happy to work for free to acquire some technical experience. Long stretches of the film are silent, meaning that extensive costs for sound editing and additional dialogue replacement were not incurred.

Although not as widely discussed as *Stranger than Paradise*, Jarmusch's first feature is filled with the themes that would form the basis for much of his later work, notably that of the outsider adrift in a land which he vaguely recognizes through its cultural iconography, but does not understand. Unlike the films of Ferrara and Lee, whose characters are from 'the neighbourhood', the Jarmusch's protagonists are often alien to their environment, or disconnected from it. *Mystery Train* is set in Memphis, USA, yet two of its story strands focus on foreigners, a Japanese couple who speak little English and a widowed Italian woman; while the title character in *Ghost Dog – Way of the Samurai* is a native of his environment, but his moral philosophies are derived from ancient Japanese teachings. Although Jarmusch appears to derive more inspiration from European and Asian film-makers, he is exploring classic American themes, albeit those of a literary rather than cinematic nature.

The first third of his breakthrough film, *Stranger than Paradise*, was shot over a long weekend, with the scenes being captured on black-and-white film stock 'donated' by Win Wenders, who had just completed his feature *The State of Things* and had some unused resources to spare. It was this first third that was screened as a short film at both the Rotterdam and Hof Film Festivals where Jarmusch was honoured with the critic's prizes. At this juncture, the German producer Otto Grokenberger was so impressed that he stepped in with the necessary funds to complete *Stranger than Paradise* as a full-length feature. With the eventual budget totalling $110,000, Jarmusch's second feature became the cheapest film to win the Camera d'Or at the Cannes Film Festival when it played there in 1984.

As with later American independent films, most notably Spike Lee's *She's Gotta Have It* and Kevin Smith's *Clerks*, the low production values and grainy image quality, which would ordinarily be considered to be sub-standard for a 'professional' feature film, worked in the favour of *Stranger than Paradise*, lending novelty value and a sense of authenticity to Jarmusch's tragic-comic story of a young Hungarian living in New York. Distribution was handled by Island-Alive, a then-successful independent company who were generating large amounts of revenue from their home video business and were investing profits in new films to ensure a continuous stream of product. With *Stranger than Paradise* they acquired a film that would likely have a long 'shelf life' if only because of its novelty value. Before its success as a home video item, however, *Stranger than Paradise* would be a cult theatrical hit, gradually grossing $2.5 million from the burgeoning art house circuit.

Jarmusch's status as an independent film-maker is not so much a result of his dependent position within the field of power, but his unwillingness to accept the terms of the field itself. He has often gone for long periods without making films, with the five years between *Dead Man* and *Ghost Dog: Way of the Samurai* being his longest stretch of exile, although he remained active in this period, acting in the independent features *Blue in the Face* and *Slingblade*, whilst also developing some of the short films which would feature in his compendium *Coffee and Cigarettes*, eventually released in 2004. His one experience with studio financing occurred when Miramax paid $4 million at the 1995 Cannes Film Festival for the distribution rights to his surrealistic western *Dead Man*, probably because Jarmusch had secured the bankable Johnny Depp to play the title role. Unfortunately, the studio was not happy with the oblique tone of the piece, with Harvey Weinstein demanding that Jarmusch cut the film down to what he perceived to be a more marketable length. As Jarmusch had final cut on the film, he refused to change a frame, leading Miramax to 'dump' the film, releasing it in a few cities and investing little money in the home video version.

For Jarmusch, the defining quality of an 'independent film' is the autonomous control that is enjoyed by its director. For him, such factors as subject matter, style, genre, critical and commercial perception and reception are irrelevant when assessing the 'independent' status of a project. As he observes,

> Independent films are completely controlled by the film-makers artistically, and commercial films are to some degree controlled by financial investment. That's the difference. And it's not about quality because there are great films that are commercially orientated – *Blade Runner*, *The Terminator*, *Lawrence of Arabia* – and there are a lot of bad independent films.[11]

Perhaps Jarmusch's greatest achievement is the influence that his work has had on the field itself. With his idealistic approach to the control of his work, and the ability to tell stories in a miniature form which not only suits his limited resources but makes a virtue from them, Jarmusch has inspired other independent film-makers who may have lacked confidence with regard to their technological knowledge and storytelling practices. Spike Lee has admitted that

> For me, the defining moment of film school was when Jim Jarmusch's *Stranger than Paradise* became a hit. All of a sudden, we all felt that making films was now doable. When you're studying the masters – Hitchcock or Scorsese or Coppola – film seems remote, distant.[12]

At the 1996 New York Critics Circle awards, a dryly humorous Jarmusch claimed that his film *Dead Man* had been seen more in private screenings than it had in public exhibition. In this sense, he is very much a producer for other producers, his work resonating most within the film-making, or artistic, community.

5.4 Spike Lee

As noted, Spike Lee is the director in this study whose economic ties to the corporate giants make him questionable as an 'independent film-maker'. Jarmusch has disavowed the Hollywood system entirely, while Sayles and Ferrara have occasionally worked as a screenwriter and director-for-hire respectively to finance their own projects. Lee, however, has received at least partial financing and full distribution from the Hollywood studios since working with Universal on his third feature, *Do the Right Thing*, in 1989 and has taken his projects to such studios as Warner Brothers, Twentieth Century Fox, Columbia, Disney, and the mini-major New Line which had become a Warner Brothers subsidiary by the time Lee secured the financing for *Bamboozled* in 2000. In addition to his film-making activities, Lee has directed pop videos for such multi-million sellers as Michael Jackson and Beyonce, and advertising spots for international brands like Nike and Pepsi. Of the four, Lee is the industry 'player', a director who not only openly acknowledges the importance of marketing and media exposure, but has also sought control of these elements to the extent that he has verged on becoming a 'brand' in his own right.

Having graduated from New York University and completed a number of short films, Lee financed his first feature, the sex comedy *She's Gotta Have It*, with $600,000 borrowed from credit cards. Much like Jarmusch's *Stranger than Paradise*, Lee's debut offered novelty in its studiously grubby production values, but whereas Jarmusch's film was intended to be visually expressive, Lee's was a vehicle for his racy dialogue, which contained a sexual frankness that is rarely found in the films of the studio system. 'You so fine, baby, I'll drink you in a tub of bathwater', and 'girl, I get plenty of what you need, the throbbing inches of USDA, government inspected, prime cure, grade-A tube steak' were amongst some of the quotable exchanges in Lee's self-penned screenplay, and the controversy which his dialogue generated proved to excellent publicity material for the independent production.

Unlike Sayles, Jarmusch, and Ferrara, who prefer the audience to 'find' their work, Lee has championed his films in the media, and has done so since *She's Gotta Have It*, generating press for himself before the film was completed and attracting enough attention for distributors to become interested in the project. Released by Island-Alive in 1986, Lee's first feature grossed $7.1 million, an unheard of amount for an independent film at the time and over twice as much as *Stranger than Paradise*, Lee's conceptual model. Lee was swift to establish his business credentials, setting up his own production company, 40 Acres and a Mule, which has since diversified across the related markets of film, television, music, documentary, and fashion.

She's Gotta Have It is the one example of Lee as a 'guerrilla' film-maker, as all his following films have benefited from corporate finance. However, he has ensured control by employing methods from the independent world, such as working with actors who have yet to achieve a commercial breakthrough and paying low salaries, or even industry scale, to cast and crew. He shares with other independent film-makers an ability to address large-scale social problems on a relatively intimate scale, often locating and shooting his films on geographical territory so specific that many of his productions have only required the use of one or two city blocks. Widely regarded as his masterpiece, *Do the Right Thing* utilized one block of Brooklyn to examine the theme of race-relations between African-Americans and Italian-Americans, showing how a series of interrelated circumstances can lead generally reasonable human beings to commit violent actions. Aside from *Malcolm X*, the budget for which came to almost $50 million due to the length of the piece and the cost of recreating periods of American history, Lee's films have rarely cost more than $16 million, approximately half the cost of the average Hollywood feature film.

Despite his cost-conscious approach to film-making, it is Lee's relations with people in dominant positions within the industry that have enabled him to retain his independence. He has diversified his own industrial network to include not just those in positions of economic capital, such as Hollywood studio executives, but those with great cultural capital and social influence, most notably celebrity actors, musicians, and athletes. When *Malcolm X* ran over-budget and Lee was pressured by Warner Brothers to make creative compromises, he instead pursued private finance from black celebrities who he believed would have an interest in investing in a film about a major figure in dissenting African-American culture. During the post-production of *Bamboozled*, when New Line were reluctant to provide additional funds, Lee secured a private donation from Phil Knight, the CEO of Nike, for whom Lee had directed a number of advertising spots featuring himself and the basketball star Michael Jordan.

However, Lee has drawn criticism for his efforts to achieve a more dominant economic position, particularly his chain of clothing outlets and his commercial assignments for Nike, a company whose history of 'sweat shop' working conditions appears to be at odds with Lee's own social and political stance. Writing for the *Village Voice* in 1991 about the apparent hypocrisy of maintaining an 'independent stance' as an artist and engaging directly in commercial enterprise, George argued that

> In the face of modern corporate infotainment monoliths, the most realpolitik counterstrategy is to be in business with as many as possible. Diversifying protects you against co-optation by any single corporate entity or industry. With revenue flowing in from commercials, books, music videos and merchandising, Spike has some major cushion should Hollywood get tired of his methods or his mouth.[13]

The business model that Lee has adopted is that of the entertainment industry as a whole. Taking himself as the product, Lee has established himself as a cultural touchstone, ensuring economic capital from the financial revenue generated by his various enterprises and cultural capital from his association with such enterprises. This success stems from Lee's ability to recognize growing areas of the media and retail market where his own 'brand' can be appropriated.

For the latter part of the 1980s, Lee was the only 'black director' to be working at his level of production. As such, he had an exclusive audience, and a unique position within the media. However, by the early 1990s, Hollywood had identified the black audience and was aggressively pursuing it with films which offered more commercially identifiable attributes, namely guns, sex, violence, and hip-hop music. Films such as

New Jack City, *Set it Off*, and *Menace 2 Society* were mining inner-city strife for dramatic value and economic profit. Lee presents black American life as a part of a greater social whole, his characters interacting and occasionally conflicting with other races but essentially existing as a section of an overarching moral economy. The 'black films' that were developed by Hollywood fit into more restrictive generic forms and allowed for little outside perspective. *Juice* and *New Jack City* are particularly confused in that they have a contradictory moral vision with regard to violence, as they view it as both a problem and the solution to the problem. Lee's films fall outside the Hollywood template, in that they begin with questions and end with further questions, denying the audience the expected catharsis.

Unfortunately, the proliferation of such violent 'hood' films, followed by more humorous portrayals of black life in such studio films as *Barbershop* and *Are We There Yet?*, has reduced Lee's cultural credit to the point where he can make the films he wants to make providing they do not go beyond a certain budgetary level. By creating, or at least identifying, a burgeoning market, Lee has ultimately become subservient to the ceiling of that market, as Hollywood has developed its own formula for how much a 'black film' will cost and return. Lee's response to this has been to broaden his social-political scope by taking on recent projects like *The 25th Hour* and *The Inside Man*. These films focus on protagonists of mixed ethnicity and deal primarily with crime-related scenarios, but also examine America's social fabric.

5.5 Independence In Practice – How Loyalty to the Rhetoric Sustains an Autonomous Sector of American Cinema

With the exception of Lee, who has tried to adjust his independent vision to the field of large-scale production, with some early success followed by the gradual neglect of the mass audience, the directors discussed in this chapter have pursued the independent path and experienced a growth in their cultural currency at the expense of their economic viability. However, the rise of their cultural currency, which has often been as a result of their lack of economic power, has endeared them to the 'cinephile set', a small but loyal audience comprised of fellow film-makers, artists, and members of the public with a serious interest in, and passion for, film. As Bourdieu notes,

> The progress of the field of restricted production towards autonomy is marked by an increasingly distinct tendency of criticism to devote itself to the task...of providing a 'creative' interpretation for the benefit of the 'creators'...And so, tiny 'mutual admiration societies' grew up, closed in upon their own esotericism, as, simultaneously, signs of a new solidarity between artist and critic emerged.[14]

A large number of film-makers use independent film as their stepping stone to the field of large-scale production, working on Hollywood projects with big stars, big production values, and potentially big commercial returns. As such, directors like Sayles, Jarmusch, Ferrara, and Lee are essential to the American independent sector because they are making a sustained contribution to its political, social, and moral economy, acknowledging the power and rewards to be found within the studio system, but choosing to ignore its advances, unless the work offered is in line with their own terms and not a negative impediment on their autonomy. It is their cultural credit which is most vital to a sector which, for the film-maker if not the financier, is about the moral profit to be gained from having work recognized by a peer group that has the intellectual capacity to interact with film through nuanced understanding of the director's oeuvre and their socially informed reading.

Independent cinema continues to exist because there are film-makers who are able to make films that the studios cannot, and because some of these films achieve a level of excellence and critical recognition that makes them a cultural necessity, making any economic evaluation, such as the number of tickets sold, or DVDs, rented, or tie-in products produced, quite irrelevant. This is not to say that all American independent cinema should be appreciated in this way. As discussed, many independent features are really studio pictures that have been made through a different financial arrangement and are intended as commercial rather than cultural products. However, there are some film-makers whose truly independent stance is evident in their work, and that work has achieved a cultural prominence as a result, even if it has been at the expense of economic gain.

The intuitive, often esoteric, approach of independent film-makers is not one that courts immediate acceptance through the exploitation of popular sentiment or the melodramatic insistence of unrestrained argument. It is a rhetoric that emphasizes the spirit of the individual, a great American theme especially within the corporate age, and finds merit in the way that spirit is embodied in the working process and eventually expressed through the finished film. The audience is presented with a unique perspective on modern society, one that is open to interpretation and can be filtered through the social experiences of the viewer, as the independent film-maker explores subject matter that the Hollywood system often chooses to ignore, subject matter that exists somewhere between the ordinary and the extraordinary.

Notes

1. Bourdieu P, *Distinction – A Social Critique of the Judgement of Taste*, p. 41, London, Routledge & Kegan Paul, 1979.
2. Jarmusch, J, interviewed by Dalton, S, *Uncut*, p. 62, 11/2005.
3. Jarmusch, p. 63, 11/2005.
4. Bourdieu, p. 76, 1993.
5. Andrew, G, *Stranger than Paradise – Maverick Filmmakers in Recent American Cinema*, 1st edn, p. 72, London, Prion, 1998.
6. Sayles, J, *Thinking in Pictures – The Making of the Movie Matewan*, 1st edn, p. 17, Boston, Houghton Mifflin Company, 1987.
7. Sayles, p. 36, 1987.
8. Andrew, p. 103–104, 1998.
9. Johnstone, N, *Abel Ferrara – The King of New York*, 1st edn, p. 1, London, Omnibus, 1999.

10. Interview with Modine, M by Hemblade, C, *Empire*, p. 64, 03/1998.
11. Jarmusch, p. 62, 11/05.
12. Lee, S, quoted by Aftab, K, *Spike Lee – That's My Story and I'm Sticking To It*, 1st edn, p. 21, London, Faber & Faber, 2005.
13. George, N, quoted by Aftab, p. 117, 2005.
14. Bourdieu, p. 117, 1993.

6

Graduating Class: American Independent Cinema as Finishing School

The directors studied in the previous chapter represent a loyalty not only to a particular form of cinema, but a specific methodology with regard to bringing that cinema to the screen. It is a loyalty and methodology that has become as much of a characteristic of their work, as it is a statement of industrial intent, as they have continued to work within the independent sector, rarely dealing with the major studios or actively pursuing the participation of 'A'-list actors. However, for every Jim Jarmusch or Abel Ferrara, there are a great number of film-makers who have started in the independent sector, but willingly gravitated towards the studio system for future projects and opportunities. These are the 'independent graduates', film-makers who have used low-budget cinema as a means of developing their craft and providing a 'calling card' to mini-majors and studios who can provide them with greater resources and public exposure. Through industrial analysis and four case studies, this chapter will argue that such progressions are necessary and, in some cases, beneficial to both film-makers and the film industry, although this will also entail the question of whether such 'independent film-makers' can claim the cultural legitimacy. The key stages in the careers of most 'independent graduates' are as follows:

(1) Film school / short films
(2) Debut Feature – usually independently financed.
(3) Second Feature – financed by a mini-major or studio.
(4) Third Feature – financed by a studio.
(5) Consolidation of industry status – formation of Production Company, diversification into television, music videos, advertising.

In this sense, American independent cinema can be seen as a 'finishing school' for young film-makers, offering them the chance to hone the skills they have developed as 'students' of the medium, either through academic pursuits or their own intuitive resources. Their services then become available to the corporate giants, who are looking to renew their product through the assimilation of fresh talent, and to enhance their cultural cachet by being seen to work with young film-makers who may provide them with critically celebrated cinema. How entrenched in the studio method of film-making these directors become is usually up to them. Some, such as Bryan Singer and Doug Liman, have embraced the opportunities offered by big-budget genre films and the 'A'-list stars that come with them, while others, such as David O'Russell and Alexander Payne, have been altogether more cautious. Payne had no shortage of offers for finance when trying to set up his mid-life crisis comedy *Sideways*, but refused to compromise on his casting of character actors as opposed to movie stars, even though major studios were willing to assign him a larger budget should he select one of the more bankable actors who were vying for roles.

According to Levy, Hollywood and independent films represent two parallel industrial networks, but this is not the case with regard to 'independent film-makers' who desire to cross over to the Hollywood mainstream, or at least develop projects with studio funding. These directors are not 'independent' in the fiscal sense, and obviously have no aspirations to be. Their willingness to work within the studio system, regardless of the commercial demands and creative compromises that come with such assignments, is indicative of either a frustration with the resources available to independent film-makers, or an open acknowledgment of the unrivalled opportunities that the corporate giants can offer those who can accept its restrictions, or navigate the unconventional elements of their work through more mainstream waters. For all their critical acclaim and cult-like followings, the films of such resolutely independent film-makers as Jim Jarmusch, Robert Altman, John Sayles, and Greg Araki have rarely achieved the social-political impact that their creators may have been straining for. By contrast, directors such as Oliver Stone, Paul Thomas Anderson, Steven Soderbergh, and Spike Lee, whose works exhibit an independent sensibility, yet are frequently funded and distributed by major corporations, have enjoyed the attention of the mass audience without visibly compromising their cinematic ambitions. As Caves notes,

> Great works of art may speak for themselves, as connoisseurs declare, but they do not lead self-sufficient lives. The inspiration of talented artists reach consumer's hands (eyes, ears) only with the aid of other inputs – *humdrum inputs* – that respond to ordinary economic incentives. The question of how contracts work between art and commerce thus is nested within the larger question of why artists and humdrum inputs choose to structure their relationships as they do.[1]

This is to say that the deals that are brokered between film-makers and the Hollywood studios are necessary, as without such arrangements, it would not be possible for films to reach a wide audience. Mottram has claimed that modern American cinema is currently enjoying a second 'golden age', as directors of rare social insight and aesthetic vision are being allocated studio resources to develop films. However, it can also be argued that, although many of these films are satisfying cinematic experiences, they are not too far removed from mainstream Hollywood product. As Biskind argues,

> There's a price to pay for making 'indie' films inside the system: namely, the gradual assimilation of studio values that increasingly dictate star casting, script choices, and which 'properties' are appropriate. The deafening applause for Oscar-nominated indie films over the last decade has drowned out the truth that many acknowledge but few will speak: while most of these films are interesting, and certainly different and preferable to the big-budget wannabe blockbusters the studios churn out, they are not, with a few glaring exceptions, very exciting.[2]

Biskind is not opposed to the films of the 'independent graduates' but he is keen to stress that he does not consider them to be as vital as lower-budget works with a greater sense of autonomy. Bourdieu is keen to stress the division between the two forms of production. As he claims:

> The opposition between legitimate and illegitimate, imposing itself in the field of symbolic good with the arbitrary necessity as the distinction between the sacred and the profane elsewhere, expresses the different social and cultural valuation of two modes of production: the one a field that is its own market, allied with an educational system that legitimises it; the other a field of production organized as a function of external demand, normally seen as socially and culturally inferior.[3]

This is to say that genuinely independent films are largely made by and for their particular sector and core audience, an audience that is intelligent and informed, and thereby capable of comprehending alternative media. By contrast, 'independent' films that have been made within the studio system can be seen as being of less social and cultural value, as they are the products of a system of mass production that adheres to the rules of the market. However, to divide the current American independent scene into these two culturally opposing camps would be a mistake, as the production of 'independent' features within the studio system is an altogether more complex process. Many 'independent graduates', are trying to forge a third form of production, one that is financially sustained by the economic power of the corporate giants, but artistically progressive and free of compromise. Others have been happy to adapt to making studio pictures, crossing over into what Bourdieu refers to as the field of 'external demand' where the interests of the mainstream audience and the corporate sponsor take precedence over the artistic ambitions of the film-maker. Despite the potential creative minefields and commercial compromises that come with working within the studio system, there are a number of key advantages which explain the decision of many 'independent graduates' to work for the corporate giants:

(1) Opportunity to work on a larger scale (i.e. – bigger budgets, access to unlimited studio resources).

(2) Opportunity to reach a 'wider' audience (i.e. – wide release of films, marketing campaigns, guaranteed theatrical and ancillary distribution).
(3) Further 'access' within the industry (i.e. – development deals and serious connections to stars and producers).
(4) Financial rewards/protection against risk (i.e. – higher earning potential, less investment of private funds, near-continuous employment).

What each of these advantages builds towards is the consolidation of a director's status within the industry. Independent film-makers such as Altman, Jarmusch, and Sayles have taken care of business by forming production companies and pursuing private financing. However, the 'companies' that they have built have been of a short-term nature, a necessary step towards completing one particular picture, before moving on to the next project. By contrast, the 'graduates' of the independent sector have sought more long-term financial stability, enabling them greater flexibility in terms of developing and financing projects. This has been achieved through a series of deals with the Hollywood studios, accepting representation by major creative talent agencies, and the formation of production companies in order to continuously have projects in development. In fact, audiences who have enjoyed the 'independent' films released by mini-majors such as Miramax and New Line, and specialist divisions like Focus, Fox Searchlight, and Sony Pictures Classics should be as grateful to the faceless executives who have shepherded such pictures through the production and distribution process as they are to the 'independent' film-makers who usually claim sole authorship of their endeavours. As Hirsch notes,

> It is commonplace in most lines of economic endeavour that those who process raw materials, transform them and merchandise the finished product receive the lion's share of economic rewards. The field of cultural endeavours is relatively unique in that we strongly desire to reward our creators, commune with their audiences, but avoid or ignore the organizational middlemen linking each to the other.[4]

As Hirsch observes, Hollywood plays the 'key role of gatekeeper and distributor',[5] a role that is 'critical in connecting the artist/creators to audience/consumers of mass culture.'[6] Without the Hollywood majors subsidizing the popular form of 'independent cinema', opportunities for film-makers would be more limited, and audiences would be bereft of many worthwhile pictures. However, it could also be argued that Hollywood only allows artistically autonomous production within its production factory as a means of seducing talent that has the potential to be employed to greater economic gain on its more traditional blockbuster fare. As Bourdieu asserts,

> The artists and writers who are richest in specific capital, and most concerned for their autonomy, are considerably weakened by the fact that some of their competitors identify their interests with the dominant principles of hierarchization and seek to impose on them even within the field, with the support of temporal powers.[7]

This is to say that the film-makers whose work has attained critical, but not necessarily commercial, success are vulnerable to the demands of the market, and may willingly or unwillingly sacrifice their values to get work produced. However, there are directors who have been able to stay true to their vision, either through being fortunate enough to achieve some commercial success. Woody Allen has maintained a career free of compromise, working with United Artists in the 1970s, the now-defunct mini-major Orion in the 1980s, and Dreamworks in recent years. His contract stipulates that he has final cut, complete control over casting and locations, and even the option of re-shooting the entire film if he is so inclined. Few of Allen's films have been commercial successes in the United States, and of a filmography that comprises thirty titles, *Annie Hall*, *Manhattan*, *Hannah and her Sisters*, *Crimes and Misdemeanours*, and *Match Point* stand out as his only substantial hits at the American box office. However, Allen is a 'prestige' film-maker, a director who is widely acknowledged as a modern master by critics. As such, studios have continued to provide finance because association with such a well-regarded film-maker brings them a level or class and exposure. Such an association also sends out a message to the creative community – talent should want to work with the studios. David O'Russell had worked with independents prior to his third feature, *Three Kings*, but had no qualms about developing a heavily politicized piece with Warner Brothers because he was aware of the controversial films that the studio had produced with Oliver Stone, such as *J.F.K.* and *Natural Born Killers*. Bourdieu suggests that such individuality cannot flourish within the system because the audience for more commercial work is unable to decipher the meaning of art of a more esoteric nature:

> Original experimentation entering the field of large-scale production almost always comes up against the breakdown in communication liable to arise from the use of codes inaccessible to the 'mass public'.[8]

However, the rise in popularity of the DVD has allowed film-makers a valuable tool in developing their relationships with audiences. Tarantino's *Reservoir Dogs* grossed $3 million during its 1992 theatrical release in the United States, but became one of the countries most rented titles when it reached the video market. By the time *Pulp Fiction* was released in 1994, an audience who had discovered the earlier film on video was eager to see the second offering from Quentin Tarantino. *Pulp Fiction* opened at number one and went on to gross over $200 million worldwide. Such independent films as *The Usual Suspects*, *Memento*, *Clerks*, and *El Mariachi* also flourished in the video market, where audiences who had been oblivious to their existence on theatrical release, or unable to see them due to limited distribution, were able to appreciate their qualities in the comfort of their own homes. Even superior examples of studio film-making have failed to find an audience. The Twentieth Century Fox production *Fight Club* returned only $34 million of its $70 million product budget upon theatrical release in the United States, and was swiftly withdrawn from screens following indifferent reviews and controversy regarding its seemingly anti-social content. However, it developed a 'cult' reputation and was a sensation on DVD where it became the most successful home entertainment title in the history of Fox, outselling pictures that grossed four times as much at the domestic box office. For directors who are willing to work within the Hollywood system, this technology has been a major advantage, allowing their films an immediate 'afterlife', where audiences can adapt to their cinematic rhythms and learn more about their creative process through the special features options that only DVD can provide, such as 'making-of' featurettes, director's commentaries, and anatomy-of-a-scene discussions.

With audiences more receptive than ever to 'independent' cinema, the relationship between studios and 'independent graduates' has become twofold – directors find financing and distribution, while studios attain cultural prestige and positive press, even if this sometimes means making a small loss, although sensibly budgeted pictures will usually recoup costs through DVD. Eager to compete with Miramax and its patronage of Quentin Tarantino, the mini-major New Line Cinema purchased Paul Thomas Anderson's script for his third feature, *Magnolia*, without having read it, even though the director's previous film for the company, the porn industry drama *Boogie Nights*, had struggled to turn a profit.

Therefore, it could be argued that the combination of artists who have succeeded in the field of restricted production, and the economic means of the field of large-scale production, could be combustible enough to produce a third form of production, a synthesis of the two fields where an artist is able to work with, and benefit from, the production and distribution resources of major studios and maintain a level of control that ensures their vision is not compromised. As Caves observes,

> The romantic ideal explains why the artist and dealer agree on the long-term joint venture that we commonly observe. The artist enters into a protracted partnership with the dealer. The dealer will display the artist's work and articulate its problem-solving context and evolving meaning to collector's and others.[9]

However, it is debatable as to whether the integrity of the 'independent graduates' can actually transcend corporate influence. While the bigger-budget works of 'independent' film-makers find their directors operating at a high level stylistically, the social and intellectual content of the films is often trite and redundant. Unlike the films of John Sayles and Abel Ferrara, which provide the overarching world view of their directors, the films of the independent 'graduates' are most commonly identified by their aesthetic – visual motifs, casting choices, music, preference of genre. When such choices are so specific and recurrent, they can be seen to constitute a particular 'style' or 'sensibility', although they can also be seen to be substituting for content. The films of Quentin Tarantino, particularly *Pulp Fiction* and *Kill Bill 1 & 2*, are derived from the director's love of 'B'-movie cinema. Any attempts at social critique or moral perspective, such as the feminist stance of *Kill Bill* and its theme of motherhood, feel self-conscious, as his work is more a celebration of the history of exploitation cinema and pulp literature than an exploration of the human condition.

The following case studies will examine the works and careers of Steven Soderbergh, Bryan Singer, David O'Russell, and Doug Liman, each of whom has moved from independent to studio production within several films, directing Hollywood features with considerable production and marketing budgets whilst still claiming 'independent' status as film-makers.

6.1 Steven Soderbergh

The career of Steven Soderbergh has seen him self-financing his own artistic endeavours, yet also delivering smoothly engineered mainstream crowd-pleasers within the Hollywood system. This could lead to comparisons with John Cassavettes, who worked regularly in Hollywood to fund his own films on his own creative terms, but Soderbergh's relationship with the studio system is more complex, his independent work being more of a psychological and emotional reaction to his experiences within the cinematic mainstream. Unlike such independent film-makers as Jarmusch, Sayles, and Ferrara, Soderbergh's films do not follow any strict thematic or narrative arch, with the director preferring to focus on whatever material interests him at the time and then adopting the appropriate visual style. This is not to deny any original qualities within his oeuvre, as Soderbergh is certainly not a plagiarist, or even an expert forger. Instead, he is able to adapt and develop the aesthetic sensibilities of earlier film-makers, providing them with an organic extension, rather than a slavish imitation. This approach is best exemplified by his meditative crime thriller *The Limey*, which stars Terrance Stamp as a London crook who travels to Los Angeles to unravel the mystery behind his daughter's death. At once alluding to the cinema of Alan Renais and Richard Lester, the film also incorporates footage of Stamp from Ken Loach's 1968 drama *Poor Cow*, suggesting links between not only the actor's earlier characterization, but the director and his cinematic lineage.

After getting his break by making avant-garde pop promos, Soderbergh became an 'overnight' sensation when his debut feature, the provocatively-titled *Sex, Lies, and Videotape* stormed the Cannes Film Festival in 1989. Soderbergh was branded 'the new Woody Allen' when the film walked away with the coveted Palme d'Or. Miramax purchased the picture for $1 million and ended up with a domestic box office haul of $24 million, an unheard of figure for an independent feature in 1989. In retrospect, *Sex, Lies, and Videotape* is less than the sum of its parts. As independent features go, it has less production value than even the most shoestring Greg Araki project. Not only does the film feature only a few locations, but these locations are barely designed – houses, apartments, the bar and commercial office that feature are adorned with the bare minimum of set dressing, failing to convince the attentive audience member that people genuinely live or work there.

It is, however, impossible to deny that *Sex, Lies, and Videotape* is the film that changed the way that Hollywood perceived independent cinema in the early 1990s, if only because of its box office gross. Soderbergh himself was thrown into a state of flux after the surprise success of his debut, describing it as a fluke, and famously quipping, 'it's all downhill from here' when accepting the prize at Cannes. It is possible to draw parallels between *Sex, Lies, and Videotape* and *Easy Rider*, both independent films from the fringes of the Hollywood system, which became break-out hits. Just as *Easy Rider* spawned a wave of less successful biker movies, the healthy returns generated by *Sex, Lies, and Videotape* were enough to have producers pumping money into talk-heavy films about philosophical yuppies, films about characters who talk about a wide variety of subjects and personal obsessions, but rarely get around to actually doing anything. However, in its quartet of central protagonists, Soderbergh's film represents the fractured psyche of a conservative America, left adrift at the end of the yuppie era. As Andrew observes,

> The movie cannily reflected a zeitgeist of a world in which AIDS had made 'liberated' sex problematic, while never resorting to reactionary dogma or solemn didacticism.[10]

This is to say that Soderbergh's film exists outside the Hollywood mainstream in that it refuses to judge its characters, or provide any sense of emotional closure. It was a semi-autobiographical piece that asked questions about the nature of human relationships without offering answers, and Soderbergh was keen to emphasize how close he was to the material, suggesting that the writing of the screenplay as a form of therapy for him after a period of self-destructive behaviour. As he recalls,

> I was involved in a relationship with a woman in which I was deceptive and mentally manipulative. I got involved with a number of other women simultaneously...there was one point at which I was in a bar, and within a radius of about two feet there were three different women I was sleeping with...I just became somebody that, if I knew them, I would hate.[11]

After being over-praised for his first feature, Soderbergh found that his subsequent and arguably superior films were largely ignored by audiences and critics alike. Stepping back from the intense self-examination that had inspired his debut, *Kafka*, infuriated both cultural camps by being shot in stark black-and-white and using the famed writer of *The Trial* and *Metamorphosis* as the central protagonist in a convoluted mystery story derived from his own works, as opposed to being a straight biopic. It took two years for *Kafka* to be released in every major territory, an absurd state of affairs when Soderbergh had made a unique mix of thriller and biography, which referenced everything from Kafka's own writing to the films of Fritz Lang and Hammer Horror.

Better received by critics was *King of the Hill*, a beautifully observed rites-of-passage story set during the Depression, while Soderbergh's fourth feature, the neo-noir *The Underneath*, is probably his most ill-conceived offering, a thriller which employed multiple time frames to tell a redundant crime story about a compulsive gambler who becomes involved in an armoured car robbery. The attitude of many critics towards Soderbergh around this time reflects not only a lack of appreciation for the director's experimentation and ambition, but also a noticeable change in the critical consensus regarding how to define 'independent film-making', as the figurehead of

1990s independent cinema was losing his lustre as a critical subject by refusing to move in more commercial circles.

Returning home to Baton Rouge, Soderbergh wrote and directed *Schizopolis*, a project which he also financed, often using funds from his less-documented sideline as a Hollywood script doctor. Following in the footsteps of John Sayles, he lent his talent to rewrites of such forgettable genre fodder as *Nightwatch* and *Mimic* as a means of economic survival when his directorial career seemed to be stalling. Loosely documenting the disintegration of his own marriage, *Schizopolis* was shot by a crew consisting of just five people, with Soderbergh taking on two acting roles himself and scenes being written and re-written on a daily basis. There was no official schedule, and other actors were often cast at the last minute depending on whose friends or acquaintances were available and suitable for the parts.

An audacious example of cinema as self-examination, *Schizopolis* frequently breaks the formal rules of American cinema by attempting to shatter the 'third wall' that exists between film and audience, with Soderbergh engaging in a discussion with his audience. This is best exemplified by a sequence in which Soderbergh himself appears on screen and pretends to 'take' questions from the audience, allowing time for questions to be asked, and then simply answering 'yes' to them. Sequences such as this one undoubtedly contributed to all major distributors passing on the film, despite early interest in a new piece about human relationships from the director of the 'groundbreaking' *Sex, Lies, and Videotape*. The success of Soderbergh's debut film still carried enough cultural currency for Miramax to offer to buy *Schizopolis* without having seen it, and for rival distributors to hastily request screenings, but, ironically, the 'independent' companies ultimately rejected a true guerrilla production on the grounds that they did not know how to sell it to an appropriate audience.

Most articles about Steven Soderbergh take a negative look at this stage of his career, observing that, though he made a few worthwhile films, he was failing to play the Hollywood game. However, it should be noted that two of these films were financed through Gramercy, the 'art house' arm of Hollywood studio Universal. It is a measure of what a good 'employee' Soderbergh was that, even after three features that failed to break $2 million at the domestic box office and a fourth that struggled to find distribution, he was still hired by Jersey Films and Universal to direct the comparatively starry *Out of Sight*, the adaptation of the Elmore Leonard novel that was to be his 'comeback'. Acknowledging the balance that can exist between the artist and his benefactor, Soderbergh described *Out Of Sight* as 'the perfect blend of what I do and the resources a studio can provide.'[12]

A near-perfect marriage of director material, *Out of Sight* plays gently with the much practiced narrative forms of the heist thriller and the romantic-comedy, without entirely subverting, or conforming to, audience expectations. On paper, this is a routine caper about a career criminal (George Clooney) who escapes from prison, taking a federal marshal (Jennifer Lopez) captive in the process. These social opposites discover an immediate mutual attraction, one that threatens to hinder their respective goals, as the crook plans a diamond heist and the marshal attempts to bring him to justice. In practise, however, Soderbergh uses Leonard's crime story to comment on the fleeting nature of human relationships, the social divisions that exist between outlaws and conformists, and the economic hierarchy that is present within the criminal world itself, as white-collar crooks are presented as possessing more economic and social mobility than their blue-collar equivalents. The theme of time running out is alluded to through visual motifs, the camera only just capturing his actors as they move swiftly out of the frame, setting aside more personal matters in favour of professional pursuits.

Out of Sight was far from an unqualified commercial success in that it returned only $37 million of its $48 million outlay at the domestic box office. However, the film was well liked in industry circles, particularly for its transformation of George Clooney from television star to serious film actor, and Soderbergh became a hot director, taking on the Julia Roberts vehicle *Eric Brokovich*, and using his newfound clout to set up *Traffic* with fledgling independent USA Films. He also formed the production company Section 8, with the ambition of bringing more 'independent' directors into a position where they could work with studio resources without being artistically compromised. Although some of the output of Section 8 has been questionable, particularly its reliance on remakes of well-regarded foreign films such as *Insomnia*, *Solaris*, and *Nine Queens*, it has succeeded in delivering a steady slate of films that have offered entertainment for the more discerning cinemagoer. His attempts to return to his 'independent' roots, however, have met with mixed results. The Hollywood satire *Full Frontal*, with its industry in-jokes, was more alienating than provocative, while his digital video project *Bubble* was more notable for being the first film to be released simultaneously to theatres and DVD than it was for its actual cinematic qualities. Acutely aware of his dual positions as an 'A'-list director and an 'independent' film-maker, Soderbergh has successfully balanced both forms of production, although it is perhaps with such studio productions as *Ocean's 11* and *Eric Brokovich* that his film-making seems most relaxed and confident.

Bryan Singer

At the end of 1995, whilst conducting their annual round up of the year in cinema, *Empire*, Britain's biggest-selling and most industry-affiliated film publication, awarded Bryan Singer the honour of Best Debut Feature for his crime thriller *The Usual Suspects*. The film was a labyrinthine caper picture that had succeeded in delighting audiences and critics alike. It drew comparisons to Tarantino's iconic debut *Reservoir Dogs* in that the action took place within the crime genre and the film featured no obvious male lead, preferring an ensemble of established actors and rising talent who excelled under Singer's succinct direction, revelling in the cryptically quotable dialogue that he had co-written. Shot for $5 million, *The Usual Suspects* grossed $23 million in the United States and proved a popular choice on the home rental market. As far as both critics and the paying public were concerned, Singer's film was a major debut. Unfortunately,

The Usual Suspects was not actually Singer's debut feature – his first film was actually the barely distributed Public Access.

The film, which Singer co-authored with his childhood friend Christopher Maguire, follows the effect a socially reserved loner has on a small town community when he sets up his own public access television programme. Titled Our Town, his show is much like an American independent feature in that it is low on production value but high on controversy, as the host 'invites' residents of the sleepy suburb to phone in and complain about whatever is bothering them about their neighbours and their community as a whole, ultimately leading to an act of violent action.

By borrowing the narrative device of Soderbergh's Sex, Lies, and Videotape, the notion of a mysterious stranger moving to a small town and using media as a means of social analysis and then provocation, and imposing the languid pacing found in the films of David Lynch, Singer is more clear about who his influences are than what his film is actually about. Public Access is never sure if it is a suburban satire, a meditation on the pervading power of modern media, or a slow-burning thriller. However, it made enough of an impression at the 1993 Sundance Film Festival, where it shared Grand Jury Prize at the Sundance Film Festival with the altogether gentler Ruby in Paradise. It says much about the need of modern film critics to justify their position as predictors of popular taste, and discoverers of new talent that a director's first feature can be so conveniently overlooked when the need for an 'overnight success story' arises. Singer, however, was happy to play along, rarely mentioning Public Access when promoting The Usual Suspects, while his real debut feature is now largely consigned to the bargain-basement section in most DVD emporiums, having failed to secure a theatrical distributor, either domestically or internationally.

The Usual Suspects is a great technical leap forward from its predecessor and also a satisfying piece of upscale entertainment. A gang of crooks are rounded up by the New York police to be interrogated for a crime they have not committed. Upon release, they band together to pull off a series of 'jobs', only to attract the attention of Keysor Soze, an underworld mastermind who is widely feared, yet never seen. Although the paranoid mood of the film owes much to such 1970s classics as The Parallax View, Marathon Man, Night Moves, and Klute, it never aspires to their psychological complexity. By focussing on a group of characters as opposed to a lone protagonist, Singer is able to treat his narrative framework as a chessboard and his criminals as the pieces, setting one up against another and ultimately employing some merely as narrative red herrings rather than individual psychological constructs.

Unlike the thrillers of the 1970s, Singer's film does not take place in the 'real' world, or reference social-political events, preferring instead to operate in a criminal vortex where innocent crusaders are notable by their absence. As with Pulp Fiction, this is a world that is populated by those in on the 'action', crooks and cops, lawyers and informants, all engaged in a dangerous game that seems to have no end or purpose, except to keep everyone in varying states of play. As such, events and actions are largely without moral consequence and the film has no social-political context. Without a moral crusader or innocent bystander at its centre, *The Usual Suspects* is emotionally remote, with Gabriel Byrne's brooding love for his remarkably understanding attorney a somewhat pat concession to the 'need' for a romantic element. Therefore, *The Usual Suspects* is another 'movie-movie', a film whose plot reflects on the nature of plotting itself, with no social-political relevance.

Singer then spent a few years developing the disturbing Stephen King adaptation *Apt Pupil*, the slow-burning story of an American teenager (Brad Renfro) who discovers that one of the elderly citizens in his suburban community (Ian McKellen) is actually a former Nazi, responsible for sending Jewish families to their deaths in prisoner of war camps during World War II. *Apt Pupil* has much in common with both Singer's earlier films in that it occupies similar geographical territory to *Public Access* and examines what can be hidden away in sleepy Middle America, yet it also follows *The Usual Suspects* in its examination of the nature of evil. A return of $8 million on a budget of $14 million made *Apt Pupil* a commercial failure, but by no means a disgrace, as critics generally agreed that Singer had handled complex material in a mature manner, while Ian McKellen's unflinching portrayal of an ageing yet still lethal Nazi was riveting to watch, but it would be Singer's next project that would see him fully graduate from independent 'school' to the Hollywood 'A'-list.

Singer's *X-Men*, released in 2000, was the big screen version of the phenomenally popular Marvel comic book, the story of a band of mutant superheroes that have been exiled from society, but are still noble enough to save mankind from destruction whenever evil rears its ugly head. Although he had been entrusted with a budget of $75 million, Singer was keen to maintain his status as an 'independent film-maker' and, addressing claims that he had eagerly jumped on to the studio bandwagon by making an expensive superhero movie for the summer season, he stated that

> Firstly, we didn't have an extraordinarily large budget...And secondly, we shot in Canada, so even thought we were making a studio picture, it was a severely independent studio picture and I could still approach it the same way I approach all my films.[13]

What Singer considered to be a 'severely independent' approach could be translated as 'severely inexperienced'. *X-Men* is structurally uneven, with not-so-special effects and an ending which feels more like an afterthought. Given that a Special Edition DVD, released some years later, contained a number of alternative and deleted scenes, it is apparent that *X-Men* is a heavily compromised film, the result of a director trying to make a faithful adaptation, but having to adhere to the demands of a studio expecting a summer blockbuster. If his 2003 sequel, *X-2*, felt more confident, it was perhaps a result of not just Singer's increased technical competence, but also his acceptance of the requirements of a studio 'event' movie. Once more, the director looked to other populist material for guidance and cited the second *Star Wars* movie, *The Empire Strikes Back*, as his conceptual model.

Singer has not ventured back into the 'independent' world since his success with *The Usual Suspects*. However, his consistent choice of spectacular popcorn pictures derived from source material firmly established in 'pop' culture suggests that this state of affairs is not so much a creative compromise, but a position that the director has been working towards throughout his career. The luxuries afforded him by big studio productions such as *X-Men* and its sequel also appear to have affected his judgements regarding material and sources of finance. He was scheduled to direct *Confessions of a Dangerous Mind*, a script from *Being John Malkovich* scribe Charlie Kaufman about the 1960s American television personality Chuck Barris and his claims of being enlisted as a CIA hit man. However, budgetary disputes led to Singer leaving the project, which was later directed by George Clooney. Other rumoured 'self-generated' projects, such as compendium film of science-fiction stories, also came to nothing. Having established himself as a producer, he has become involved in television, overseeing production of the successful medical drama *House MD*.

6.3 Doug Liman

As with Bryan Singer, Doug Liman does not appear to have any concrete views about the nature of independent film, and has effectively used the sector as a stepping stone to more lucrative Hollywood productions. Perhaps this explains why his definitions of independent cinema verge on the banal. He insists that

> First and foremost, when I think about independent films, I think about them being as character and script driven.[14]

Like Singer, he gained recognition not with a 'ground-breaking debut', but with his second feature. Also like Singer, he has rarely discussed his first film, *Student Body*, a privately financed 1994 comedy-thriller which failed to find distribution. Over the course of five films, Liman's work has become increasingly commercial, more concerned with courting a mass audience. His most recent film, the action-comedy *Mr & Mrs Smith*, is a particularly dispiriting exercise in bombastic studio film-making, far removed from the social subtleties of his earlier offerings, *Swingers* and *Go*.

Regardless of Liman's questionable notion of what constitutes an independent film, it cannot be denied that his second feature, *Swingers*, was made outside the Hollywood system. Privately financed, shot on locations without the required permits, and filmed without a distribution deal in place, it was a truly guerrilla operation. The screenplay was written by Jon Favreau, who co-starred alongside his friend Vince Vaughn. Both had been working in Hollywood for some years, picking up small roles in studio productions and television series, sometimes finding that their supporting roles had been edited down to mere background characters. While Liman was responsible for the visual style of *Swingers*, it was Favreau's 'voice' at the heart of the piece. The film was based on his experiences of being an unemployed actor in Los Angeles, and his screen friendship with Vaughn was a reflection of the bond they shared in real life, while the film's most distinctive quality was its quotable dialogue, a key characteristic of independent features since Spike Lee's *She's Gotta Have It*. For his group of 'swingers', Favreau had invented a lexicon derived from outmoded examples of popular culture, with the expression 'you're so money' becoming much used by impressionable males and ironic cineastes.

The anecdotal plot of *Swingers* focuses on Favreau, who has moved from New York to Los Angeles to pursue a career as a comedian, but is struggling to get by professionally, and spending his evenings hanging out with a group of fellow wannabes led by Vaughn. Such a summary of *Swingers* suggests that it is another independent talkfest in the mould of *Sex, Lies, and Videotape*, but that is without mentioning the infectious spirit of the piece. The men in *Swingers* are on the bottom rung of the ladder, but instead of wallowing in self-pity, they try to emulate their rat pack heroes by going out and hitting the most fashionable, out-of-the-way night spots. Eventual distributor Miramax used the standard release pattern for an independent film by debuting *Swingers* in select cinemas in New York and Los Angeles, targeting a select audience that would spread the good word amongst their friends. Such word-of-mouth marketing is common in independent film distribution, but many films fall off the radar before they are given a chance to go on to greater success. *Swingers*, however, kept on playing, and in Vaughn it had an instant celebrity whose presence in magazines kept the film's profile high in the face of more expensive opposition.

As much as he was probably proud of the film he had made, Liman was more enthusiastic about the deal he brokered single-handed with Miramax. Although turned down by the Sundance Film Festival, screenings were arranged and Miramax showed interest. Initially offered a small sum that would cover production and negative costs, Liman refused, confident that *Swingers* was of greater commercial value, and that Miramax, now owned by the Disney corporation, could afford to pay a higher price. He was to be proved right. As Liman explains, 'I sent a fax to my parents saying, "Miramax. $5.5 million. Doug." A very good feeling.'[15]

For his next feature, Liman followed in the footsteps of Bryan Singer with a movie that had an independent feel about it, and yet had enough commercial elements to become a breakout hit. Sadly, his edgy teen flick *Go* did not become the box office smash that studio backer Columbia was hoping for, but its $15 million return on a $5 million budget, and healthy DVD revenues, made it a profitable investment. The budget was slim when you consider the amount of production value on the screen, with the story jumping between Los Angeles and Las Vegas and the director pulling off an extended car chase through the streets of the gambling capital. *Go* may appear to be a superficially 'dark' comedy, detailing three interconnecting stories over one day, and its structural device gave some critics the impression that it was simply a lightweight distant cousin of *Pulp Fiction* and *Mystery Train*, but there is much more going on in *Go* than they gave Liman and screenwriter John August credit for.

Go is a movie about the youthful members of society who are not well represented in modern cinema. While mainstream Hollywood portrays people in their late teens or early twenties as college kids or youthful high fliers, *Go* shows the reality. Some are working dead-end jobs in convenience stores, putting in exhausting hours over the Christmas period to avoid eviction. Others are bored and seek quick, cheap thrills through a lad's weekend to Las Vegas, while the most 'successful' characters in the movie in material terms are a neighbourhood drug dealer and a pair of gay actors. It is also a movie which offers no moral stance on the actions of its characters. They go out, get drunk, get high, get into trouble, suffer the consequences, and then get up and do it all over again. Liman and August do not judge their protagonists; they simply show how a lot of young people are escaping from their otherwise mundane lives. Even the drug dealer is a multi-faceted creation. He tries to kill the checkout girl who double-crosses him over a deal, but he also acts like a gentleman when an attractive young woman is left at his apartment as 'collateral' for twenty hits of ecstasy.

Eager to move into the big-budget arena, Liman directed the $75 million spy thriller *The Bourne Identity*, an adaptation of the 1980 best-seller by Robert Ludlum which grossed $122 million at the domestic box office. Although the novel is aimed at a more mature audience, Liman keeps things youthful by casting Matt Damon as an amnesiac spy, and the German actress Franka Potente as his unlikely ally. Like *Go*, this is a movie about young people thrown into the adult world and forced to deal with its dangers. This is most evident in the first half, which plays with genre expectations, although the second half reverts to type. As with *X-Men*, this is a case of a talented but crucially inexperienced film-maker struggling to find his feet within the Hollywood mainstream. Keen to score a big success, Liman accepted studio demands for re-shoots following unsuccessful test screenings, and was also happy to cut away at scenes involving celebrated character actors Chris Cooper and Brian Cox. As he recalls, 'Nobody cared. The audience just wanted to follow Matt and Franka.'[16]

If *The Bourne Identity* had a rough-and-ready aesthetic to distract the more discerning viewer from its 'airport thriller' plotting Liman's fifth feature, *Mr & Mrs Smith* altogether jettisoned any pretence of reality. Aside from its implausible concept of two international assassins who marry and set up home together without knowing what the other does for a living, this film shows scant regard for logic or character psychology, with Liman falling back on two of the most reliable attributes of the Hollywood blockbuster – big stars and even bigger bangs. Brad Pitt and Angelina Jolie are worshipped by his camera, photographed from the most flattering of angles at all times and relied upon to keep the film afloat when the narrative takes another ridiculous turn. This is the kind of expensive action-extravaganza where the 'stars' can be hit, kicked, stabbed, slapped, thrown, and shot at, yet only sustain minor bruises, grazes or cuts, wounds that are artfully placed by the make-up department.

After falling behind schedule on *The Bourne Identity*, Liman found himself under close supervision and was not allowed to direct all of the logistically challenging action sequences himself. Liman's lack of control over narrative direction, obvious in the cases of *The Bourne Identity* and *Mr & Mrs Smith* as each had alternative endings and supporting characters who were cut out at the last minute, is characteristic of 'independent graduates' who do not generate their own material. While Liman possesses a distinctive visual style, and a knack for bringing quirky performances from Hollywood players, he is ultimately a 'director-for-hire' who has parlayed his good fortune with *Swingers* into a lucrative career as a director of expensive star vehicles. To consolidate his status as an 'A'-list talent, Liman has co-founded Hypnotic, a company specializing in feature films, television, and advertising. Obviously keen on diversification, his profile on the company website mentions his success with feature films, but is equally keen to promote his commercials for Levi's, Sony, and particularly his Nike spot with champion golfer Tiger Woods. He has also developed several television series and directed the pilot for the successful teen drama *The O.C.*

6.4 David O'Russell

Of the four directors studied here, Russell is the closest to Caves's romantic ideal of an artist working within the system without compromising his ideals. Like Woody Allen, he writes his own material and does not try to set up the financial structure of his projects until he is satisfied with his completed screenplay. Also like Allen, he has managed to attract stellar casts for his films and negotiate shooting and editing schedules that are more flexible than those of the average studio production. These are significant achievements for a director who has managed only one commercial success, and whose films are eccentric and occasionally controversial. Unlike Soderbergh, Singer, and Liman, he has remained a detachment from the industry, often retreating to an almost monastic existence between projects and has not formed his own production company, moved into television, or worked as a 'director-for-hire'.

While the first features of Singer and Liman can be viewed as stepping stones, Russell's first feature, *Spanking The Monkey*, has more in common with Steven Soderbergh's *Sex, Lies, and Videotape*, in that it is a film that is financially and culturally independent – a story that is filtered through the perspective of its creator, with a semi-autobiographical tone and few concessions to the demand of the mass market or festival selection committees. The script was originally titled *Swelter*, and Russell wrote it whilst serving seven days of jury duty in Manhattan. Detailing the incestuous relationship between a college student and his bedridden mother, the project had the hallmarks of an independent production in that it would utilize simple, affordable locations and a small cast.

Russell's only real industry contact at the time was his girlfriend, a low-level executive at New Line Cinema, who managed to bring Russell's screenplay to the attention of her senior colleagues. Despite reservations over the content, New Line took out an option on the screenplay for $2,000 and proposed a budget of $1 million on the condition that Russell could secure the services of a movie star whose presence would somehow 'legitimize' the unsavoury subject matter and bring in a mass audience. This condition appears to be a not-so-subtle example of studio politics with New Line executives not wanting to dismiss promising material out of hand, but also not willing to grant it the elusive 'green light'. There are few, if any, actresses in Hollywood who are old enough to convincingly portray the mother of a college student and bankable enough to guarantee an audience, and after Faye Dunaway declined the role, Russell found himself having to finance the film independently. His creative process mirrors that of Steven Soderbergh with *Sex, Lies, and Videotape*, as his screenplay, whilst not entirely autobiographical, alluded to aspects of his own life, something that Russell was keen to discuss when promoting the film. As he recalls,

> There was something in me that felt compelled to do it. It was autobiographical, except the extremeness of it...I remember feeling very liberated when I wrote it...And there were still great feelings of liberation in making the movie, by making your own point.[17]

The financing for *Spanking the Monkey*, as the film was later re-titled, came from two grants, one from the National Endowment for the Arts, the other from the New York State Council of the Arts. The two grants totalled $80,000, while an additional $1,000 was raised by selling the film off as shares to friends and family. In the tradition of true independent cinema, the film that was shot in guerrilla style, with real locations and non-professional actors being utilized, while the subject matter was candid and controversial. Whilst on location in upstate New York, Russell would frequently lie to local residents about the plot of the movie, through fear that some would object to the theme of incest and force the production from the location. Although New Line had rejected the film at script stage, they bought the completed picture through their 'art house' division, Fine Line, after it won the Audience Award at the Sundance Film Festival in 1994, and *Spanking the Monkey* eventually grossed $1.3 million.

As with the other directors studied here, Russell has always intended his work to play to as wide an audience as possible, regardless of its subject matter. Although he did not become actively involved in producing and marketing, he did intend his second feature, the black comedy *Flirting With Disaster*, to cross over to people who did not see *Spanking The Monkey*, either because of its limited release, lack of marquee names, or difficult subject matter. *Flirting with Disaster* was a broader piece, concerning an uptight executive trying to find his natural parents after discovering that he was adopted. With Ben Stiller, Tea Leoni, and Alan Alda in the cast, it also benefited from some 'star' value, and an episodic narrative concerning an incident-filled road trip, a staple of 'independent' cinema since *Easy Rider*, *Five Easy Pieces*, and *Two Lane Blacktop*, ensuring that it was a more cinematic proposition than Russell's debut. Although it grossed $12 million at the domestic box office, Russell felt that his backer and distributor, Miramax, had soft-sold the picture, particularly on the video market, and that he could actually be better served by a major studio.

Developing an action script entitled *Spoils of War* about three soldiers who attempt to pull off a gold heist in the final days of the Gulf conflict, Russell entered into a contract with Warner Brothers to deliver a $45 million adventure movie that would need to connect with a mass audience if it was to be a profitable venture. Always ambitious with regard to casting, Russell favoured Clint Eastwood or Dustin Hoffman for the lead role, a jaded military commander who would lead the rouge operation. When Eastwood failed to show interest, and the studio refused to cast Hoffman based on the poor box office record of his 1990s films, Russell pursued Nicolas Cage instead but eventually settled on George Clooney. As with Soderbergh and Liman, Russell is a film-maker who is acutely aware of the benefits of 'star' casting, With the right star, financing falls into place more easily, and the film-maker is more 'protected' in the sense that the studio is less concerned over their investment in potentially difficult material now that it has some commercial value involved.

The working methods of David O'Russell belie an independent sensibility, in that he operates intuitively, constantly re-writing, encouraging improvisation, making last-minute changes, and sometimes scrapping whole sequences. Unfortunately, these are working methods that can rarely be adopted in the independent sector, where time is always of the essence, and strict budgets and schedules force the kind of creative compromises that Russell is unlikely to be willing to make. Regarded by those who have worked with him as a 'control freak', Russell may struggle to find financing from studios should the 'A'-list talent he has so far managed to attract tire of his working methods, or his films continue to deliver merely modest box office returns.

6.5 Natural Progression – The Necessity of 'Studio Recruitment'
One might question if it is necessary for directors to progress so quickly to studio movies, with bigger stars and budgets when there are directors like Sayles, Rudolph, Schrader and Jarmusch making movies independently and finding an audience for them. It should, however, be noted that these are rare film-makers who have managed to balance art and commerce, or had the nerve to take a few years out between projects when producers were reluctant to back the films that they wanted to make. They have also found different subject matter to tackle, re-inventing themselves with each project. For every Altman or Sayles, there is a whole host of one-trick ponies, directors who have one terrific movie in them, who then make the same movie again. This can be because of their own reluctance to do something different, or because doors do not open to allow them to diversify their output, but either way it eventually stalls their careers, meaning that today's indie wonder boy could be wandering tomorrow's indie wasteland.

David O'Russell, by contrast, has made four distinctly different films, but has done this by maintaining his own acerbic point of view. *Spanking the Monkey* satirizes the roots of American culture by putting the suburban family unit under the microscope; *Flirting with Disaster* takes aim at the fragmented family culture that has come to be as a result of the problems addressed in the earlier film; *Three Kings* questions another important American unit in the form of the military; and *I Heart Huckabees* places classic philosophy within the context of capitalist America. Although each of these films shows a growth in the cinematic sensibility of their creator, they also find him broadening the appeal of his work, moving from a $200,000 incest drama seen by a curious few on the art house circuit to a $10 million Miramax comedy with a mid-range cast to an explosive, Warner Brothers-backed action picture which grossed $60 million at the domestic box office, and back to a more personal film, but one made with greater confidence and resources than his first.

Despite the achievements of these 'independent graduates', particularly Soderbergh and Russell, it is debatable as to whether they can still be considered 'independent film-makers', purely because their work is now reliant on studio financing, industry deal-making, and the key commercial attribute of 'star' casting. As Bourdieu notes,

> Intellectual labour carried out collectively, within technically and socially differentiated production units, can no longer surround itself with the charismatic aura attached to traditional independent production.[18]

This is to say that the 'independent graduates' have become key players in the Hollywood system, bringing fresh perspectives to contemporary American cinema, but existing firmly within the mainstream and relying on studio resources. Hollywood's subtle absorption of such talents has effected how 'independent cinema' is regarding by the paying public. To mainstream cinemagoers, the term 'independent' has come to mean a certain type of film, as opposed to a certain method of production. When films financed and distributed by mini-majors and specialist studio divisions, such as *Lost in Translation*, *Sideways*, and *Eternal Sunshine of the Spotless Mind* are described as 'independent', it is a description that is being used to succinctly sum up the core attributes of the films themselves, not their production backgrounds. The term is referring to the classy casting, the possibility of a major star, such as Jim Carey or Bill Murray, playing against 'type', the tasteful cinematography, the fashionable soundtrack, the collectable DVD, the possibility of awards and, therefore, social legitimacy.

Therefore, the 'independent' cinema that is practiced by directors now working within the system, finding funding from mini-majors, studios, and specialist divisions, has come to be characterized by its aesthetic choices, rather than its inherent social-political stance, becoming increasingly conventional in the process as directors come to terms with the constraints of being in the employ of the corporate giants. Although this can be seen to compromise the value of 'independent cinema', it cannot be denied that moving forward is necessary in any industry, and it would be wrong to criticize any director for taking on a big studio project, simply because he or she has come up through the independent world.

Making an independent movie has become a way to get noticed. Many of the young film-makers probably harbour dreams of going to Hollywood, making a runaway smash, and working with 'A'-list superstars and debuting with an impressive independent feature is the first stage in their quest to achieving this dream. The likes of John Sayles and Abel Ferrara can remain in the independent world, because that is the best place for them to tell their stories, but not all directors are as personally involved in their projects in the way that Sayles and Ferrara are. Sayles regularly puts his money where his mouth is and invests his own earnings to bring his stories to the screen, while most other directors would prefer to have the comparative security of being a 'director-for-hire' and signing a development deal with a major studio that would guarantee them work for many years to come.

Notes

1. Caves, p. 73, spring 2003.
2. Biskind, P, review of *The Sundance Kids: How the Mavericks Took Back Hollywood* in *Sight & Sound*, p. 95, 06/2006.
3. Bourdieu, p. 130, 1993.
4. Hirsch, P, *Cultural Productions in the U.S.: Do Changes in Ownership Matter?*, p. 36, 1985.
5. Hirsch, P, 'Cultural Industries Revisited', *Organization Science*, 11:3 (May-June 2000), p. 356.
6. Hirsch, p. 356, May – June 2000.
7. Bourdieu, p. 41, 1993.
8. Bourdieu, p. 129, 1993.
9. Caves, pp. 73 – 74, 2003.
10. Andrew, p. 263, 1998.
11. Soderbergh, S, quoted by Greenberg, J, 'Sex, Lies, and Kafka', *Connoisseur*, 11/1991.
12. Soderbergh, S, quoted by Johnston, S, 'The Flashback Kid', *American Independent Cinema – A Sight & Sound Reader*, (ed. Hillier, J), p. 268, London, BFI, 2001.
13. Singer, B, quoted by Fischer, P, 'X2 Director Has Something to Sing About', www.filmmonthly.com by Topel, Y, 04/07/03.
14. Liman, D, quoted F, 'Behind Bourne', www.actionadventure.about.com, 2002.
15. Liman, quoted by Daly, S, 'Liman on Liman', www.ew.com, 14/05/2006.
16. Liman, quoted by Daly, 14/05/2006.
17. O'Russell, D, quoted by Spines, C, 'Who Let the Underdogs Out?', *Premiere*, 10/2002.
18. Bourdieu, p. 131, 1993.

7

A CULTURAL COMPARISON: BRITISH INDEPENDANT CINEMA AND ITS RELATION TO ITS AMERICAN COUNTERPART

American independent cinema does not exist in a cultural or economic void. As discussed, it succeeds as a mode of cultural expression because it occupies a position, however financially subservient it may be, within the industry of mass production. With its own corporate hierarchies, methods of production, distribution, and promotion, not to mention a reliance on stars and media exposure, the American independent sector has become a marketable brand, easily identifiable through its key characteristics. This has been achieved through its industrialized nature, which has enabled producers to project the image of a freewheeling artistic movement, whilst at the same time ensuring that profits are maximized, and industrial relations are finely balanced. To fully comprehend how the American independent sector benefits from being an economically small, yet creatively significant, part of the industry of mass production, it is necessary to look at its less successful British counterpart.

This chapter will provide an outline of the independent feature film production sector in the UK. The British independent sector is one that is best exemplified by its fragmentation, with production companies lacking relations to one another, or to any of the monolithic corporate giants that characterize the American field of cultural production. While this comparatively ad-hoc approach to business makes it difficult to apply the term 'industry' to British film production, it does qualify many productions as 'independent', a status which even lower budget American efforts fail to achieve due to their carefully concealed financial ties with the Hollywood giants.

Any attempt to define what is meant by the term 'British independent cinema' is as inherently problematic, as it raises the usual questions of whether it is sources of funding or intellectual content that warrant such status. However, while those cultural commentators looking for a straightforward analysis of American feature film production can simply cite the distinction of perceived 'studio' and 'non-studio' film-making as a means of distinguishing the 'independent' sector from its more corporate cultural parallel, this is simply not applicable to Britain as the country does not have a studio system, or rather a number of companies with enough financial capital and industrial resources to develop, make, and distribute feature films.

7.1 Cinema in Cycles – Modern British Feature Film Production and the Failure to Sustain an Independent Sector

Feature film production in the UK since 1960 has been of a cyclical nature, with three notable periods when British film-making seemed to be at a critical and commercial peak, at least from a non-industrial perspective. Firstly, the American studios chose to establish London production bases during the period of 1963 and 1964, mainly to capitalize on the 'Swinging Sixties' scene that was attracting so much attention overseas, a scene which owed more to the fashion and music than it did to feature films. This resulted in a run of 'British films' that were financed by American studios, such as *Alfie*, *Tom Jones*, and *The Italian Job*, a scenario which was to be repeated in the late 1990s with the success of American-funded but British-flavoured films like *The Full Monty*, *Bend It like Beckham*, and *Shakespeare in Love*.

As the 1960s came to a close, and fashion and media focus shifted elsewhere, the American majors moved out of London leaving the 'industry' in a dilapidated state. Although Britain won many critical plaudits for its feature films in the 1960s, the profits that are crucial to sustaining an industry and production were sent overseas to the Hollywood majors, while the talent that the scene produced, the movie actors, directors, writers, and designers, were mostly lured, or forced, to Los Angeles where they continued to work for the Hollywood majors on American soil. One of the few production companies to survive was EON Productions, whose output was exclusively that of the James Bond franchise, and whose distribution deal with United Artists and international appeal of its product gave them economic stability. However, constant cultural shifts, particularly those which affected changes in cinema and the action-adventure genre of which the Bond franchise is a prominent example, meant that the company had to develop its films within the creative constraints of the American studio system in order to ensure their longevity as a commercial property.

The second upswing in British feature production occurred in the 1980s, when the industry found itself energized by a combination of city money, entrepreneurial spirit, and some genuine film-making talent. The UK production companies of the 1980s were financed with British, and also European, capital that was often sourced through city investment and the ancillary markets of major corporations such as record labels and television networks. However, such companies did not have the financial capital to sponsor more than a few productions at a time, a situation that both government and private film initiatives have since failed to rectify. This meant that each production was essentially an informed gamble, the success or failure of which would determine how much the company would have to invest in its next project. Two companies in particular, Palace Pictures and Goldcrest, attempted to defy the rules of independent production by operating as studios, embarking on a slate of films with simultaneous production schedules. Goldcrest invested particularly heavily, spending £90 million over the period of 1980 to 1987 in British film and television production.

Palace Pictures survived much of the 1980s for the same reason that its American counterparts, such as Vestron and Island Alive, managed to last most of the decade – it maintained ownership of its product, gaining crucial revenue from the home video and television profits generated by such films as *Mona Lisa*, *The Company Of Wolves*, *Scandal*, and the notorious horror film *The Evil Dead*. The growth rate of the VCR market in the UK was rapid, outpacing other European countries and even North America. In 1985, it was estimated that 42 per cent of the population of the UK owned a VCR, with the figure rising to 54 per cent in 1988. Palace succeeded in financing their theatrical releases by maintaining the rights to their films within the burgeoning home entertainment market, which also included soundtracks, but like its American counterparts, Palace ultimately found itself overextended and was forced to auction the rights to the most successful titles in its library, providing short-term production funds but ultimately costing the company an essential revenue stream.

Goldcrest befell much the same fate, only more swiftly so, as the company invested in large-scale productions such as *The Mission*, *Revolution*, and *Absolute Beginners*, films that rivalled the American majors in terms of logistical ambition. With their financially problematic combinations of big stars, foreign location shooting, period settings, and global marketing costs, Goldcrest ultimately declared bankruptcy, having amassed debts of approximately £20 million. Goldcrest's downfall was to mimic the studio system in its development of feature films that aimed to court both audiences and awards. However, the Hollywood majors regularly invest in smaller scale films in more affordable genres, making immediately marketable fare such as horror films, romantic-comedies, and suspense-thrillers, films that are essentially entertainments without any aspirations to the higher social value that Goldcrest was aiming for with such historical epics as *The Mission* and *Revolution*. These smaller productions are more representative of Hollywood's annual production slate than their 'event' movies, and steady revenues from such genre filler is effectively used to cushion the blow of the failure of a bigger project. *Absolute Beginners* cost Goldcrest £8 million, going 30 per cent over its initial budget prior to prints and advertising, while *Revolution* also overran and eventually cost £9 million, and *The Mission* came in at £17 million.

Each project underperformed commercially, failing to 'break even' and earn back its production cost at the international box office. Scathing reviews for *Absolute Beginners* and *Revolution*, and general audience apathy towards both films, meant that they grossed around one-third of their respective costs. Significantly stronger critical response to *The Mission*, and its success at the Cannes Film Festival in 1986 where it was awarded the

Palme d'Or, failed to translate into profitable returns and the film stalled at a gross of £8.5 million. Goldcrest ultimately struggled because it tried to balance the spectacle and mass-audience appeal of the Hollywood studios, with the artistic principles of 'auteur' projects, more commonly found in European cinema. By signing over creative control and economic responsibility to film-makers, Goldcrest was forever running the risk of allowing directors to indulge in artistic and economic tangents, at the expense of the company's bottom line. The contract between director John Boorman and Goldcrest for the 1985 production of *The Emerald Forest*, a project that the company co-financed with the American independent Embassy, is one example of their leniency towards 'prestige' film-makers, providing the writer-director with the status of 'producer', and therefore allocating all creative and economic decisions to him. As Goldcrest was also providing the completion guarantee, they had to continue providing funds when the film went over-budget, as under no circumstances could Boorman be removed from the picture since, under his capacity as director-writer-producer, he 'was' the picture.

The ultimate failures of Palace and Goldcrest, and the gradual withdrawal from the business of other brief 'players' such as Virgin and Thorn-EMI, illustrates the economically variable nature of feature film production, and the high level of risk which is necessitated by investment in the industry, especially when production is not always equated with distribution. With the large debts that were amassed by Palace and, particularly, Goldcrest, city investment was less forthcoming, with corporations preferring to pursue opportunities in other areas of the leisure, retail, and lifestyle market and banks reluctant to extend the loans necessary for production companies to establish themselves on an international scale. This lack of major companies has made the independent British film sector what it is today – a fragmented group of small-time operators, chancing their arms on half-developed projects that appear designed to ride on the coat-tails of another film which has found recent commercial favour.

As with American independent cinema, not all British independent films are made under the same circumstances or for the same cost. It is also the case that they do not all benefit from the same methods of distribution. However, much of the feature film production in the United Kingdom is still very much independent in the financial sense.

7.2 Perception is Everything – British Independent Cinema since 1990
The early 1990s found Britain entering another perceived 'renaissance' in feature film production with a 'British film' becoming a notable media focus, often aligned with the popular myth of 'cool Britannia', an amalgamation of film, music, and the politics of the New Labour government. As Tony Blair stated,

> Some still see Britain as it was two decades ago: in decline; others as no more than a relic of the past, a theme park of castles and villages. We do not reject our heritage, but we also need to be a forward-looking country...Our task is to replace a myth of an old Britain with the reality of the modern Britain.[1]

In cinematic terms, the 'reality of the modern Britain' was better presented by the 'relics of the past', remarkably prescient films such as Nicolas Roeg and Donald Cammell's *Performance* (1970), Mike Hodge's *Get Carter* (1971), Robin Hardy's *The Wicker Man* (1973), and Franc Roddam's *Quadrophenia* (1979). During the mid-1990s they received belated re-releases and re-appraisals and were adopted as a form of 'alternative heritage', with such 1980s offerings as *The Long Good Friday* and *Mona Lisa* attaining cultural credibility for largely superficial reasons, such as their location within the fashionable gangster milieu and the presence of iconic British actors Bob Hoksins and Michael Caine. From this 'new' ancestry, it was possible for British independent cinema to re-imagine itself, to reinvent a more modern sensibility, casting off the perceived shackles of the 'heritage film', the Merchant-Ivory costume dramas that, ironically, had long proved to be the saving grace of the British film industry, maintaining its international profile and cultural identity through their success in the overseas market.

Like the New Labour government, British independent cinema in the 1990s was a calculated public relations exercise on the part of producers and distributors. With films becoming more youth-orientated, courting teenagers and students, and offering opportunities to first-time directors, British audiences were presented with home-grown examples of that most enduring commercial identifiable attribute – the star. Perhaps, for the first time since the 1960s, Britain had an acting community whose star glamour could if not rival that of the Hollywood elite at least emulate it. While the earlier era had brought Michael Caine, Terrance Stamp, Julie Christie, and David Hemmings to international attention, the British cinema of the 1990s 'discovered' Jude Law, Ewan McGregor, Kate Winslet, Kiera Knightly, Daniel Craig, Robert Carlyle, and Johnny Lee Miller, faces of glamorous, yet oddly classless, youth.

The British film 'industry' has previously been seen as a collection of roving talents, travelling the globe in search of opportunities, mainly in the United States and Europe. However, the supposed 1990s revival of British film-making seemed to promise an investment in sustaining a sector which would not only stand as a national industry in its own right, but also become part of the international entertainment market, allowing talent to build the kind of cultural capital which would eventually bring economic prominence back to the British sector. Unfortunately, much of the new 'talent' would soon be in the employ of the American giants, making films within the studio system. It should also be noted that such media hype concerning a re-emergence of British talent was generated through the media outlets of multinational corporations with an interest, not necessarily in legitimate British feature film production, but in 'Britishness' as a marketable commodity, an internationally recognized stamp of culture and quality that they could appropriate as a means of marketing and diversifying their own feature film product.

The combined revenues of British feature films and British television productions from the American market between 1993 and 1997 totalled £330 million, a not unimpressive sum, but not enough to sustain an industry that intends to compete on an international scale. When the average cost of a Hollywood studio production is £30 million, and the average cost of an American independent film has risen to £5–10 million, it becomes apparent that such revenues are not sufficient to fully finance the range of product required. A look at some successes at the British box office from 1996 onwards would indicate that British film production, and its independent sector, were riding a wave of good fortune, with such films as *Bend It like Beckham*, *Lock Stock and two Smoking Barrels*, *Sliding Doors*, *Emma*, *Trainspotting*, *The Full Monty*, *Bridget Jones's Diary*, *East is East*, and *Shakespeare in Love* winning the approval of critics and the adoration of audiences. However, a closer examination at the production credits on these box office hits reveals that they have mostly been financed by American companies. Of the aforementioned titles, the only one that can lay claim to the status of British film is *East Is East*, as it was developed, financed, and distributed by Film Four. The current investment in 'British cinema' by Hollywood seems to suggest that 'Britishness' is not only almost a genre in itself, but also a marketable one, and a commodity that has been recognized by the American giants.

Crucially, the British independent sector lacks the entrepreneurial spirit that makes the American independent sector such a talking point. Considering the fact that British cinema lacks the vertical integration that is commonly associated with the term 'industry', it is perhaps ironic that British cinema has a rigidly industrious structure as far as recruitment, promotion, opportunity, and allocation of production funds is concerned. There is still an emphasis on academic qualification, something that is not possessed by a large number of American independent film-makers, who are largely self-taught, and this causes creative stagnation by delaying, or outright preventing, the development of potentially exciting talent. As Ogborn observes,

> The most common route into the industry now appears to be a degree in film or media followed by work as a freelancer within the corporate, commercial or television industry, paralleled by film-making on microscopic budgets, the achievement of a higher profile through a television broadcast or festival screening, and then, hopefully, the 'lucky break'.[2]

There also exists a genuine tension between the need to develop a viable economic sector that can ensure employment through the entertainment of the masses, and an altogether more altruistic aim to ensure the longevity of a national and local cinema that provides an informed commentary on the social fabric of British life. This is a tension that is not as evident in the independent cinema of the United States, wherein such commentary is often effectively intertwined with a strong narrative sensibility that makes such material accessible to both domestic and international audiences. The roots of these problems lie in the fragmentation of the industry. A government report conducted by the Department of National Heritage in 1995 found that

> There is an absence of significant investment in film companies and productions by general investors, private individuals and corporations which are not engaged in producing or

distributing films. This is because film production is generally regarded as an industry where the risks are high and the returns are volatile and unpredictable. The absence of vertically integrated structures linking production to distribution and exhibition and the fact that most UK production companies are single film companies means that the profits from successful films are not, on the whole, available to cushion the losses suffered by investors in unsuccessful films.[3]

The financing methods behind British independent cinema vary to an extent from production to production, but there are two near-constants. Firstly, production is rarely equated with distribution with most production companies being just that, in that they make feature films but lack the internal and external resources, and financial acumen, to release their product into the arena of popular consumption. Secondly, there are usually a number of financiers involved in an independent British film, some of which are public, others of which are private. At present, there is no shortage of these independent companies operating in Britain. Unfortunately, they are unable to finance film at moderate-to-high budget levels, raising sums or £1–2 million for each production via loans from private investors and pre-sales. As a 1998 government report discovered, 'Typically, companies are established to develop, finance, and produce a single film, and then start again from scratch on their next project.'[4]

The key issue that is raised by these two constants is that of fragmentation. Production companies and independent financiers are not vertically integrated, and are therefore disenfranchised from distribution companies. Producers have to go back to the drawing board every time they embark on another feature film production, with no guarantee of recouping their costs or ensuring distribution for their projects, while the financiers are only able to fund films up to a relatively low, budgetary level, resulting in product that is often lacking in such immediately identifiable and automatically marketable commercial attributes as stars and visual spectacle. This situation prevents producers from being able to consistently produce and release feature films, crucially preventing them from building up a library of titles, sustained revenues from which would enable them to invest in multiple as opposed to single productions.

Although there may be some logic in the basic notion that if the film is made cheaply enough, it will be easy for it to recoup its profit, this is not the case as low-budget productions rarely offer the escapist glamour and high-level production value that the audience expects of a theatrical release, meaning that such offerings are largely ignored by audiences. For production companies to flourish and break out of the cycle of low-budget, low-return feature films, there must be a level of risk investment that is, to an extent, comparable to Hollywood and even the American independent sector. As the renowned producer David Puttnam has commented,

Making a film for £200,000 is no guarantee that you're going to return £200,000 and that's been one of the tragedies of low budget production. I would like to see the balance corrected in favour of medium-sized pictures, because those are the pictures that have a chance of going out, breaking out, making a great deal of money and making small, medium and *large* budget pictures possible.[5]

The low box office returns of many British independent feature films is not the only major problem facing producers – there is also the complex matter of distribution, and how it denies them access to much of the profits from their cinematic endeavours. The following chart shows the revenue stream of a film industry that does not possess a distribution network, or a system where short-term loss is covered by long-term profit, as the profits that are eventually allocated to producers are too small to be successfully re-invested in feature film production. The majority of profit is left with the distributors, usually corporate offshoots and American subsidiaries, who often view an investment in a British feature film production as a 'one-off' opportunity when the fluctuating laws of the market come to favour their economic needs, rather than a long-term business enterprise.

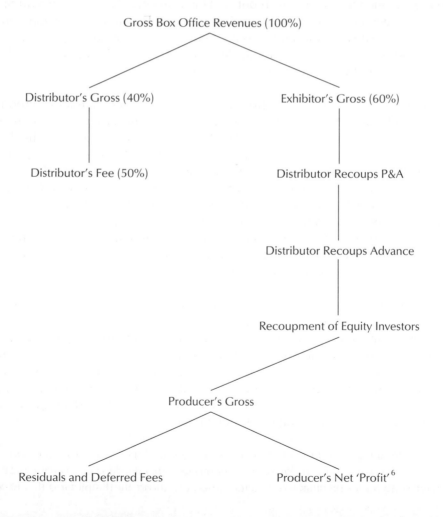

Gross Box Office Revenues (100%)

Distributor's Gross (40%) Exhibitor's Gross (60%)

Distributor's Fee (50%) Distributor Recoups P&A

Distributor Recoups Advance

Recoupment of Equity Investors

Producer's Gross

Residuals and Deferred Fees Producer's Net 'Profit'[6]

As this chart shows, very little of the estimated £1.6 billion that is spent by British consumers on the film industry finds its way back to producers, as it is often only possible for them to get the film made by selling off the rights which represent the eventual profits. This allows the distributors to enjoy enormous power over producers, limiting their source of future funds and, to an extent, influencing their choice of projects through their own preference for particular generic and cultural trends.

By means of further illustration, it is given that from the box office gross revenues of any feature film 60 per cent will go to the exhibitor, with the distributor receiving the remaining 40 per cent. From that 40 per cent, the distributor will immediately absolve 50 per cent to cover its fee, then take from the remaining 50 per cent to recoup their prints and averting cost, plus any 'advance' paid on the acquisition of the film. The remaining amount, which could be anything from 15 to 25 per cent of the amount allocated to the distributor will go back to the original producer, who will then have to use his relatively small share of the profits to take care of any residual or deferred fees owed to others involved in the production process, such as writers, director, actors, and technicians. Whatever remains is the producer's net profit, and this is rarely enough to fund another feature film. This explains the cyclical nature of the independent productions in the UK since the mid-1990s, such as the romantic-comedies which followed the success of *Four Weddings and a Funeral*, and the stream of gangster films which were rushed into production after *Lock, Stock and Two Smoking Barrels* proved to be a surprise hit at the domestic box office.

It should be also noted that UK independent cinema is operating on shoestring budgets when compared with its American counterpart. British independent films are rushed through production at an average cost of £1 million. As a means of budgetary comparison, consider the respective costs of the following offerings from the American independent sector – *Lost In Translation* cost $4.5 million, *My Big Fat Greek Wedding* cost $5 million, *Monster* cost $10 million, and *21 Grams* cost $20 million. Each was financed by an independent with a vertically integrated business strategy, either through its own in-house distribution division or via a deal with a major studio, meaning that there was a guarantee that the film would be distributed theatrically before a frame of footage was shot

7.3 Aspiring to the American Aesthetic – Appealing to the Mass at the Expense of National Identity and the Independent Vision

Vertically integrated productions that have set their aesthetic and commercial ambitions at a more 'American' level have largely failed to excite audiences or justify their financial expenditure. In 1993, Polygram Filmed Entertainment, one of the few vertically integrated companies of the era, invested £3 million in *The Young Americans*, a visually imposing but emotionally empty 'cop movie' with an imported American star in Harvey Keitel and a plot which, although located within the heart of London's club land, never appeared to aspire to offer any actual social insight into its moody milieu. Aside from a series of sequences set inside some of the capital's trendiest nightspots, *The Young*

Americans was essentially an old-fashioned gangster movie, building to a showdown between the cops and the mobsters, with a few morally conflicted and very good-looking teenagers caught in-between. Similar problems also hindered *Shopping*, the 1993 action-drama that focussed on young ram-raiders, and which was also produced by Polygram. On a superficial, level, the film is concerned with the wayward youth of Great Britain, its disregard for social order and its preference for visceral thrills over economic viability. However, it is also located in a London which is barely recognizable, with little sense of the social reality of its characters as everyone is reduced to generic archetype – the 'cool' rebel, the 'troubled' girlfriend, the 'absent' father, the 'concerned' cop. In addition, the youth culture and vaguely futuristic society portrayed are framed by images borrowed liberally from American movies and rendered aesthetically and intellectually stillborn, lacking in independent sensibility, or national identity.

Such commercially minded, but culturally stale cinema is representative of much of the annual output of Britain's independent sector. Unlike the American independent sector, art and commerce rarely seem to meet on screen, with a great chasm existing between generic comedies and thrillers and the more socially 'elitist' work of Mike Leigh, Ken Loach, and Peter Greenway. By contrast, the American independent sector is less easily divisible and more culturally elusive. Compare the work of New York-based independent film-makers (Abel Ferrara, Spike Lee, Jim Jarmusch) with their Los Angeles counterparts (Paul Thomas Anderson, David O'Russell, Quentin Tarantino) or more rural contributors (John Sayles, David Gordon Green) and one discovers a veritable kaleidoscope of modern film-making, encompassing a wide range of cultural themes and genuinely intuitive visual sensibility.

The reason that these directors have been able to develop their talents is that they have been largely supported by a vertically integrated industry that has allowed for such experimentation and development providing that it has adhered to a broad narrative structure and met with approval from audiences and, to a lesser extent, critics. Before a British independent film can begin production, it must be marketed to its prospective financiers, often through some association to earlier, successful films. In this sense, the British independent sector operates much like the Hollywood mainstream, or any other industry of mass production, in that it evaluates the potential profit and loss of any investment against previous endeavours. This is at odds with its American independent counterpart that is more focussed on finding fresh material with some novelty value for its loyal audience. Admittedly, the American independent sector does also recycle itself, with the slew of gangland dramas that followed Tarantino's success with *Reservoir Dogs* and *Pulp Fiction* being the most obvious example, but the British sector is particularly notable for favouring formula over innovation, a preference which has perhaps alienated or outwardly discarded directors who may have made films to rival their American counterparts.

7.4 Political Representation in British Independent Cinema – A Social-Political Comparison of Two National Film-makers

Even in its lower-budget, non-Hollywood form, American cinema is still very much an 'international cinema', one that is familiar to audiences around the world through its employment of certain characters, themes, cultural iconography, and the American narrative tradition, all of which have come to constitute much of what is excepted from the 'movie-going experience', hence Hollywood's dominance of the feature film market. This is particularly true in the case of the sector's politics, which, although frequently expressed through the films that it produces, are presented as being secondary to the more immediate matter of narrative. It is also important to note, especially when comparing the US independent scene with that of the UK, that American independent cinema is extremely indebted to Hollywood – not necessarily the economic power of present-day Hollywood or its filmic output, but the glories of its past, its storytelling legacy, and the cultural values which are associated with the films of earlier eras. American independent cinema is as focussed on story and the classic characters of the American narrative tradition, such as law enforcement officers, drifters, loners, criminals, and aspiring heroes, as present-day Hollywood, but differs greatly in its presentation of these stories and characters, employing alternative approaches to narrative subtle psychological deconstruction of its protagonists.

It would seem that British independent film-makers are able to exhibit a greater political freedom than their American counterparts. While many American 'independent' productions are subsidized by the studios, and therefore relatively conservative, British independent cinema operates outside the boundaries of such corporate politics by seeking finance from European sources. Territories such as France and Italy, which have a great tradition of social-realism within their own national cinema, and strong leftist politics, have proved to be loyal supporters of British directors, particularly those who are perceived as 'auteurs'. Mike Leigh's *Secrets And Lies* was funded by the French company Ciby 2000, while Ken Loach's *Land And Freedom* was put together through a three-way production deal which included money from BBC Films, one of Germany's public funding bodies, and the Spanish branch of the French cable television company Canal Plus.

This balance of art and commerce is familiar from discussion of the films of the American independent director John Sayles. He sustains audience interest through a carefully cultivated narrative formula, burdening his protagonists with social-economic obstacles that they must overcome. The politics of his work are inherently socialist, but are secondary to the story and the fulfilment his narrative, even though it is Sayles's overriding moral and political vision that is revealed by the end, unifying both themes and plot strands. The supporting characters in his films perform the twin functions of servicing plot needs and providing a social-economic perspective on the events of the story and their effect on the fabric of the concerned environment.

Possibly the closest British equivalent to John Sayles is Ken Loach. As with Sayles, the leading characters in Loach's films are people who would be supporting players, or mere extras, in a Hollywood production – union workers, single mothers, unemployed grafters, and low-level soldiers, amongst others. As much as Sayles is interested in those citizens, legal or illegal, who were not intended to prosper under the Reagan or Bush administrations, Loach focusses on those Britons who were left behind economically by the Thatcher government. However, there are crucial differences between the two film-makers, their narrative and aesthetic approaches, and the representation of their political ideologies. While Sayles very much favours a 'slow burn' approach in terms of establishing character, environment, and, most importantly, politics, Loach chooses to drop his audience into a particular social-economic situation, such as the sudden loss of employment in *Raining Stones* or the illegal border crossing in *Bread and Roses*.

While Loach has earned praise for giving a cinematic 'voice' to the British working class, this is often at the expense of the other social groups and classes presented in his work. Employers in positions of power are portrayed as penny-pinchers who derive pleasure from the economic misery that their employees endure, while government-affiliated figures such as social workers and employment officers are presented more as social obstacles than social functions in that they misunderstand the people they are trying to help. His working-class characters are not glorified, and Loach often shows that their lack of will and long-term commitment stands in the way of changing their circumstances for the better, but he does seem to believe there is value in their habit of their taking complex problems and issues and condensing them into reductive, simplistic, sentiment, and mundane nuggets of 'homespun' wisdom.

A crucial difference between Sayles and Loach, and a reason why the former may have achieved a more unified critical response than the latter, is their method of presenting their respective political values. Sayles ensures that his characters are ultimately defined by actions rather than by words. The protagonists in *Lone Star*, *Matewan*, and *Silver City* may be adrift in circumstances of cultural change and political upheaval, but they also conform to the classic idea of the American hero, in that they are men who bide their time, avoiding any obvious political affiliations, and ultimately act in accordance with their own deep-rooted personal beliefs. Their motivations stem from long-term concerns, and their actions cannot always be viewed within the context of a specific situation.

Loach, however, chooses to give his characters an outer, rather than inner, voice, often employing them as mouthpieces to express his own arguments, ironic considering that he frequently chooses to focus on the most inarticulate of protagonists and social groups, thereby restricting his own ideology to the verbal limitations of people with a narrower, less learned, viewpoint. While Sayles shows people dealing with everyday instances of social and economic injustice within the confines of a fictional narrative, it is Loach who is more of a documentarian in terms of his aesthetic sensibility, who often allows his work to give way to passages of dialogue that are both heavily expositional in terms of the politics and emotions they express.

The 1995 production *Land And Freedom* found Loach employing the story of a lower-class British worker who volunteers to fight in the Spanish Civil War of the 1930s as a means of tackling the subject of socialism and the dangers of propaganda, but despite the period setting and occasional bursts of action as soldiers are gradually wounded and even killed, Loach stalls the narrative momentum for a sequence in which his key themes are debated at length during a political meeting. Like Sayles, however, he is determined to make films that, even when located within specific historical periods, exhibit a contemporary attitude and relevance towards their subject matter, as opposed to being self-consciously marooned by the requirements of a genre such as the war epic. Loach approaches the subject matter in much the same way as his contemporary pieces, with 'action' coming in short, abrupt bursts, and attention given to the day-to-day routine of life in the trenches, where any sense of overriding political vision was often lost as idealism gave way to the kind of time-killing which can be found in many aspects of modern life.

7.5 The Small Screen Surrogate – British Television as an Alternative Method of Independent Production

The BBC and Channel Four are the closest Britain has to the American conception of the film industry in terms of possessing the resources of production and exhibition. In the 1990s, they were joined by BskyB and the three companies have managed to develop new talent and produce films that can play to national and international audiences. A number of their feature productions, such as *Truly Madly Deeply*, *Saving Grace*, and *Mrs Brown* were developed as small screen films, but received worldwide cinema releases when it became apparent that they could not only play successfully theatrically, but also increase their future television audience by doing so through the exposure that is achieved by critically acclaimed big screen exhibition. This creates the impression of an industry where the differences between cinema and television are not as significant as in the United States, an impression that is further compounded by the fact that British films that have been intended as theatrical features, such as *The Nephew*, *The Serpent's Kiss*, and *Bullet To Beijing* have received their public debuts on the small screen, either as television films or straight-to-video releases.

While industry personnel in the United States is often characterized by working within either film or television, with feature film talent operating in both independent and studio production, but rarely in small screen enterprises, the industry personnel in the UK is more likely to move from television to feature films and back again, for reasons both economic and cultural. Firstly, work within the British television industry is more plentiful, artistically varied, and often more financially lucrative. Secondly, it is also likely to reach a much larger audience in a country where television viewing is not only the most popular leisure activity, but one that dwarfs cinema in terms of its ability to consistently attract and entertain audiences with material that is both financially and culturally British.

Notes

1. Blair, T, *Britannia's Committee for Cool*, BBC News UK, website (www.news.bbc.co.uk), 01/04/1988.
2. Ogborn, K, 'Pathways into the Industry', *British Cinema Of The 90s* (ed. Murphy, R), 1st edn, page 65, London, BFI, 2000.
3. *The British Film Industry*, Department of National Heritage report, 1995.
4. *A Bigger Picture – Film Policy Review*, March, 1998.
5. Puttnam, D, quoted in *The British Are Coming*, Bloom, P, *Empire* magazine, p. 56, 08/1990.
6. Brookes, J *'The Rise Or Fall Of The British Film Industry? A Critical Overview Of UK Film Making In The 1990s*, discussion papers in mass-communications, p. 9, University of Leicester Press, 2002.

8

SELECTIVE EXHIBITION: THE SUNDANCE FILM FESTIVAL AND ITS SIGNIFICANCE TO THE INEPENDENT SECTOR

Film festivals occupy a space between the completion and distribution of a motion picture, a space which could be termed 'selective exhibition' as it is where films are screened for an audience, but in an environment which finds the director, producers, and distributors still holding some control of their work, not quite giving it over for popular consumption. Within the festival circuit, the film-maker and his producers still control over the film and its point of cultural inception, which entails some choice in the selection of the festivals that their work is screened, and the type of audience who is likely to see it. Festival screenings are not a part of a film's general release, meaning that they are not immediately beneficial financially, as they do not represent box office takings. However, they do serve to generate publicity and provide feedback on work that is usually beyond alteration, although some festival screenings have resulted in last-minute adjustments to films prior to general releases.

Venice is the world's oldest film festival, with Cannes firmly established as its arch rival. Although outwardly a celebration of cinema, Cannes was actually created to lure attention away from Venice and increase France's international profile as both a contributor to the arts and a tourist destination. Although the Cannes festival runs for less than two weeks, it earns £50 million per annum in tourist revenues alone, while it is estimated that more than £200 million worth of movies are bought during the festival's twelve-day duration. Other festivals have sought to emulate its success. Major cities such as London, Berlin, and New York offer major festivals, which attract famous names, major premieres, and coverage from the mass media. By comparison, smaller cities and towns, such as Karlovy Vary, Calgary, and Edinburgh, play host to festivals which benefit from some celebrity attendance, but rarely attract the kind of media coverage to secure screenings of big Hollywood features, instead offering audiences new independent features and timely retrospectives.

In 2002, over six hundred film festivals were reported worldwide, which has much to do with the availability of corporate sponsorship for such events. As Wasko notes,

> Even film festivals are becoming for commercialised, as more businesses are offering sponsorship for the events. Because the presumed impact of traditional advertising is weakening, festivals offer companies with expensive products access to an ideal audience.[1]

If the international box office charts, reported weekly across the entertainment news media, are the key indicator of commercial success and audience spending, it is the film festivals that represent shifts in artistic supremacy, as directors of previous eras fade into the background, making way for new film-makers. Indeed, the cinematic lifeline of many film-makers can be traced through their relationship with the festival circuit, in terms of how their works and attendance have been prioritized by organizers, and how their own roles within the industry hierarchy have shifted over periods of time. The following is a time line that represents the careers of those directors who have enjoyed much of their exposure through the film festival network.

Stage 1	Stage 2	Stage 3	Stage 4
First Feature – Some acclaim and media attention, possibly resulting in distribution deal. Critics may regard film-maker as part of a new 'wave' in popular film-making.	Follow-Up Films – More media attention, and critical interest, possible awards. Regarded as a 'current' film-maker, representing the international cinema.	Later Films – Included in festival out of 'respect' for body of work. Films have become a reference point for younger directors who may now be more critically favoured.	Elder Statesman – Involved in festival in 'critical' capacity as jury member, speaker, or screening of works as part of retrospective. May no longer be active in film-making at this stage.

The critical reaction to films in the festival environment is often seen to either usher in or cast out an era of film-making, whether it be through the 'overnight' success of new directors, or the fall from grace of a more seasoned veteran, whose latest works are perceived to fall short in comparison to their earlier 'masterpieces'. In a sense, the shifting positions of directors reflect how recognized they are by the cinephile audience, that is to say, regular viewers with a keen interest in the trajectory of cinema who regard previously celebrated directors as bookmarks and reference points in the lineage of modern film, and younger film-makers as more likely to deliver works that offer social-political relevance. Although the films of new directors are often seen to be seeking to emulate, or pay 'homage' to, those of the previous generation, they also strive to move cinema forward through the adoption, and then the reinvention, of earlier techniques. Such artistic practice brings renewed vigour to seemingly exhausted concepts and genres, however, it does suggest a struggle between the old and new guard of popular culture. As Bourdieu states,

> It is the continuous creation of the battle between those who have made their names and who have struggling to stay in view and those who cannot make their own names without relegating to the past the established figures, whose interest lies in freezing the movement of time, fixing the present state of the field forever.[2]

Only the film-makers themselves know if they have intentionally set out to make motion pictures which will relegate those directors they have respected and even idolized, but in terms of breaking into an industry which is inherently competitive, whether it be for funding, distribution, or securing additional talent for prominent roles, such battles for prominence are frequent and unavoidable. It is also common for critics to 'discover' new talent, particularly in festival venues such as Sundance, and to proclaim them exciting new voices in cinema. To justify such claims, critics must effectively discard film-makers of the previous generation, who had been equally championed, although they can rarely praise young directors without referencing those they are supposedly 'replacing'. Quentin Tarantino's 1992 debut *Reservoir Dogs* gained comparisons to the early works of Martin Scorsese, such as *Mean Streets* and *Taxi Driver*, because of the gutter-level authenticity of its explicit violence and salty dialogue and the presence of Scorsese alumnus Harvey Keitel in one of the lead roles. Paul Thomas Anderson's *Boogie Nights* and *Magnolia* were likened to the 1970s output of Robert Altman, due to his fondness for multi-stranded narratives and preference for casting actors 'against type' in unflattering roles.

Achieving the necessary funding, distribution, and talent for their films, especially in the independent arena which offers fluctuating commercial rewards, is often a result of a director's cultural capital, the amount of recognition and acknowledgment that his or her work has received, and the prestige value that it represents. Film festivals serve as a forum for achieving, maintaining, and emphasizing this cultural capital, as festivals themselves were initially intended as a means of celebrating works and film-makers that were perceived to be the 'best' within their field. As Bourdieu notes,

> The names of the schools or groups...are pseudo-concepts, practical classifying tools which create resemblances and differences by naming them; they are produced in the struggle for recognition by the artists themselves or their accredited critics and function as emblems which distinguish galleries,groups and artists and therefore the products they make or sell.[3]

This is to say that events such as film festivals bring great prestige to artists by placing them within an 'elite' group through their inclusion. The selection for a film in a festival such as Cannes or Venice is almost as much a means of categorization as the actual genre that the film occupies, as it suggests the work is one of sufficient quality, a film that is of the highest standard and worthy of international attention and acclaim. It also positions the film towards a certain consumer, an audience that would be regarded as 'highbrow' for its leanings towards works that have been bestowed with critical approval. An award from a festival, or merely inclusion in such an event, provides an image of distinction that seems to elevate what is essentially product to a higher level of social standing, making it infinitely more desirable to a particular section of the audience than it would be without such recognition.

With so many promotional opportunities, festivals have become a part of the industry, a venue for unveiling new films and related products, whilst also celebrating the industry itself by declaring its cultural diversity and liberal politics. If festivals like Cannes, Venice, and Berlin represent present-day Hollywood and its corporate European equivalents, the Sundance Film Festival represents the future of the studios, as it is where they look for signs of where film-making and audience trends are heading, before deciding how such trends can best be adopted to their system of mass production. Amy Taubin, a critic for the *Village Voice*, noted that

> Sundance is certainly kind of a crucial institution in the rise of indies. Or let's put it this way: a crucial institution in the *institutionalisation* of indie.[4]

This is to say that Sundance, as with other festivals, has become a part of the Hollywood machine. How this came to be, and how reluctant festival organizers were to their event's integration into the Hollywood system of mass production, will be examined in this chapter. However, it must first be noted that Sundance is a prime example of how commercial industry will always catch up with, and eventually absorb, any other method of commercial production and exhibition that can be considered to be independent, peripheral, or marginal, providing that it offers the opportunity for the field of large-scale production to renew itself. As Sundance chairman Robert Redford recalls,

> When the first studio people showed up, I dragged them off the street and into the screening rooms...Eventually, and this caught me by surprise, people began flocking here because they were interested in the wonderful, diverse menu of films we were screening that started with *El Norte* and gained stream with *Sex, Lies, And Videotape*. Sundance was suddenly so cool that Hollywood simply couldn't ignore it. In fact, Hollywood wanted to be 'in' with it. When Hollywood came, the merchants came. And when the merchants came, the media came and voted, Sundance was part of themainstream.[5]

In an age when the average Hollywood feature film doubles its production cost through marketing and distribution, festivals such as Sundance have become an invaluable platform for launching product into cultural circulation. While some festivals, particularly those centred around independent cinema, have been reluctant to accept this fact, they have been amenable to the corporate sponsorship that has both kept them financially afloat and maintained their cultural profile.

Like many other aspects of feature film business, the film festival can be seen as a 'high risk' venture, particularly for films that have already developed a 'profile', meaning those films that have attracted media coverage and audience expectation whilst in production. A positive festival reaction, which would entail favourable reviews, press attention, and enthusiastic audience response, can increase a project's chances of commercial success by adding to its profile. Unfortunately, a negative reaction, such as poor reviews, minimal media coverage, and bad word of mouth from audiences will effectively derail a film's commercial prospects for the same reason in that the general public will form the perception that the film is a 'failure'. Such negative reaction at festival screenings have even sent some directors back to the editing room to try and 'fix' their films, while films that have played at festivals without distribution have struggled to secure a release after poor audience response.

It is important to note that, for all the supposed bohemian spirit of festivals, particularly those like Sundance, Raindance, and Slamdance that favour independent productions, attendance at these events is dominated by industry 'players'. Even those individuals who comprise the 'general audience' are people who exist on the fringes of the film industry, as the majority of screenings, workshops, and accommodation is booked up long in advance of the opening night. The following is a list of social types commonly found at film festivals:

(1) Industry Talent – Established directors, actors, actresses, producers, screenwriters, and other key contributors with films in the festival, or using the festival as a venue to promote their projects.
(2) Fringe-Industry Talent – Directors, actors, producers, screenwriters, and other key contributors from the independent sector, usually with a first or second feature in festival, vying for both prizes and distribution, or look for further work opportunities.
(3) Industry Personnel – Distribution reps, agents using the festival circuit as a 'talent pool' and a means of sourcing choice acquisitions.
(4) Corporate Sponsors – PR representatives of major companies and recognized brands who 'sponsor' films and events as part of their vertically integrated promotion strategies (e.g. – Hugo Boss, Dolce & Gabana, Absolute Vodka, MTV, HBO, Ralph Lauren, Orange).
(5) Media – Journalists from news media covering the event, some under the employment of the Hollywood majors or Sundance itself and gathering material for promotional purposes to be used at a later date, often in ancillary ventures such as television and DVD.
(6) General Moviegoers – Usually only those who are 'connected' enough to the industry to gain access to events and admission to screenings.

The Sundance Film Festival is the most important event of it type in the United States, and perhaps the world. All the major international film festivals, from Cannes to Venice, from New York to London, generate enormous media attention and prove themselves annually as the best venues to launch new movies, whether they be the artistic films that play as part of a festival programme, or the Hollywood pictures that use up every available piece of advertising space in the vicinity. A list of significant independent pictures of the last two decades would include such titles as *Reservoir Dogs*, *Sex Lies and Videotape*, *Clerks*, *Stranger than Paradise*, *Go Fish*, *Slacker*, *Ruby in Paradise*, *House Party*, and *The Blair Witch Project*. Apart from transcending their low-budget origins to cross over to a mainstream audience, what all of these features have in common is that they were 'discovered' at Park City. Without playing to such a rapturous response from Sundance audiences, some may not have been picked up by distributors and pushed into the cultural mainstream through aggressive marketing and enthusiastic reviews from critics caught up in audience euphoria.

It is possible that even without Sundance, films of the high calibre of *Reservoir Dogs*, *Stranger than Paradise*, and *Go Fish* would have found distribution, either through an alternative festival or as a result of the enterprising nature of their producers. However, it is unlikely that their debut features would have made such a cultural impact without Sundance as their launching pad. Although Soderbergh's *Sex, Lies, and Videotape* is now more famous for winning the Palme d'Or at Cannes than it is for winning the Audience Award at Sundance, it was the response that his debut feature generated at Park City that prompted Miramax to purchase the film and submit it for competition at Cannes. Such is the prominence of the Sundance Film Festival within the American, and international, film industry, that even scholars such as Levy cannot resist resorting to hyperbole when describing it:

> Every major city in the United States has a film festival, but there is little doubt that the Sundance Film Festival is the premiere showcase for new American indies. Indeed, as far as industry heat and exciting discoveries are concerned, Sundance now ranks second only to Cannes on the film map. Celebrating new talent, Sundance has become a Mecca for aspiring independents.[6]

What follows are the five key benefits of securing a slot at such an event:

(1) **Prestige –** By submitting a film to a prestigious festival (e.g. – Sundance, Toronto, Locarno), the project will benefit from press and industry coverage. Even if the film comes away 'empty-handed', with no awards and little press, being selected will still have long-term benefits as the 'Official Selection Of...' status can be a marketing tool for both theatrical and ancillary release.

(2) **Distribution –** Film festivals are the best chance that a production has of securing distribution, due to the presence of industry personnel plus industry-affiliated audience members, whose positive response can enhance interest from distributors. It could be argued that the prizes given at festivals are superficial awards, as the real

prize is securing distribution. The Cannes film festival tries to divide the practices of art and commerce by screening films 'in competition' and in the buyer's market, whereas the definition of 'success' at festivals such as Sundance and Raindance is more ambiguous due to the fact that most films are competing for both awards and distribution.

(3) **Reviews and Press Coverage** – Festivals are an important means of generating publicity, especially if the film is not immediately picked up for distribution. In addition, the audience for independent cinema uses media to inform its viewing choices, so reviews and press coverage will immediately bring a film to the attention of its core audience. Independent cinema gains much of its awareness via the Internet. Popular movie websites such as the Internet Movie Database have sections devoted to independent film, while there are other sites, such as Indiewire, which specialize in coverage of non-studio features, and providing advice on production resources.

(4) **Contacts** – Film festivals are attended by industry professionals, with the general public being low on the list for access, so such events present a perfect opportunity for industrial 'networking'. This can lead to future opportunities in terms of financing, casting, distribution, and exposure.

(5) **Research** – Festivals provide directors, producers, and distributors an opportunity not only to see how well their film 'plays' with an audience, but to see other independent films, which are perhaps rivals to their own. Reactions can lead to changes in the way the project is handled in terms of marketing, and could also result in additional editing or even re-shooting. Festivals are an ideal research tool for distributors and producers because their selection choices effectively represent the next year's worth of independent films, and suggest trends and turnarounds that may affect their own investment choices.

8.1 From Park City to the Popular Conscious – A Brief History of Sundance

The initial incarnation of the Sundance Film Festival was The US Film Festival, the brainchild of film professor Arthur Knight, a zealous supporter of the independent film movement. Knight convinced festival director Sterling Van Wagenen that an event to emphasize the work of independent film-makers would be of importance to both the future of the American film industry and the social-political fabric of its industrial culture. The location of Utah was then chosen, perhaps for reasons both emblematic and geographical. Images of Utah conjure up a more 'grass-roots' feel, the simplified notion of 'natural development' that could be applied as much to young film-makers as the local environment, while the distance between Utah and Hollywood was enough to put some cultural distance between the festival and the corporate workings of the studio system, but not enough distance that the event would be inaccessible to producers and distributors. The choice of Utah as the location for the festival is also an early indication of the inherent compromises that were necessary to bring Knight's ambition to fruition, in that festival publicist John Earle wanted to bring large-scale Hollywood productions to the state, using feature film and television projects as a means of supplementing local economy. It was this aim, however, which helped to attract the backing of the Utah

Film Commission, as well as the potential boost to the local tourist industry through the exposure that the festival would bring.

The first festival was held in Salt Lake City in 1978, with Hollywood productions completely absent from the schedule and a wide range of legitimately independent features showcased. Although the festival was intended to be a non-competitive event in order to emphasize the communal nature of independent film, awards were introduced with a Grand Jury Prize and a Special Jury award being allocated. This was perhaps a means of increasing awareness in a festival and generating a certain cachet with audiences when the winning films were released commercially. As independent production was sporadic during this period in American cinema, the USFF sometimes had problems filling all of its slots, meaning that retrospectives and talks were arranged when a sufficient number of feature films was not available. However, the festival possessed an energy and enthusiasm which became infectious. Tom Bernard, an executive for Sony Pictures Classics, remembers that

> You had all these wild people who'd watch movies at night and ski all day, party with the filmmakers all night long, and it was a real spontaneous-combustion kind of place for filmmaking...movies came out of this mixture of people, that's how the Sundance labs came to be later...There was a purity about it. It wasn't about awards, it was about people looking for what was new in filmmaking.[7]

Despite this atmosphere of geniality and creativity, a continuous struggle for financial stability and a need for publicity meant that the USFF had to invite some Hollywood glamour to the festivities, with On Golden Pond and Sophie's Choice being two of the studio features to play at the festival in the early 1980s. However, compromises and did little to undermine the festival's reputation as a home away from home for new film-makers. While the present-day Sundance Film Festival is essentially a whirlwind programme of new features, with an awards ceremony at its close, the USFF was closely constructed around seminars and workshops, with classes being integrated with the screenings and guest speakers to maximize their educational potential. The workshops were designed to enable young film-makers to learn from veterans of the independent sector, while panel discussions allowed enthusiastic audience members, who now find it very difficult to gain access to the festival, to ask questions of film-makers who could then benefit from immediate feedback.

The atmosphere that the USFF offered in this period was one of sociability, a place where existing work could be discussed, and advice on how bring ideas to fruition could be sought. It was an environment of cultural and educational, if not necessarily industrial, opportunity. While independent film-makers are now known to structure their production and post-production schedules around the Sundance submission dates, and base their creative choices on what they perceive to be necessary to make an impression on audiences and buyers at Park City, the films that the festival attracted in the early-to-mid-1980s were a more eclectic bunch. During this period it was quite common to find the festival screening marginal, experimental, or localized productions, the kind of films that are often not intended for an audience outside the festival circuit. For many of these films, the USFF was the end of their cinematic journey in terms of finding an audience, while in today's market, festival screenings represent the beginning of their cultural consumption. By the early 1990s, a film that left Sundance without distribution was considered a failure, at least in industrial terms, whereas in the festival's earlier days, distribution deals were not common or instantaneous enough for them to be the principal reason to submit a feature for inclusion in the line-up. As Michael Barker of Sony Pictures Classics recalls,

> There still weren't a lot of movies you wanted to pick up. It was a place you wanted to check out...New directors came, but they struggled to fill a slate. They had premieres where they'd bring some big names in, linking the studio and independent worlds, but a lot of people with the hottest films in the festival didn't get distribution.[8]

Behind the scenes, the Hollywood presence was already being felt. Sydney Pollack, the director of such studio fare as *Tootsie* and *The Firm*, was a competition juror for the 1979 festival and saw potential for providing a crossover in the interests of independent and studio film-making. The festival had floundered in 1980 when the event was cancelled due to a combination of poor weather and a $40,000 deficit, at which point Pollack suggested that that proceedings should be moved from Salt Lake City to Park City, which would be more economical and less affected by adverse nature conditions. He also recommended holding the festival during the lucrative ski season, a time of year when many Hollywood executives take their vacations in the era, offering industry types the chance to engage in the combined activities of skiing on the slops and discovering new film-makers. Around this time, the festival began screening studio films and hosting industry parties, although in the early years at Park City, such socializing was largely confined to the main street of town, rather than the remote and exclusive ski lodges which are used for such occasions today.

The festival was still struggling financially, with the extension of the event from seven to ten days in order to accomadate more films and workshops putting a strain on the budget. At this stage, Robert Redford, the festival's most public patron, would enter the picture. Redford had been involved in organizing the festival in the late 1970s but had parted ways from the USFF to develop the Sundance Institute, a workshop that enabled film-makers to develop ideas in an organic, less commercially conscious environment. After being approached for financial aid by the USFF, Redford agreed to sponsor the event on the condition that control of the festival's direction would be handed over to him, starting in 1984, with the USFF officially becoming the Sundance Film Festival in 1991. Redford's reason for becoming involved again was of a practical nature, as he wanted to provide a forum for the film-makers that he had been nurturing through his Sundance labs.

Under the guidance of Redford and chief programmer Geoff Gilmore, Sundance maintained a balance between art and commerce, screening independent features, with some Hollywood productions generating media interest and corporate sponsorship. Crucially, this was a time when deals for distribution rights to films were not done at Sundance, but taken care of afterwards, with the sale of the lesbian drama *Go Fish* to the Samuel Goldwyn Company for $450,000 in 1994 marking the first occasion that bidding on a feature was conducted during the event. It could be argued that this was out of some respect that the industry felt towards the event as an emblem of the independent film movement, but it is more likely that the studios were waiting patiently, observing the financial progress of previous Sundance 'favourites' before incorporating it into its business model.

8.2 Getting Seen at Sundance – The Selection and Exhibition of the Festival

Sundance can be seen to be representative of the American independent film sector, as it finds thousands of features competing for screening space, critical attention, and audience time. As much as the continued existence of independent cinema is indicative of a need within both the audience and the industry for novelty, it is also apparent that there is only room for so much diversity within a culture of mass production and consumption. The rigorous selection process for the Sundance Film Festival is indicative of exactly how many independent feature films fall by the wayside every year, whether for reasons commercial, technical, or thematic.

Although the Sundance Film Festival runs for only two weeks, it is a year-long operation in terms of submissions and building up a final slate of films which will, in theory, represent the best that independent cinema has to offer. International festivals which trade in established talent, such as Venice and Cannes, have occasionally had their reputations tainted by perceived lobbying for the inclusion of certain titles based on the promised appearance of various stars and celebrities, while the festivals themselves have engaged in their promotional campaigns to be the event to host the latest works of film-makers of international renown.

Film festivals and major studios have an uneasy yet symbiotic relationship, mainly because the stars and products that the entertainment companies can provide attract enormous media coverage, and such coverage attracts corporate sponsors with interests in vertically related markets that festivals need in order to survive financially. As the majority of films screening both in and outside of competition at Sundance are by unknown film-makers and feature actors who are either unknown, or low in the Hollywood pecking order, there is less competition between the festival organizers with their counterparts with similar events, and more aggressive lobbying on behalf of producers and distributors to secure their film a place in the line-up.

According to the New York Times, all films submitted for Sundance must go through the following process of elimination and selection before finding their place in the festival.

Submissions – 1004 American feature films **(7459 Projects** 936 Foreign feature films **submitted for** 4311 Short films

2005 Sundance 760 American documentaries **Film Festival)** 448 Foreign documentaries

Viewing – A dozen or more Sundance staff divide up the submitted films and write reports on each one, rating them on a scale of 1 to 5. Some films are viewed more than once.

First Elimination – Films that have received a low rating are 'dismissed' from the selection process.

The Debate – A core team of five

Outside Voices – The team of Programmers, led by core programmers has claimed to Geoff Gilmore, review be open to the opinions of those and discuss the films industry figures who have an that have 'survived' association to Sundance and the first elimination. the US independent sector.

Second Elimination – The films that the core team are not passionate about, and those that have also not received any outside support, are 'dismissed' from the selection process.

Final Decision – In late November, the final slate of approximately 120 independent feature films and documentaries that will be shown in the festival in February is announced.

Once selected, it is decided which films will be screened in competition, with around 32 usually being selected, and the remaining films being screened out of competition. Competition and non-competition films are then placed in the following categories as a means of best organizing screenings:

Competitive: Dramatic Competition
Documentary Competition

Non-Competitive: Frontier
Premiere
World Cinema
Midnight American Spectrum

Screenings are usually introduced by the director, who will conduct a questions-and-answers session afterwards. Sundance labs run throughout the festival, providing directors and writers with the opportunity to develop their ideas with assistance from more established film-makers and scribes. An awards ceremony takes place at the end of the festival, with the following categories being honoured:

Grand Jury Prize (Best Film)
Directing Award (sponsored by the Director's Guild of America)
Cinematography Award (sponsored by Eastman Kodak)
Freedom of Expression Award (sponsored by the Playboy Foundation)
The Waldo Salt Screenwriting Award
Audience Award for Dramatic Film
Audience Award for Documentary Film
Best Short Film

The selection process for Sundance has often been scrutinized, particularly by Biskind, who has suggested that the event is now openly in competition with other festivals, such as New York and Toronto. While it is apparent that Sundance has no shortage of applicants, it has been suggested that the festival will still resort to underhanded measures to secure films. Such practices can actually be traced back to 1984, when the independent producer Jeff Lipsky was contacted about the possibility of 'submitting' Jim Jarmusch's *Stranger than Paradise* for inclusion in the line-up.

> They called me to get *Stranger than Paradise* and I turned them down. I don't remember who the artistic director was at the time but he virtually said to me, 'Look, if it goes in, I can almost assure you it's going to win'. I said, 'Fine, OK, I'll enter it.'[9]

Representatives for the Sundance are obviously keen to refute any charges of using the rewards that their event offers as a means of maintaining leverage over producers and film-makers. Their most common defence is to portray Sundance as an institution that is symbolized by its integrity, and to assert that it is actually fledgling film-makers, opportunistic producers, and an overbearing mass media that is trying to use its influence to sway programming selections. As Gilmore claims,

> Integrity is a huge part of Sundance's success. Because if we don't have integrity, we don't become the festival we've become...One of the things I learned is that there is very little value in showing films that don't work.[10]

It could, however, be argued that Gilmore's idea of 'films that don't work' can be read as 'films that don't work in the marketplace', as throughout the 1990s, Sundance began to provide more screening opportunities for films that were made within, or at least on the fringes of, the Hollywood system. Some selections from the Hollywood production line were enough in keeping with the lineage of the festival that their inclusion was acceptable, such as The Hudsucker Proxy, which played at the 1994 festival. Although a $40 million Warner Brothers venture, it was written and directed by Joel and Ethan Coen, whose 1984 debut Blood Simple had been a great influence on the independent sector, if only for the enterprising manner in which it was funded. However, with 1994 also marking the first year that distribution deals were struck during the festival, the combination of Hollywood product in the programme and money changing hands, suggested that Sundance was gravitating towards a more commercial position, positioning itself closer to Cannes and Venice as a major industrial event. Answering such concerns, Gilmore claimed,

> It's not like I'm trying to become Cannes West here...To some degree the distinction between studio films and independent films is becoming more and more grey, and we're reflecting that.[11]

However, this can be seen as an example of Sundance becoming a part of the Hollywood machine. The original intention of the festival was to provide a forum for film-makers whose work was resolutely outside the system, films that may not otherwise be seen, whereas the present Sundance Film Festival is catering to a need that is twofold – the need of director's to gravitate towards a long-term Hollywood career, and the need of the studio system to find talent and films that it would not have developed through its own cycle of mass production.

8.3 Power Play in Park City – Has Sundance 'Sold Out' to Hollywood?

There has been much discussion about whether Sundance has changed Hollywood, or if Hollywood has changed the Sundance Film Festival; first by accommodating it, and then by absorbing it as a means of meeting its own cultural and economic needs. To examine this debate, it is necessary to look at Hollywood's use of, or reliance on, the festival and how Sundance has responded to it. In the early-to-mid-1980s, Sundance struggled because there was simply not a wide enough range of American independent films to screen at the festival. Therefore, the festival sought assistance from Hollywood in terms of attracting publicity through the screening of big studio films, and from visits by high-profile celebrities and prominent industry figures. At this juncture, Hollywood's involvement in Sundance was beneficial because it helped to generate publicity for more socially worthy productions, whilst also providing an opportunity to scout film-making talent that might be put to use on big-budget productions. However, the purchasing of said talent's independent work was not an option at this stage, as there was still a clear divide between 'independent' and 'studio' production, while the Hollywood majors had yet to identify the long-term benefits of investing in the distribution of independent features.

Throughout the 1980s, independent films continued to pique the interest of critics and niche audiences, although even the most successful low-budget productions of the period, such as *Stranger than Paradise, Blue Velvet, The Brother from Another Planet*, and *She's Gotta Have It*, failed to gross $10 million domestically, making such pictures insignificant to an industry that was developing an insatiable appetite for $100 million-grossing blockbusters. Independent films were still regarded as a talent pool for directors, but it was not yet considered a good career move for talent to go back to the independent sector after working on studio productions. Therefore, the sector lacked the star 'glamour' that it acquired in the mid-1990s when established Hollywood names began to take substantial pay cuts to work on independent films which would add impetus to their careers through critical acclaim and cultural capital.

As with *Easy Rider* in 1969, the commercial rejuvenation of the independent sector, and, therefore, the repositioning of the Sundance Film Festival in relation to the entertainment industry, came about because of the financial success of one film. *Sex, Lies, and Videotape* was financed independently through a video distribution company and shot for around $1 million by the young writer-director Steven Soderbergh. After picking up the Audience Award at Sundance, then still operating under the banner of the United States Film Festival, in 1989, it was purchased by Miramax and entered for the Cannes Film Festival where it beat a number of a higher profile films, such as Spike Lee's incendiary *Do the Right Thing*, to win the coveted Palme d'Or. To the studios, the awards that were showered upon *Sex, Lies, and Videotape* were irrelevant to the fact that it grossed $25 million in the United States, and $80 million worldwide, showing a superior cost-return to any Hollywood production of recent years.

Like *Easy Rider, Sex, Lies, and Videotape* is not as audacious as it first appeared and Soderbergh had made compromises to get the film made. He had intended to shoot in black and white, but changed his mind when financiers threatened to pull out, while the plan to use unknown actors was dropped when the script attracted James Spader, Laura San Giacaomo, Peter Gallagher, and Andie MacDowell, a quartet of second-division Hollywood acting talent whose names would at least guarantee the sale of the film for overseas video and television. Ultimately, the film is a tease, a morality tale structured as a chamber piece, dressed up with some frank sexual discourse and a title so enticing that it has become part of the modern vernacular. Even Soderbergh has admitted its shortcomings, whilst also suggesting why it was successful. Discussing the film in 2004, he stated that

When I look at it now, it looks like something made by someone who wants to think he's deep, but really isn't...the fact that it got the response it did was indicative of the fact that there was so little else to latch on to.[12]

However, the Hollywood system was impressed enough by the box office returns of Soderbergh's debut to take a greater interest in Sundance as a source of acquisitions, while many impressionable independent film-makers set out to emulate the success of *Sex, Lies, and Videotape* with their own low-budget features about the nocturnal admissions of seemingly straight-laced, upper-middle-class suburbanites and professionals. This short-lived trend followed the brief craze for youth-orientated stories which appeared after *Easy Rider*, and was soon replaced by the guys-with-guns cycle in the wake of Tarantino's *Reservoir Dogs*, another debut film that was discovered at Sundance, and even developed with assistance from the Sundance Lab. It is perhaps not surprising that independent films began to adhere more to generic constraints and the perceived rules of the market when the potential rewards became so great. As Harvey Weinstein commented, 'It's not like they can just go make a home movie. The stakes are a little higher now that there's a forum for it. This really is a world stage.'[13]

Geoff Gilmore appears to be comfortable with the sudden rise in profile of the festival and is keen to stress that

Sundance was being written about as a national institution, and was being regarded by people inside the industry as playing an important role in setting the agenda for the independent universe.[14]

Unfortunately, the agenda of Sundance and the agenda of American independent cinema are not the same thing. If the agenda of American independent cinema is to continue to make films that are interesting, challenging, socially conscious, and aesthetically adventurous, the agenda of the Sundance Film Festival is altogether more complicated. While it has become a part of the American film and entertainment industry, Sundance is also an industry in itself. Aside from the festival, the Sundance banner encompasses a wide variety of vertically related and integrated avenues of business, such as the Sundance television channel, which screens independent films, documentaries, and shorts. This, in turn, promotes the Sundance Institute and festival, which draw attention to the locality of its event and its appeal as a tourist destination.

The agenda of Sundance is to make sure that independent cinema remains fashionable and commercially viable, in order that the festival and its divergent interests continue to prosper. A look at its list of screening categories also indicates this, as films that are felt to have more popular appeal are placed in the main competition, or other slots that will lead to publicity, whereas the more rural, indigenous productions that the USFF was established to celebrate are restricted to regional sections, suggesting that the selection committee is including such films for social-political reasons, but acknowledging that they are unlikely to find an audience outside the festival circuit.

What has not changed about Sundance is that its most immediate beneficiaries are the independent film-makers, although their benefit can be at the expense of overeager buyers. Some film-makers have succeeded by creating an aura of celebrity around themselves, often through their 'war stories', convoluted accounts of how they managed to make their features with limited fiscal and physical resources, which can be alternately amusing and horrifying. The media's preference for such 'underdog' stories has meant that some young directors have received more press and attention than the actual films that they have struggled to complete. As Kevin Smith observes,

> Independent films punched through based on the salesmanship of the distributors that were repping them and the personalities of the people who made the films, and not even so much the personalities as the backstory.[15]

Sundance is an ideal stage for recounting such stories. A humble but entertaining 'performance' when introducing screenings, giving interviews, or participating in panel discussions can gain favour with both the popular media and serious critics, who will be looking for a new 'discovery' to champion as a means of fuelling their own reputations as commentators of the culture zeitgeist. Robert Rodriguez, whose debut feature *El Mariachi* won the Audience Award in 1992, recalls his time spent discussing his film at the festival, and endearing himself to critics and audiences,

> An audience member asked the big question: 'so what if you were asked to direct *Lethal Weapon 4*? Would you take it?' We went down the line, everyone saying they wouldn't take it. You could feel the 'yeah right' vibes coming from the audience. So when it came to me, I said, 'Damn right I'd take it!' Cheers from the audience. That's what they wanted to hear. But I added, 'the studio would give me a $50 million budget, but I would really make it for one million, and I bet you the studio would never know the difference. I'd then take the rest of the forty-nine million and I'd save a country with it.' Big laughs, great audience. At fifteen bucks a ticket for these panels, you've got to try and give them their money's worth.[16]

With such crowd-pleasing behaviour winning over audiences and journalists, it is easy for distributors to make mistakes when purchasing festival films. The audience at Sundance is a very particular one, comprised of certain professionals with particular relation to the film industry, while the individuals who make up the general audience are enthusiasts of the type of cinema that Sundance offers. For this audience, attributes that may be commercially problematic for distributors, such as confrontational subject matter, non-linear narratives, or a lack of star names, are expected, accepted, and encouraged.

The street drama *Hurricane* was purchased by United Artists for $1 million following a strong audience response, but unsure of how to market their purchase, UA left the film on the shelf for eighteen months, losing any momentum from its success at Sundance. Eventually released and re-titled *Hurricane Streets*, the film grossed a meagre $334,041 domestically, followed by a swift trip to the video rental market where it was 'lost' amongst superficially similar offerings about gang violence. *The Spitfire Grill* was more commercially successful, returning $12 million domestically. However, the real success story concerning *The Spitfire Grill* was not its box office gross, but the fact that the financiers exceeded their own expectations by selling the film to distributor Castle Rock for the sum of $10 million. With the additional cost of prints and advertising, Castle Rock's investment in *The Spitfire Grill* would total an estimated $20 million, giving them a domestic loss of $8 million. The film itself is something of a hybrid, representing both 'old' and 'new' Sundance in that it is a rurally located, social-conscious piece, but also produced technically to industry standard with a narrative driven by melodrama.

Hollywood has not so much changed Sundance, as changed independent film, which in turn has changed the festival. With the mass media offering regular accounts of the financial rewards and career opportunities which are offered by Hollywood to film-makers from the independent sector, Sundance has become the obvious place to take a low-budget film with commercial aspirations. It should also be noted that experience and atmosphere which is offered by Sundance, at least in the festival's early years, has had little impact upon the Hollywood mainstream as the festival's intended emphasis on the low-budget, do-it-yourself ethos of independent film-making is hard to find in the never-ending stream of bloated Hollywood blockbusters.

Although many of these studio productions offer gainful employment to talent that blossomed in the independent sector, whatever qualities distinguished their early work are often hard to find once they have been institutionalized and set to work within the Hollywood machine. In terms of Hollywood's investment in the independent sector through acquisitions, many of which are handled at Sundance, the interest of studios has had a negative impact in that they have forced the smaller, genuinely independent distributors out of the market by making offers that they simply cannot match. If Sundance has had an economic effect on Hollywood, it is to make the studios realize that there is a potentially lucrative niche market for independent cinema, providing that purchasing, advertising, and distribution costs are kept in line with a film's projected box office return. Unfortunately, this in turn has had an economic side effect on independent film by marginalizing distributors who were already operating on the fringes of the industry, and forcing first- or second-time film-makers to compete for distribution by catering their work towards the Hollywood mainstream.

Notes

1. Wasko, p. 208, 2003.
2. Bourdieu, p. 106, 1993.
3. Bourdieu, p. 106, 1993.
4. Taubin, A, quoted by Anderson, J, *Sundancing – Hanging Out and Listening In at America's Most Important Film Festival*, p. 15, Avon Books, 2000.
5. Redford R, quoted in article 'Turning an Industry Inside Out: A Conversation with Robert Redford', *Harvard Business Review*, 80:5, (May 2002).

6. Levy, E, *Cinema of Outsiders – The Rise of American Independent Film*, 1st edn, p. 39, New York, New York University Press, 1999.
7. Bernard, T, quoted by Anderson, p. 17, 2000.
8. Barker, M, quoted by Anderson, p. 18, 2000.
9. Lipsy, R, quoted by Anderson, p. 18, 2000.
10. Gilmore, G, quoted by Clark, J, 'The Soul of Sundance's Machine', *The New York Times*, 05/12/2005.
11. Gilmore, quoted by Nelson, R, 'Safe at Sundance', *Metro Active Online Edition*, 21/02/1997.
12. Soderbergh, interviewed by Biskind, p. 41 2004.
13. Weinstein, H, interviewed in *The New York Times*, 13/12/1992.
14. Gilmore, quoted by Anderson, p. 21, 2000.
15. Smith, K, quoted by Biskind, p. 23, 2004.
16. Rodriguez, R, *Rebel Without A Crew, Or How A 23-Year-Old Filmmaker with $7,000 Became a Hollywood Player*, p. 178, London, Faber & Faber, 1996.

9

The Business of Art: Miramax Films and the Cultivation of the Niche Market

This study has looked at the efforts of independent film-makers and how their methodologies are embodied in their work. It has also looked at the distribution and marketing of non-studio feature films, and how these methods contrast with those employed by the studio sector. However, an analysis of how distributors not only identify but expand the core audience for their product is crucial to understanding the workings of the American independent sector and how it mirrors the hierarchies of the Hollywood, whilst also operating in a potentially more competitive field.

After the completion of a feature made outside the Hollywood system, and a tour of film festivals and buyer's markets, the picture is purchased for distribution, either by an independent company or the specialist division of a major studio. The company then acts as a bridge between the film-maker and the audience, making the work available to the public by booking it into theatrical venues, promoting it towards the target audience, and later guiding the film through ancillary markets. Kracauer claims that works of art are social objects that are willed into a temporal state by an audience that subconsciously requires them as a means of explaining the workings of the world and its cultural changes. This has some legitimacy in explaining how film-makers come to create cultural products, as they respond to movements of popular feeling and attempt to encapsulate public concern and sentiment within narrative constructs. However, it does not explain how these films are made available to the audience. Bourdieu argues that cultural products only come to be seen and appreciated when enterprising businessmen maximize their value through skilful promotion:

> The ideology of creation, which makes the author the first and last source of the value of his creation, conceals the fact that the cultural businessman (art dealer, publisher, etc) is at once and the same time the person who exploits the labour of the 'creator' by trading

in the 'sacred' and the person who, by putting it on the market, by exhibiting, publishing, or staging it, consecrates a product which he has 'discovered' and which would otherwise remain a natural resource.[1]

This is to say once again that the romantic notion of the artist being a self-made individual who enjoys a unique connection with his audience is, in fact, a fallacy, as the artist requires the economic support of a middleman, or company, to place their work in circulation. They are also reliant on the strategic practices of these middlemen, or mediators, as they are able to identify key markets for their artistic endeavours. If, as Bourdieu claims, the true artist has to have a disinterested nature, he or she has little capacity for connecting with the audience, and therefore requires the fiscal intervention of individuals and companies with interest of a predominantly economic nature, if only to sustain their activities as a practitioner of the creative arts.

It is actually not the film-makers that drive the market, but the distributors who select what they judge to be the most marketable films from festivals and buyer's markets, leaving the rest to gather dust. Caves suggests that contracts between art and commerce can exist in a manner that is mutually beneficial, sustaining the romantic ideal of the creatively autonomous artist and the supportive benefactor. However, this is rarely the case in the world of feature film distribution, where the artist's involvement with his or her work effectively ends once the picture has been signed over and sometimes even before it has been completed.

Miramax Films and American independent cinema are synonymous, so synonymous that Biskind has devoted an entire tome to the company's dominance of non-studio feature film production and distribution. While he has provided a candid account of the inner workings of the company as it grew from independent upstart to studio subsidiary, he has not analysed Miramax in relation to the market, and most importantly has neglected its cultivation of the niche as a means of gaining and maintaining a financial foothold in a high-risk business. This study has concentrated on the accumulation of cultural credit of the independent film-maker, and how that credit translates into autonomy from the mechanics of the system. Miramax Films, however, incorporates that credit into its marketing mix to attract a cultivated audience, making the pedigree of the film-maker a commercially identifiable attribute in itself. This is a key characteristic of the art house or 'specialist' film business, where marketing towards the niche audience is an altogether subtler and more time-consuming process than that of selling product to the masses. As Bourdieu notes,

> It can be seen that, although the opposition between the short cycles of product which sell rapidly and the long cycle of products which sell belatedly or slowly is found in each of the arts, they differ radically in terms of the mode of profit acquisition and therefore because of the connection that is made between the size of the audience and its *social quality*, in terms of the objective and subjective relationship between the producer and the market.[2]

While its status as an independent is questionable, especially after being bought by Disney and producing feature films with budgets north of $80 million, Miramax has continued to trade on its 'outsider' status, presenting itself as an alternative source of finance for film-makers, whilst employing commercially identifiable attributes and recognized business practises as a means of furthering its industrial status. Although Miramax has existed since the late 1970s, it was not until the late 1980s that it would enjoy its commercial breakthrough. *Sex, Lies, and Videotape* grossed $24 million in the domestic market, almost 24 times that of its production budget. Miramax consolidated its success with the strong performance of a number of acquisitions, before being bought by Disney in April 1993. Whilst operating as a genuinely independent enterprise, Miramax honed their marketing mix, targeting specific audiences, but doing so in a manner that appeared tasteful and unobtrusive. As Bourdieu observes,

> But the law of this universe, whereby the less visible the investment, the more productive it is symbolically, means the promotion exercise, which in the business world take the overt form of publicity, must here be euphemized. The art trader cannot serve his 'discovery' unless he applies all his conviction, which rules out 'sordidly commercial' manoeuvres, manipulation and the 'hard sell', in favour of the softer, more discreet forms of 'public relations' (which are themselves a highly euphemized form of publicity) – receptions, society gatherings, and judiciously placed confidences.[3]

In the independent sector, credibility is maintained by avoiding crass commercialism. The niche audience is not opposed to marketing, but does not respond positively to the kind of blanket promotion that is characteristic of the studios. Miramax has benefited from the cultural inception of its brand name and the values that the name is supposed to represent – quality, class, culture, at once traditional and progressive. Their films have been promoted through culturally legitimized forums such as print media and film festivals, where the emphasis on the social importance of cinema has largely eradicated any sense of salesmanship.

9.1 Selling to the Selective – Identifying and Capturing the Niche Market

'**Niche (neesh)** n **1** a recess in a wall for a statue or ornament...**3** of or aimed at a specialist group or market.'[4]

Like other independent distributors, Miramax occupied a niche within a large market, at least in its pre-Disney incarnation. A niche is considered to be a small market that entails an individual customer, or a small customer group, with similar cultural needs, and personal characteristics, such as age, gender, race, interests, abilities, disabilities, income, or occupations. It is a market that needs to be specifically targeted, but creatively so, as it is likely to be alienated by the aggressive strategies commonly found in mass marketing. A niche market should have one or more of the following –

(1) Sufficient size to be profitable and sustainable.
(2) A lack of competition or lack of attention and customer care from other companies.
(3) The potential for manageable growth.
(4) The right level of income.
(5) Self-definition, to self-consciously avoid categorization amongst the 'mass'.
(6) Opportunities for new companies to succeed based on instinctive knowledge of the market rather than pure financial acumen.

Commercial companies operating in niche markets must remain financially prudent whilst also delivering cultural products that are of a high quality and tailored specifically to the needs of their customer base. Within the film industry, this financial prudence entails that companies operating in the independent sector must only invest in pictures that can return a profit on their cost by playing purely to a niche audience. This also explains why the market is driven more by acquisitions than by production, with companies becoming involved at the later stages when a film can be more sensibly assessed as a commercial product. By isolating consumer segments, they keep their marketing expenditure in check, as they acknowledge that blanket mass marketing is unnecessary for their product, and do not invest in promoting their films beyond the core demographic, unless they display signs of crossing over to a wider public. Dalgic and Leeuw claim that;

> Niche marketing could be viewed as the implementation of the marketing concept, in that niche marketing requires a customer/market-orientated organization which is customer focused, competitor orientated, responsive, anticipative and functions in balance with the market and with internal resources; in pursuit of long-term relationships and sustainable profitability. Niche marketing is a continuous process.[5]

This is to say that niche marketing represents the roots of promotional strategy, as it involves the sale of a specific product to a specific consumer group, but then develops that sale into a long-term relationship, adapting its products and marketing strategies in accordance with market changes and instinctively anticipating those changes to maintain an advantage over rival niche suppliers. Kotler observes that there are four key marketing principles. This applies to both mass and niche marketing:

(1) Concept (Necessarily innovative, based on an interpretation of market needs).
(2) Strategy (The targeting of specific customers and other groups of influence, such as critics, festival programmers, and award committees).
(3) Methods (Word-of-mouth marketing, media exposure).
(4) Market Knowledge (Accumulation of information through research and development, often pure managerial chat and speculation).

However, the two sectors approach these principles from different perspectives. Niche companies, such as independent film distributors, operate what is termed the 'bottom-up' strategy, meaning that they start from the needs of a select group of customers and gradually increase their clientele until they have a larger share of the market, with their monopoly of a certain product allowing them to expand the market at their own terms, providing that rival niche marketers or opportunistic mass-marketers do not try to emulate their success. With regard to maintaining their customer base, long-term relationships are the key, with the company avoiding the loss of business through mutually beneficial transactions and generating new business through reputation. The bottom-up approach has two major advantages: Firstly, it requires less fiscal resources, and secondly, it is more flexible and easier to implement. By clearly identifying a specific customer base, less capital has to be spent on research and development as more instinctive choices can be made. As Kotler argues:

> Why is niching profitable? The main reason is that market nicher ends up knowing the target customer so well that he meets their needs better than the other firms that are casually selling to this niche. As a result, the niche can charge a substantial mark-up over costs because of the added value. The nicher achieves high margin, whereas the mass marketer achieves high volume.[6]

An independent financier may invest $5 million in five feature films per year with the aim of returning $50 million, while a studio will invest hundreds of millions of dollars in around twenty films to achieve a similar cost-return ratio. The independent financier, however, has little margin for error. Given the restrictions of the marketplace, the independent distributor cannot afford many failures, and needs to maximize the commercial potential of each title. By comparison, the studio is spread-betting, aiming to achieve a significant market share through volume of product and by locking up multiplex screens and spending double its production cost on advertising. Studios can afford failures, and expect them, but are safe in the knowledge that a success rate of one in three will not only cover the losses of box office failures, but put them into profit. While the studio, will achieve its goals through economical capital, the independent, will succeed by investing in product that enhances its reputation as a specialist supplier to a limited but nonetheless upwardly mobile customer base.

9.2 From Independent to Mini-Major – A History of Miramax Films

Miramax Films was founded in downtown Buffalo, New York by brothers Harvey and Bob Weinstein in 1979. Initially they divided their enterprise into two interrelated camps, booking and promoting rock-and-roll concerts, whilst also distributing concert films and re-issues of foreign films. *The Secret Policemen's Ball*, *Pelle the Conqueror*, *The Thin Blue Line*, and *Working Girls* were amongst their successes in the mid-1980s, with the company acquiring each title for around $50,000 and promoting them to their niche markets to achieve grosses of $1.5–$2 million each. *Working Girls* was the template for many of their later hits in that it took potentially exploitative subject matter, the business of prostitution, but presented it with a stark aesthetic and which led to critical support and interest from more upscale audiences. *The Thin Blue Line* was a haunting documentary by Errol Morris concerning the case of a man on death row for the murder of a police officer, a crime that the convicted party claimed not to have committed. Adding drama to the Miramax advertising campaign, Harvey Weinstein declared, rather tastelessly, 'Never has Miramax had a movie where a man's life hangs in the balance.'[7] Fresh evidence presented by Morris's film prompted a retrial and an acquittal, while Miramax were able to celebrate another successful acquisition. At this time, many independents were going out of business because they were investing too heavily in production and suffering losses when their product failed to perform at the box office. Miramax, however, were targeting niche markets and handling only a few films per year, focussing intensely on wringing every last possible dollar out of each title.

While the sexually explicit content of *Working Girls* and legal controversy surrounding *The Thin Blue Line* were certainly risky, they were calculated risks in that Miramax had already gauged the market for each film and spent only the amount required to capture the niche audience that would appreciate their formal innovations and social-political perspectives. While earlier independents, such as Vestron and Island-Alive, had been overly reliant on the VHS market, Miramax acknowledged the importance of big screen success to achieving a healthy ancillary life. Strauss Zelnick, former president of Twentieth Century Fox, states that

> Because video is released after theatres, the success in video tracks the success in theatres like every other market. Certain pictures outperform in video, but that would never induce you to make a picture because if it fails at the box office, video will not 'fix' the failure. A movie will perform in accordance with its performance at the box office which means you won't make enough money to justify the decision.[8]

Although Miramax also moved into production, it did so cautiously with low-budget co-productions, whilst also acquiring films for distribution to bring value to their library. In this sense, they embraced the 'speciality' aspect of the business, operating more like a gallery or small publishing house in their accumulation of titles by prominent directors. This enhanced the cultural credibility of the company, winning favour with critics, art house bookers, and niche audiences. In 1988, Miramax secured a $25 million debt/equity package from Midland Montague Ventures, a division of the London-based Midland Bank. Early forays into production failed miserably, with in-house projects lacking the distinctive style of the company's acquisitions, but *Sandal*, a co-production with Palace Pictures in the UK starring Ian McKellan, John Hurt, and Joanne Whalley, was a definite turning point. The film detailed the British defence minister John Profumo's affair with the teenager Christine Keeler, and proved to be an international success, grossing $30 million worldwide on a $7 million budget. It was, however, their purchase of Steven Soderbergh's debut feature *Sex, Lies, and Videotape* which truly put the company on the map, and led the entire industry to re-assess its economic perception of independent cinema now that the commercial ceiling had been raised to an entirely unexpected level.

What is often ignored in recounting the history of Miramax is that the company actually had nothing to do with the evolution or production of Soderbergh's film. It was co-financed through RCA Home Video and Virgin, with video rights being divided between the two parties, and the producers left to sell the film for theatrical distribution. Harvey Weinstein did not actually see *Sex, Lies, and Videotape* until it premiered at the US Film Festival in February 1989, and he acquired the rights a few weeks later at the American Film Market in Los Angeles. It was entered into the Cannes Film Festival, and won the Palme d'Or, enabling Miramax to capture the attention of the press and promote Soderbergh as a major new film-maker. The film opened in the US in May, building on excellent reviews and strong word of mouth whilst playing on 350 screens. It gradually expanded into national release in August, just as American critics were bemoaning the lack of quality films as the Hollywood majors unleashed their annual summer blockbusters. *Sex, Lies, and Videotape* became a talking point even the mainstream audience could not ignore.

The success of Soderbergh's film established a formula for Miramax – the acquisition of a film by an established film-maker or new talent, followed by festival and critical exposure, then a limited release to capitalize on niche markets, followed by a wider release once the film had entered the mainstream. In 1993, Miramax was the distributor of not one but two Palme d'Or winners, as Jane Campion's *The Piano* and Chen Kaig's *Farewell my Concubine* shared the top prize at Cannes. Both pictures proved to be popular at the American box office and in ancillary markets. *The Piano* also gave Miramax its first taste of success in related media, as its haunting Michael Nyman soundtrack crossed over into the album charts. However, the Weinstein brothers, Bob in particular, were aware that it was taking time to recoup investment through their slow release patterns and reliance on award seasons and festivals for media exposure. Their main rival in the independent market was New Line Cinema, a company that had been established in the late 1960s, but flourished in the late 1970s and early 1980s. The main business of New Line was exploitation movies and popcorn pictures. Their biggest success came with the acquisition of a cheap children's adventure film, *Teenage Mutant Ninja Turtles*, while the *Nightmare on Elm Street* franchise provided a steady revenue stream with its annual instalments. Seeking to emulate the success of New Line, but without tainting the prestige of the Miramax label, the Weinsteins established Dimension in 1993, an offshoot that was to specialize in genre fare, with recognizable actors and instant commercial appeal.

As with their art house investments, Miramax did not initially make their own product, instead acquiring films that could be released under the Dimension banner. Their first pick up was *The Crow*. The film was regarded as 'damaged goods' in the industry. It had been left incomplete when star Brandon Lee was killed on set when a stunt went tragically wrong. Bob Weinstein invested in additional post-production to tie up the narrative loose ends that had been left by Lee's passing and secured a fashionable alternative-rock soundtrack. *The Crow* opened at number one with $12 million and eventually grossed $51 million. With an opening weekend take that surpassed the overall gross of many of their art house releases, and a final gross that set an in-house record, Miramax had tapped into an instant cash flow, a means of sustaining the company in between critically adored but commercially risky art house pictures. However, a film released the following year would combine the artistic and the commercial in a manner which would prove irresistible to critics and audiences alike.

Quentin Tarantino's *Pulp Fiction* gave the company its first $100 million hit in 1994, winning the Palme d'Or at the Cannes Film Festival and an Oscar for Best Original Screenplay. If *Sex, Lies, and Videotape* had redefined the commercial possibilities of independent cinema, Tarantino's $8 million film set a new benchmark, achieving the 'blockbuster' status usually reserved for studio productions. Miramax had first dealt with Tarantino when they purchased his debut feature, *Reservoir Dogs*, for distribution from the independent financier Live Entertainment. Although the film had performed disappointingly in the United States, grossing just $3 million, it became a success on video and overseas, particularly in England. Unfortunately for Miramax, they had only bought the domestic theatrical rights and had to settle for breaking even while Live, who had retained the video rights, made a healthy return.

Tarantino and producer Lawrance Bender had developed *Pulp Fiction* at Tri-Star, but the studio became uncomfortable with the graphic violence and bad language that seemed to dominate the piece, not to mention the sequence where a hit man would revive the leading lady from a drug overdose by plunging a hypodermic needle into her heart. Polygram expressed interest, but were experiencing censorship problems with *Reservoir Dogs* and were unable to maximize the potential of their acquisition as its video release had been indefinitely delayed by the British Board of Film Classification. While Polygram was weighing up the pros and cons of taking on another Tarantino picture, Miramax was acting more entrepreneurially. Harvey Weinstein obtained a copy of the script and reportedly made an offer to Tarantino and Bender whilst only halfway through it. Although he initially granted Tarantino complete creative control, Weinstein did try to interfere with casting, initially refusing the director's choice of John Travolta, then regarded as a has-been, for the lead role of Vincent Vega, and insisting that either Daniel Day-Lewis or Bruce Willis would make more marketable alternatives. However, he grudgingly granted Tarantino's wishes, when the director and his producer turned the situation into a deal breaker.

Although *Pulp Fiction* was loaded with Hollywood stars, Miramax pushed Tarantino into the media spotlight. Although already a celebrity in Europe following the success of *Reservoir Dogs*, his name was known only to the cinephile set in the United States. This changed, however, when *Pulp Fiction* became a media sensation. Tarantino willingly embraced everything that Steven Soderbergh had rejected, becoming an overnight celebrity. He appeared on the cover of almost every entertainment magazine, and tirelessly promoted his film, and therefore the Miramax dream. At this juncture, the media perception of Miramax shifted. No longer was this a struggling independent, courageously battling the forces of the major studios through entrepreneurialism and intuition, it was now a part of the system, a well-funded Disney subsidiary with the means of producing $100 million hits. The company also diversified, setting up a literary division and investing in the short-lived *Talk* magazine, which often seemed to be a thinly veiled means of promoting Miramax product – the first issue featured Gwyneth Paltrow on the cover, and the interview with the actress focussed on her starring roles in Miramax productions. The newfound Miramax cash flow was also apparent to actors, who would no longer accept lowly salaries now that the Weinsteins were bankrolled by Disney. Although grateful for his *Pulp Fiction* comeback, John Travolta turned down the lead role in *Copland*, which eventually went to Sylvester Stallone, on the grounds that Miramax could now afford to pay him a proper salary. Such setbacks did not have an adverse affect on production or acquisition, as Miramax set about releasing a number of pictures that was unprecedented for a studio or mini-major. The following chart displays the number of films released each year in the history of the company:

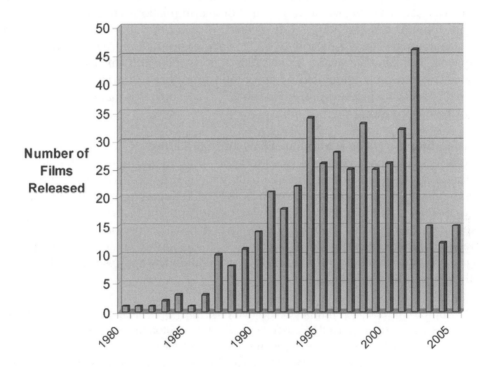

The year 2003 was the most productive in the history of the company, with Miramax releasing almost fifty feature films, a massive amount when the Hollywood majors were averaging twenty. This volume is a reflection of Miramax's desire to monopolize the art house market by inundating it with product, even at the expense of competing with itself for screen space and audience time. The art house market had become the Miramax market, with rival distributors, such as Fox Searchlight, Newmarket, and Lions Gate, having to compete not only with quality of product, but with hard dollars, as the marketing and distribution of independent cinema became less intuitive, and more scientific, much like its studio equivalent, with set formulas for release patterns and advertising campaigns. Not all of the films that Miramax acquired in this period received proper theatrical distribution, with some being released on only a handful of screens before being sent to DVD. Others missed out on a theatrical slot altogether and were released directly to the home market with little or no fanfare.

In 2005, the Weinstein brothers announced that they had sold Miramax to Disney, and that they would be leaving the company to start a new venture. Although production predictably slowed at this point, the company was still left with a slate of films, including *The Great Raid*, *Darkness*, *The Underclassman*, *Cursed*, and *The Brothers Grimm* that had been sitting on the shelf for over a year awaiting release, not to mention new titles like *Sin City* and *Hostage*. With the Weinsteins focussing their attention on life post-Miramax, little attention was paid to these pictures, with many commentators referring to their release strategies as being like a 'yard sale'. Long-term relationships with Tarantino and Robert Rodriguez ensured that *Sin City* received proper promotion, and the film proved to be a success, taking $72 million, while *Hostage* performed more modestly, grossing $34 million. The latter film was a Bruce Willis action movie and, despite its commercial potential, was severely undersold by an organization that was winding down, with a release on 1,800 screens, as opposed to the 2,500 and upwards that is usually reserved for that type of product.

9.3 Expanding the Niche – Miramax Films and Marketing

Miramax is a company that has practised the 'bottom-up' method of marketing – targeting a specialist audience and gradually widening its approach to capture more of the mainstream. As much as this explains the marketing of its most notable product, such as *Sex, Lies, and Videotape*, *The Crying Game*, and *The Piano*, it also explains the marketing of the company itself towards the overall public consciousness, moving from a label that signified a certain level of quality to the cinephile set, to an internationally recognized brand that became a shorthand for middlebrow escapism. Bourdieu claims that there are three distinct markets:

> Firstly, there is the specific principle of legitimacy, i.e., the recognition granted by the set of producers who produce for other producers...i.e., by the autonomous, self-sufficient world of 'art for art's sake...Secondly, there is the principle of legitimacy corresponding to the 'bourgeois' taste and to the consecration bestowed by the dominant fractions of the dominant class...Finally, there is the principle of legitimacy which its advocates call 'popular', i.e., the consecration bestowed by the choice of ordinary consumers, the 'mass audience'.[9]

It would appear that Miramax operates within the first of Bourdieu's three markets, specializing in highbrow product for an elite community of artists and critics. However, the company has succeeded by taking works from that community and promoting them towards the second of Bourdieu's markets, the middlebrow audience that possess substantial spending power and a need for novelty. As Perren notes,

The company broadened the audience of these movies by portraying them as what Hollywood has to offer *and more*: full of sex, violence, and risky content. This marketing sleight of hand, in which the films were at once similar and different from Hollywood, helped Miramax carve out an often financially lucrative and aesthetically viable space for independent cinema from the late 80s and into the mid 90s.[10]

In its pre-Disney incarnation, Miramax sensibly avoided the 'popular' market altogether, knowing its films were certainly not for teenagers or adults requiring undemanding escapism. However, this meant that Miramax were able to expand their portfolio of films at a time when Hollywood had rejected socially challenging material. The company acquired independent pictures at a low price, and funded their in-house productions at modest costs. These low-to-mid-budget pictures had actually become too difficult for studios who could not envision how to sell a film that featured well-known actors, but not genuine stars, solid production values, but not spectacular visual effects, and was not adaptable to synergetic marketing strategies.

Industry commentators have often cited the marketing of *The Crying Game* as an early example of Miramax's entrepreneurial, even opportunistic, approach, but there are earlier instances of such publicity-seeking. In 1983, actress Claudia Ohana was encouraged to pose for *Playboy* magazine to promote *Erendira*, while in 1989 Daniel Day Lewis was pressured to testify before Congress on behalf of the Americans with Disabilities Act, as a means of bringing attention to his performance as cerebral palsy sufferer Christy Brown in *My Left Foot*. To promote the Christine Keeler biopic *Scandal*, star Joanne Whalley Kilmer was accompanied on the interview circuit by Keeler herself. Miramax was seeking to expand the cinephile audience and make a profitable crossover into the mainstream. As Harvey Weinstein explains,

> Although we market artistic films, we don't use the starving artist mentality in our releases. Other distributors slap out a movie, put an ad in the newspaper – usually not a very good one – and hope that the audience will find it by a miracle. And most often they don't. It's the distributors' responsibility to find the audience.[11]

The audience which Weinstein is talking about could be perceived to be 'any audience', as Miramax have re-packaged many of their films, pushing their pictures beyond the art house niche and expanding the perceived social class for their product. Like the major studios, Miramax has not just employed one campaign per film, but several campaigns, running parallel to tap into separate markets. *Sex, Lies, and Videotape* had alternative posters and trailers, promoting the film as an upmarket comedy, a salacious erotic drama, and a prestigious Cannes award winner. However, its greatest coup was the trailer for *The Crying Game* in 1992. An interracial gay love story centring on a protagonist with ties to the I.R.A, it had failed commercially in the UK, despite strong reviews, but Miramax remarketed the film for the American release, cutting a trailer which eliminated any suggestions of homosexual material or reference to conflict in

Northern Ireland. They promoted the film as an action-thriller with a 'big secret', rather than as a relationship film with gat connotations.

Although *The Crying Game* has thriller elements, and ratchets up the tension in the final third, the big twist arrives early in the narrative, with the revelation being used more as a catalyst for thematic introspection than for shock value. While it could be argued that such marketing misrepresented the themes and values of the film, it did lead to a gross of $62 million and capture the attention of a mainstream audience that would not usually have seen a film that tackled the issues of terrorism and gender identity. Most film-makers, while accepting that the company has occasionally emphasized the commercial attributes of their films over their subtler, more artistic, qualities, have acknowledged that the Miramax marketing mix has broadened the audience for their work. As Kevin Smith admits,

> We just like to make the movie. After that, it's their call. When they first came up with the poster for *Chasing Amy*, my take was that it looked like a *Details* cover. But Harvey said, 'Trust me, trust me, it's very eye-catching, it'll work.' And he was right.[12]

It is, however, the advertising campaign for *Pulp Fiction* which best exemplifies the lucrative balance that Miramax has perfected between art house class and commercial appeal. The print adverts display the dictionary definition of the term 'pulp fiction', emphasizing the literary ancestry of the picture, and its victory at the Cannes Film Festival. They also feature stars John Travolta, Uma Thurman, Bruce Willis, and Samuel L. Jackson, each looking suitably iconic in black-and-white attire, posing with guns in a manner that suggests a film that will feature two of cinema's most commercially identifiable attributes – sex and violence. The trailers take the same approach, opening with mention of the film's Cannes win, and the literary definition of the title, before cutting to a helter-skelter montage of key sequences, peppered with colourful dialogue and accompanied by blistering guitar music. Miramax would later employ the same approach to Tarantino's follow-up films, *Jackie Brown* and *Kill Bill*, but this time the effect was one of familiarity, not novelty, with the audience being reminded of the signature style of a celebrated film-maker.

9.5 The Independent Benefactor – Miramax Films and Creative Relationships

The crucial difference between Miramax, and now-defunct independents such as Island-Alive, Cannon, Vestron, and Orion, is that the company has not just followed the direction of the market, but tried to control that direction. Through its 'in-house' talent, directors such as Tarantino and Rodriguez, Anthony Minghella and Lasse Hallestrom, and actors like Matt Damon, Ben Affleck, and Gwyneth Paltrow, the company has provided independent cinema with a marketable image, one that encapsulates both youth and experience, familiar to audiences, but not immediately associated with the studio system. The positive aspect of this is that Miramax have eradicated the limitations for independent cinema, establishing that there is no commercial ceiling for a movie that finds favour with audiences, and that success is possible across a wide range of genres. The negative aspect is that, in pursuit of this success, the company has forced creative compromises upon film-makers and become less ambitious in terms of its in-house productions, settling on a formula for popular approval. Discussing the Miramax production slate in 1997, in the wake of their Oscar success with *The English Patient*, senior development executive Meryl Poster claimed:

> I think we're re-inventing ourselves every day. The scripts we're getting right now are all epic romance, like *The English Patient*. Well, we did *The English Patient*, and I don't think we're going to do it again. So when some of the other companies try to emulate our formula, we'll be on to something different.[13]

However, much of the company's output from the late 1990s onwards has an air of familiarity about it, as 'in-house' production was creatively stifled by the desire to maintain a lucrative middlebrow audience. In 1999, Miramax released *The Cider House Rules* in time for Academy consideration. It was based on a classic novel, featured a cast of established stars and was directed by the Swedish film-maker Lasse Hallestrom. In 2000, Miramax released *Chocolate* in time for Academy consideration. It was also based on a well-regarded, if inherently schmaltzy, novel and again featured a cast of stars with Lasse Hallestrom directing. In 2001, Miramax released *The Shipping News*, a film whose posters were almost Academy Award consideration brochures in themselves. It was based on a popular novel, directed by Lasse Hallestrom, and featured established actors. Ultimately, audiences, critics, and Academy voters experienced a sense of *déjà vu*, as Miramax's Oscar-baiters became subject to the law of diminishing returns. *Proof* reunited the director (John Madden) and star (Gwyneth Paltrow) of *Shakespeare in Love* but received little attention, and Hallestrom's *An Unfinished Life*, with Robert Redford and Jennifer Lopez, failed to gross $10 million domestically and was not expanded from limited release.

Through its Dimension division, Miramax also mined the lucrative direct-to-DVD market, producing cheap genre pictures, usually sequels to bigger-budget films that had enjoyed some theatrical success, but not enough to warrant an expensive follow-up. Miramax understood that the DVD market thrives on brand recognition, of which the sequel is a prominent example, and the likes of *The Prophecy 2*, *Mimic 2*, and *Dracula: Legacy* did swift business on the rental market. While these investments represented the economic backbone of the company, its more public business was that of major films by major film-makers and the cultivation of media interest in festival acquisitions. Unfortunately, the mistreatment of talent, usually directors and sometimes actors and writers, has led to a media backlash, as the image of Miramax as a generous benefactor has started to erode. As Bourdieu notes,

> This is why the dual reality of the ambivalent painter-dealer or writer-publisher relationship is most clearly revealed in moments of crisis, when the objective reality of each of the positions and their relationship is unveiled and the values which do the veiling are reaffirmed.[14]

Terry Gilliam found himself in a number of combative situations over his period adventure *The Brothers Grimm*. Budgeted at $80 million, the film was bought by Miramax from the struggling MGM/UA in pre-production, and the Weinstein brothers imposed changes upon Gilliam that overruled some of the director's early creative choices, the most public being the firing of lead actress Samantha Morton and Gilliam's original composer. Problems continued in the post-production stage, with Gilliam being forced to undertake re-shoots that he perceived to be unnecessary, as Miramax tried to turn a dark, menacing fable into a rip-roaring adventure romp. Once completed, Miramax shelved the film for a year, before releasing it to indifferent reviews. It grossed a disappointing $42 million in the US, although overseas grosses put it into profit. Gilliam has since admitted that he had consciously avoiding working with the Weinsteins on other projects because of their reputation for tampering with films by even the most celebrated of directors. The stories of interference which had made Gilliam wary of Miramax have not been restricted to industry gossip, but have actually become public, as directors and producers have talked openly about their negative experiences with the company.

Charles Burnett directed *The Glass Shield* for Miramax in 1993, a police drama about a young black officer who is placed in an otherwise all-white precinct and forced to confront the issue of race both off and on the streets. Miramax was unhappy with the final cut, although it did not deviate from Burnett's approved screenplay, which portrayed the central protagonist in a morally contradictory light. Despite his adherence to the 'suggested' changes, Burnett was not compensated with a wide release or strong marketing push. His politically charged film, which would have found favour with an upscale audience, was half-heartedly promoted as if it was just another entry into the 'ghetto crime' cycle, popularized by *Menace 2 Society* and *Juice*, before being sent to video and cable.

Jim Jarmusch was less compliant when it was suggested that he make cuts to his film *Dead Man*. The project had been purchased by Miramax in mid-production, with Jarmusch's contract stipulating that he had final cut, although Miramax still threatened to stall the release should the director not bring down the two-hour running time. As Jarmusch has never had any serious interest in commercial success, and had rarely enjoyed financial fortune in the American market, he resisted the attempts to tamper with his vision and settled for maintaining his preferred cut at the expense of a wide release. However, he was still disappointed by the manner in which Miramax failed to promote the film, possibly because he felt that his stature as an independent film-maker would warrant better treatment. As he explains:

> I did not expect *Dead Man* to be a commercial success. But I wanted it handled in a classy way. And it was handled, as one critic put it, with tongs by Miramax...Ultimately, I felt punished.[15]

Such tampering has not been restricted to in-house productions, but has also been applied to critically celebrated acquisitions. The version of *Cinema Paradiso* which proved so successful in the US and the UK, was actually a whole hour shorter than the cut that had been popular in its native Italy, with Miramax removing much of the second half of the picture because they felt that the American audience would find it depressing. The Chinese film *Farewell my Concubine* was edited down by twelve minutes for the western market, even though it had shared the Palme d'Or at the Cannes Film Festival, while the Mexican romance *Like Water for Chocolate* was also subject to re-structuring before Miramax would release it in America.

Other film-makers have been more fortunate. Harvey Weinstein predicted that Tarantino's *Jackie Brown* would not reach the box office heights of *Pulp Fiction* if the director did not trim his film down, but was happy to release the picture in its full form when Tarantino retorted that it was not a priority for him to achieve another $100 million success. Miramax put their full marketing efforts behind *Jackie Brown*, which returned $42 million on a $12 million outlay, less than half the gross of Tarantino's previous film, but still an example of how the company could maintain healthy relations with talent, and turn a profit.

Aside from being increasingly reluctant to support films that lacked commercial value, Miramax was also sidestepping controversy, thereby alienating directors who felt that the company would dilute their vision. In 1989, Bob Weinstein boastfully declared, 'Some guys run from controversy. We run towards it.'[15] However, this attitude was not in evidence in 2002 when Miramax came to release *The Quiet American*, an adaptation of Graham Greene's novel concerning the strained relationship between a British journalist and a CIA agent in 1950s Vietnam, as their initial friendship turns into a battle of wits over conflicting politics and the love of a local girl. Miramax paid $5.5 million for the North American rights to the film, which was completed prior to the tragic events of September 11, 2001. Although the film was finished more than a year before Bush began arguing for unilateral action in Iraq, the events depicted in the film, and the questionable arguments of its title character, carried striking similarity. Harvey Weinstein claimed that

> You can't release this film now; it's unpatriotic. America has to be cohesive and band together. We were worried that nobody had the stomach for a movie about bad Americans anymore.[16]

It is a sign of the company's economic growth, and cultural focus, that it could pay $5.5 million for a film and not release it, when in their earlier days the Weinstein brothers had been tirelessly promoting foreign pictures they had picked up for a fraction of that amount. Ultimately, *The Quiet American* was released because of internal pressure from its star, Michael Caine, who insisted that 'I wouldn't make an anti-American movie – I'm one of the most pro-American foreigners I know. I love America and Americans.'[17]

Miramax screened the film at the Toronto Film Festival, with reviewers declaring Caine's performance to be amongst the finest of the actor's illustrious career, and predicting an Oscar nomination for Best Actor. Despite this support, Miramax released *The Quiet American* cautiously, allocating a two-week run in a few theatres in New York and Los Angeles. Caine received the expected Academy Award nomination, but lost out to Adrian Brody for *The Pianist*. Miramax did not expand the release of *The Quiet American* although critical support and Caine's Oscar nomination led to a domestic gross of $13 million, impressive for a film that had been discarded by its distributor, and indicative that it could have been a much bigger success had Miramax not lost its artistic nerve.

With the dealings of the film industry becoming ever more public, the company began to lose some of its initial niche footing as both critics and vocal audiences began to turn against the company and its ethos. Some film-makers did not wish to speak out against the company, understandable given its status within the industry. The likes of Jim Jarmusch and James Gray, whose 2000 crime drama *The Yards* was delayed and discarded by Miramax, have relied upon their cultural credit to protect them when speaking out publicly against the company. Jarmusch emerged relatively unscathed from his *Dead Man* experience. He has been respected for both his work and methodology since the early 1980s and has a seemingly never-ending line of actors waiting to work with him. Gray, however, had only one other film to his name prior to completing *The Yards*. He was regarded as an up-and-coming talent rather than a major player and did not complete another film until 2007.

9.5 The Metamorphosis of Miramax – Cultural Change within the Studio of Independence

As the company has moved from a film-by-film operation to a studio with multiple projects in various stages of production, Miramax has become more corporate in its dealings and outlook, losing sight of its core consumer base. Piercy claims that

> Being market-led is simply about putting the customer at the top of the management agenda and list of priorities. It is about focus on the customer, specialising on the customers' unique needs, finding better ways of doing what the customer values, educating and informing the customer, commitment and care.[18]

Ultimately, this is where Miramax's standards had slipped towards the end of the Weinsteins' ownership. Rather than focussing on the customer as an informed individual, the company was aiming its product at the faceless mass, investing heavily in big stars and advertising campaigns as a means of securing immediate revenue. Focus, with *Lost in Translation* and *Eternal Sunshine of the Spotless Mind*, and Fox Searchlight, with *Sideways* and *Napoleon Dynamite*, were proving more adept at handling independent pictures, employing the old Miramax model of festival and critical exposure, limiting release to niche markets, followed by expansion once strong word of mouth had been achieved. Miramax, by contrast, was operating more like a major studio, producing star vehicles and genre pictures, with a few prestige pictures lined up for Oscar consideration.

While less successful feature films have ultimately broken even through ancillary markets, the latter-day Miramax has struggled to remain at the forefront of the independent market, purely because it has alienated much of the talent it requires to deliver a stream of visionary pictures. Film-makers have become wary of dealing with the company, preferring instead to work with specialist divisions that are, ironically, more creatively flexible than their business model. Miramax acquired *In the Bedroom* and *Garden State* for theatrical distribution, but their directors, Todd Field and Zach Braff, refused to sign long-term development deals with the company, fearing a loss of control. Todd Haynes chose to make *Far From Heaven* with USA Films, and David O'Russell defected following the failure of Miramax to properly promote his second film, *Flirting with Disaster*. Relationships with more established directors such as Minghella and Scorsese have been easier to sustain, but the need these film-makers have for massive budgets to bring the lavish visions of *Cold Mountain* and *Gangs of New York* to the screen have proved a financial burden, while other independent film-makers have delivered cost-effective hits for other companies, that have been happy to allow creative control in exchange for more modest funding. The process of cultural change that Miramax has undergone is an unavoidable side effect of engaging in capitalist enterprise, as the broadening of market opportunities is sadly juxtaposed with the limiting of artistic possibilities.

Notes

1. Bourdieu, p. 76, 1993.
2. Bourdieu, p. 46, 1993.
3. Bourdieu, p. 46, 1993.
4. *Collins New English Dictionary*, p. 514, 1997.
5. Dalgic, T & Leeuw, M, 'Niche Marketing Revisited: Concept, Applications and some European Case Studies', *European Journal of Marketing*, 28:4 (1994), pp. 53–54.
6. Kotler, P, 'From Mass Marketing to Mass Customization', *Planning Review*, September/October 1991.
7. Weinstein H, quoted by Pierson, J, *Spike, Mike, Slackers & Dykes – A Guided Tour Actors a Decade of Independent American Cinema*, p. 84, London, Faber & Faber, 1995.
8. Zelnick, S, quoted by Wyatt J, 'The Formation of the Major Independent – Miramax, New Line and the New Hollywood', *Contemporary American Cinema* (Neale, S & Smith, M, eds), p. 75, London, Routledge, 1998.
9. Bourdieu, p. 50–51, 1993.
10. Perren, A, 'Sex, Lies and Marketing – Miramax and the Development of the Quality Indie Blockbuster', *Film Quarterly*, 55:2 (2001), p. 37.
11. Weinstein, quoted by Ceroe, D, 'Taking an Independent Path', *Los Angeles Times*, p. 1, 03/05/1989.
12. Smith, K, quoted by Major, W, 'To the Max', http://www.boxoffice.com, 08/1997.
13. Poster, M, quoted by Major, 08/1997.

14. Bourdieu, p. 79, 1993.
15. Jarmusch, J, quoted at http://www.imdbquotes.com.
16. Weinstein, quoted by Wiener, J, 'Quiet in Hollywood', http://www.thenation.com, 06/11/2002.
17. Caine, M, quoted by Wiener, 06/11/2002.
18. Piercy, N, *Market-led Strategic Change: Making Marketing Happen in Your Organization*, p. 26, Thorsons, 1991.

10

THE RECEPTION OF AN ALTERNATIVE AMERICANA: AUDIENCES AND AMERICAN INDEPENDENT CINEMA

The final stage in the process of feature film production is, of course, the public availability of the finished work, and its reception by members of the paying audience. Although the film remains the commercial property of its studio, private investor, or distributor, it is now also the social and intellectual property of the audience, or the public mass, a crowd that can broadly be referred to as the 'cinemagoing public', but which can, as this chapter will show, be broken down into distinct social-economic groups with their own set of positions and preferences. This is a complex process, as the reception of a film can drastically alter its social positioning. As Gripsrud states,

> The production of a film provides a raw material which regulates the potential range of experiences and meanings to be associated with it, but it is through audiences that films become 'inputs' into larger socio-cultural processes.[1]

This chapter brings together what Bourdieu terms 'the field of production' and 'the field of consumption', meaning, in this case, the film-maker and their audience. Therefore, it is necessary to provide some analysis of the relation between the two, and how their respective cultural changes may be mutually exclusive. This will be explored through analysis of audience theory, and studies of four ideal types with a certain level of interest in the cinema and the American independent sector. If, as Bourdieu claims, those who operate within the field of restricted production are interested in disinterestedness, then the field of consumption becomes something of a necessary evil, for all producers must amass enough cultural and economic capital in order to continue to secure financing for their films. As Bourdieu states,

In the cultural market – and no doubt elsewhere – the matching of supply and demand is neither the simple effect of production imposing itself on consumption, nor the effect of a conscious endeavour to serve the consumer's needs, but the result of the objective orchestration of two relatively independent logics, that of the field of production and that of the field of consumption.[2]

This is to say that the realm of popular culture, whether that be film, music, theatre, or any other form of art, exists because of two distinct yet interrelated cultural allocations – the artist creates and expresses, while the public is entertained, but also enlightened and stimulated. Therefore, the audience becomes an important part of the artistic process as their wants and requirements can change and fluctuate in preference and intensity depending on such factors as fashion, personal economy, and social awareness. The audience can effectively dictate the means, resources, and even the aesthetic and artistic direction of the film-maker by bestowing differing degrees of acceptance on particular films, thereby affecting the fortunes of their creators. Recent scholars of the American independent sector, such as Levy and Merritt, have largely ignored the relation between film-makers and audiences. Merritt is particularly reductive, dividing the audience for independent films into the categories of 'gentility and edge',[3] suggesting that the crowd favours either stately literary adaptations or visually kinetic pictures with some graphic content.

This chapter will show that, although there is a core audience of cinephiles for American independent sector, the overall audience can be much broader, depending on the type of film and its commercial appeal. Even within the field of restricted production, it is beneficial and profitable to reach a wide audience, as that audience will be receptive to works that are high in novelty value and also align themselves to their own cultural interests and social-economic conditions. It should be noted that every film does find an audience, no matter how small or insignificant it may be with regard to eventual economic profit, or how disinterested the director, or the other talent involved, may be in participating in a work of commercial value. Bourdieu's observation on this is as follows:

> As an artist put it, 'Everyone sells', meaning that painting of the most varied styles always eventually find a purchaser...this is not the result of intentional design but of the meeting between two systems of differences.[3]

These 'systems of differences' are the artistic process of the film-maker and the culturally instilled desire for visual stimulus that exists within the audience. Each makes choices with regard to their production and their consumption, and these choices, or preferences, ultimately lead the artist to the audience, or vice versa. How exactly an independent film manages to 'find' an audience, or perhaps how the audience is able to 'find' independent films, will be discussed in this chapter through an account in the changes of feature film distribution over the past fifteen years as the rise of the multiplex and the aesthetic rehabilitation of the art house have together granted American independent cinema a new accessibility. It is also important to consider what exactly the audience derives from American independent cinema, both in social and intellectual terms, and how such uses and gratifications are as much of a characteristic of the sector as the films that it produces.

10.1 Defining The Demographic – Who is the Audience for American Independent Feature Films?

The core audience for American independent cinema, by which I am referring to those viewers who actively seek out such films and attend screenings on a regular basis to the point where it almost becomes routine, is essentially the cinephile set. This crowd is one that is driven by an almost absurd love for the culture of the movies, a group of people so enamoured with the silver screen that it has informed their lives, politics, relationships, and personal philosophies both consciously and sub-consciously. This is also an audience that favours an analytic approach, essentially approaching film as a text that must yield multiple meanings and interpretations, and often views a particular film in relation to the other works of its director or author. A breakdown of the particular social types who form the cinephile audience is as follows:

(1) Students within higher education and recent graduate with relevance to visual flexible schedules to allow for cinemagoing and other social activities.
(2) Single young professionals and professional couples without children, possessing disposable income and the free time to spend it.
(3) Serious-minded filmgoers with selective taste, who prefer entertainment of a socially and intellectually provocative nature.
(4) Filmgoers with an insatiable appetite for new films and particular directors.
(5) Filmgoers who see multiple movies each month, mixing studio with independent features to satisfy their demand for visual media and novelty.
(6) Other sociable groups – Anti-literary types, possibly little background in higher education, but responsive to visual stimulus and some discussion.

To categorize this audience as being in opposition to those who favour 'escapist' Hollywood films would be incorrect, as the audience for American independent cinema is also seeking escapism, the difference being the level of engagement that takes place between the audience and the movie. Whereas Hollywood cinema offers spectacle, and in doing so overrides any attempt on behalf of the artist to enclose any subversive social-political content or context, the films from the American independent sector are generally more thoughtful, proposing questions of a social, moral, economic, even theological, nature and often leaving those questions to linger at their close. As Bourdieu notes,

> In the theatre as in the cinema, the popular audience delights in plots that proceed logically and chronologically towards a happy end and 'identifies' better with simply drawn situations and characters than with ambiguous and symbolic figures and action or the enigmatic

problems of the theatre of cruelty, not to mention the suspended animation of Beckettian heroes or the bland absurdities of Pinteresque dialogue.[4]

While Bourdieu draws a distinct divide between the 'popular' audience and those seeking works of higher social value, the reality of the American independent sector is that there is a significant crossover between the two groups, especially when such commercially identifiable attributes as stars, genre, and Academy Awards can be ably exploited by marketing teams. It should be noted, however, that this crossover in audience interest does not occur immediately, and it is the cinephile set, or at least those more discerning audience members, who are relied on to show initial 'support' to an independent feature and spread favourable word of mouth.

American independent cinema was adopted by the cinephile set following the fallout in foreign production in the mid-1970s, a period which found such directorial titans as Fellini, Truffaut, Brunel, Kurosowa, and Godard winding down their illustrious careers. To write off foreign cinema from this point would be foolish, and there are a number of directors working in world cinema who carry as much cultural clout with the cinephile set as Tarantino and Soderbergh. However, the films of Wong Kar Wai (Hong Kong), Zhang Zimou (both China), Luc Besson and Jeanne-Pierre Jeunet (France), Tom Twker (Germany), Pedro Almodovar and Julio Medem (Spain) are often extremely indebted to the American narrative tradition, with characters who are as much ciphers as those who occupy the mainstream American cinema. Other international film-makers of note, such as Ang Lee (China), John Woo (Hong Kong), and Mattiu Kassovitz (France) are now based in Hollywood, bringing their visual, but not social-political, sensibilities to American feature films, thereby supporting Bourdieu's view that the field of large-scale production must borrow regularly from the field of restricted production to renew itself. Foreign cinema is not restricted in the financial sense, but it is restricted in terms of distribution, language, and cultural barriers, and the fact that the actors featured may be huge stars in their respective territories, but not sufficiently famous to 'open' a film in the international market.

With regard to distribution, foreign films are screened in the UK every year, but few benefit from wide releases unless they prove to be popular successes, like *Amelie, Life Is Beautiful*, or *Crouching Tiger, Hidden Dragon*, films that were intended as 'blockbusters' in their home territories and lend themselves to more conventional marketing strategies. The true purpose for theatrically releasing foreign films is to increase awareness of their forthcoming DVD release. The short life of foreign films in cinemas and an over-reliance by distributors on the DVD market, is preventing international cinema from developing a serious following in both the US and UK. By contrast, American independent cinema benefits from aggressive distribution, as most of its output is handled by major distributors as opposed to the smaller outfits that are usually found to be handling foreign films on limited promotional budgets. Therefore, the cinephile audience, while still receptive to foreign films, has become more enamoured with the American independent sector as it is more accessible.

This leads to the correlation between the nature of independent film production and the lives of many of those who crave its latest offerings. A large portion of this audience is comprised of students and other young people who enjoy free time and economic flexibility. Because of these circumstances, they are frequently looking for novelty, yet their educational backgrounds and exposure to more substantial works of art across a variety of mediums makes them demanding, with a need to be surprised, challenged, stimulated, and even shocked, as well as entertained. This is a group for whom film is inherently and eternally fashionable, a medium that is both a social driver, in that it provides opportunities for group activity, yet is also suitable for more private times, when a viewer may want to be socially removed, yet still able to interact with, or relate to the mood, content and philosophy of film.

This audience has much the same attitude in its viewing choices as independent film-makers have towards their work. Young upstarts such as Paul Thomas Anderson, Robert Rodriguez, Wes Anderson, and Richard Linklater have taken advantage of the light-footed nature of independent production and the availability of new digital technology, rapidly moving from being promising film-makers to established players with impressive catalogues. Meanwhile, the previous generation, still ably represented by the likes of Spike Lee, Robert Altman, Abel Ferrara, and John Sayles, are keeping up the production pace. As much as the audience for American independent cinema is eager to try new things in a short space of time, film-makers appear to feel much the same way about their work, mixing styles and genres to assemble bodies of work almost as quickly as young cinephiles assemble collections of DVDs, posters, and soundtracks which belie their own preferences and personalities.

In addition to what could be termed the 'student crowd', American independent cinema also appeals to an older audience that has become jaded with the conventions of the Hollywood mainstream, or simply finds little studio product system that is aimed at their age group. Both the Hollywood cinema and the life of the cinemagoer are inherently repetitious, as the studio system produces the same films annually, and the regular viewer attends screenings frequently and consumes the product. However, the cinephile audience seeks to legitimize this repetition by finding novelty within it, and thereby turning a repetitious habit of consumption into a cultural devotion. The cinephile audience is not obsessed with the avant-garde, but it is seeking the 'independent spirit', the sense of a film-maker rising above the requirements of the system to deliver a more personal work. Therefore, the audience is looking for entertainment that offers strong storytelling, but also intellectual value and finds both of these elements in American independent cinema. Amongst this group of people are lifelong fans of popular cinema, people who watch both studio and independent films, but are keen to see something new. American independent films will also have some appeal to those who generally prefer studio product but may occasionally select an independent feature based on recommendations from friends, a creative advertising campaign, or enthusiastic reviews.

10.2 Finding Fortune on the Fringes – How Exhibitors Have Embraced American Independent Cinema and Expanded its Audience

The increasing accessibility of American independent cinema has much to do with the broadening of its demographic from students and cinephiles to an audience that, a little over a decade ago, would have enjoyed Hollywood blockbusters as their staple cinematic diet. The multiplex boom of the 1980s began to grow in the early 1990s when exhibitors expanded their cinemas or developed new sites to increase the number of screens, thereby also increasing the number of films showing and the range of choice available for the cinemagoer. Admittedly, many chains have often used their multiple screens to exploit the popularity of brazenly commercial Hollywood product, preferring to book additional prints, particularly those suitable for the lucrative family audience. However, it is now common to find at least two or three independent titles playing at multiplex venues, sharing screening room with major studio films. Independent and foreign programming was reserved for major cinemas in the London area, and art house venues in cities with a high-student population, but several 'word- of-mouth' hits led exhibitors to reassess their selection policies. When *Reservoir Dogs* opened in January 1992, it became an instant success in London, propelled by director Quentin Tarantino's publicity tour, and ecstatic reviews which proclaimed the director to be 'the next Martin Scorsese'. The *London Evening Standard* described the film as 'an awesome, pumping, powerhouse of a movie', a quote which was used for the poster campaign. Within weeks it was clear that this was not a success that would be restricted to the capital, as multiplex cinemas across the UK began booking *Reservoir Dogs*. When the British Board of Film Classification refused to grant *Reservoir Dogs* a video certificate, due to the graphic sequence in which a vicious sociopath slices off the ear of a police officer who is unable to defend himself, the film's theatrical run was prolonged to satisfy demand.

By the mid-1990s, independent films such as *The Usual Suspects* and *Swingers* were playing in both multiplex and art house cinemas, in some cases posting a higher screen average than their Hollywood competition. The introduction of independent cinema to the multiplex could be seen as a genuine attempt by the major exhibitors to cater to as wide an audience as possible. However, a more accurate view would be that, since multiplex cinemas began to expand to as many as twenty screens, there is simply a greater need for product to fill those screens, which is where independent films come in. While a mainstream Hollywood film will open on a large screen, and sometimes play on multiple screens at the same venue, an independent feature is more likely to open on one of the smaller screens. This reflects that, while exhibitors acknowledge that there is business in independent cinema, it is still very much a niche market. However, by bringing independent feature films into the multiplex environment, exhibitors have 'legitimized' them for the non-cinephile audience.

The major cinema chains are primarily interested in attracting family ticket buyers, as the average family visit will entail four admissions, plus the purchase of snacks and drinks. In suburban areas, most cinemas are part of an 'entertainment park', where going to see a movie is but one of the attractions, which can also include bowling, shops, games arcades, and fast food eateries. The aim of these developments is to get families, or large groups of people, on to the site and then to keep them there for the remainder of the day by providing lots of entertainment opportunities and recreational activities. By contrast, the art house cinemas, which rely on American independent cinema for a large portion of their business as opposed to just a small percentage of it, cater not to families, but to students and young professionals, individuals, and social groups with substantial amounts of disposable income, and perhaps a self-conscious attitude towards what they spend it on. No longer dilapidated structures screening rare prints of forgotten foreign features, the modern 'art house cinema' is not just about seeing movies but adopting cinema as a part of an urban lifestyle. These are places for socializing, with a trendy bar or café being an essential part of the business, and, in some cases, a book shop or exhibition. Art house venues strive to make their customers feel like they are a part of a select audience, a crowd that is intelligent enough to enjoy entertainment outside the Hollywood mainstream and also socially active.

10.3 Critical Dependency – American Independent Cinema and Supportive Media

Critics are seen to play an important role as both influencers and predictors of cultural taste. The cinephile set makes use of critics, as the films that it favours are rarely accompanied by the blanket marketing. Therefore, critics become an avenue of information and a guideline to which films are worth seeking out. However, it is debatable as to how far this critical influence extends as many independent features have benefited from critical goodwill, but have failed to cross over to a wider audience. Distributors welcome the response of critics when their words benefit their films and do not hesitate to integrate favourable reviews into advertising campaigns as a means of enhancing the prestige of their product, but ultimately critics are a marketing component that can be exploited or discarded. When reviews are not favourable, distributors will emphasize the commercial attributes of their product, such as star names, sex, and violence, and go for the 'hard sell'. In this case, though, critics act as predictors of public taste, in that films which receive negative reviews may suffer large declines as negative word of mouth circulates.

In the case of independent features, negative reviews carry a serious impact. Without marketing hype, independent film-makers are reliant on critics to 'open' their pictures through positive notices that will influence viewers in the key upscale markets, where low-budget features are usually granted their early engagements. The cinemagoing audience is a diverse one, and the range of critical sources reflects that. All news publications, from broadsheets to tabloids, carry reviews, as do fashion and entertainment magazines. There are also more specialist publications, such as *Sight & Sound*, that offer a more academic analysis than *Empire* or *Premiere*. Support from the commercial press is crucial, however, because it reaches a wider audience. Although these publications openly favour Hollywood productions, filling their pages with promotions and product tie-ins, they also seek to endorse independent pictures as a means of maintaining their cultural legitimacy. Having a quote on the poster of a successful film, and being seen as having 'influenced' the choice of cinemagoers, is also a way for the critical press to promote itself, and attract advertising revenue. Below are charts that summarize the critical reception of ten independent features, based upon the responses of critics in the United States at their time of release and a graph to show their eventual performance at the domestic box office.[8]

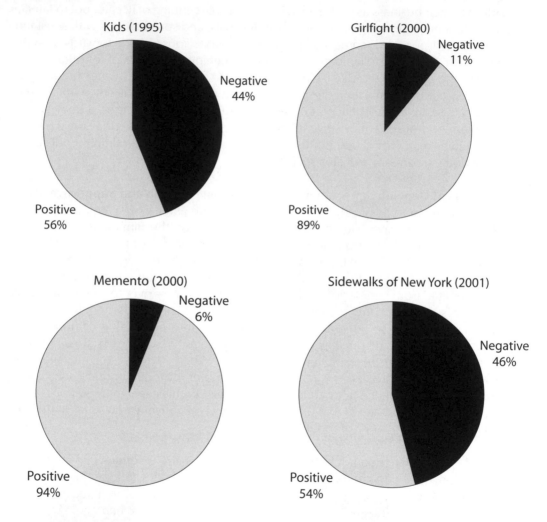

Kids (1995)
Negative 44%
Positive 56%

Girlfight (2000)
Negative 11%
Positive 89%

Memento (2000)
Negative 6%
Positive 94%

Sidewalks of New York (2001)
Negative 46%
Positive 54%

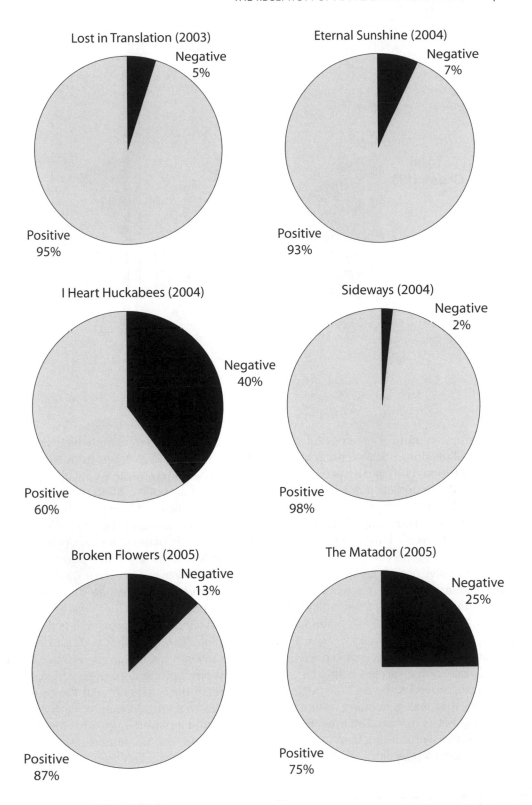

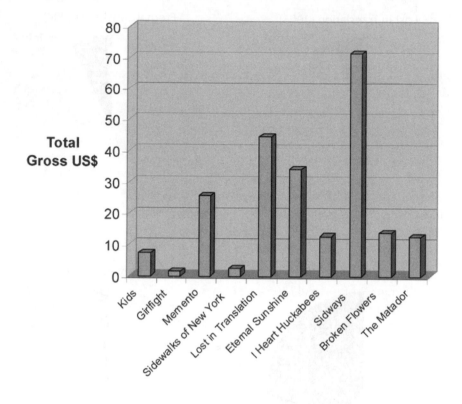

The most commercially successful of the films surveyed is *Sideways*, which grossed $71.5 million domestically and achieved a 98 per cent positive score from American critics. This could be cited as an example of an overwhelmingly positive critical response translating into audience approval. *Eternal Sunshine of a Spotless Mind* achieved a 93 per cent positive score, but grossed only $34 million. Critical acclaim contributed to its strong $8 million opening, which was not matched by *Sideways* until the latter film was in its fourteenth week, but it found a limited following outside of its niche audience. Other results suggest little correlation between critics' reviews and box office performance. Largely positive notices failed to translate into success for *Broken Flowers* or *The Matador*, while *I Heart Huckabees* achieved a similar gross to those films, despite suffering a 40 per cent negative score from critics. An 89 per cent positive score for *Girlfight* was not sufficient to arouse audience interest, and the award-winning film grossed less than the largely dismissed *Sidewalks of New York*. It is possible, however, that without positive critical support, *Girlfight* would have finished with an even smaller gross. *Kids* achieved greater box office success with a larger negative score, but the controversy it aroused may have proved to be an unexpected asset, enticing the audience with the promise of a film that was generating an unusually polarized reaction. *Memento*, with its $25 million gross, is perhaps the true critical success, in that it played in theatres for almost five months without much of an advertising campaign, but continued discussion of the film amongst significant television and print critics, particularly Roger Ebert of the

Chicago Sun Times, made it a talking point amongst more discerning audiences and a film to track down in limited engagement.

10.4 Sitting with the 'In Crowd' – Researching the Art House Audience

I frequented art house cinemas over an eighteen-month period, attending screenings of a wide range of films at different times (late morning, afternoon, evenings) to gauge the ideal types who form the audience for American independent cinema, asking viewers to participate in a survey regarding the reasons for their choice of film. These results are shown in two pie charts that show results in percentage form. In each case, chart 1 is reflective of audience demographic, and chart 2 is reflective of reasons for selection. Each chart uses the following keys to denote groups and reasons for selection –

Chart 1: A = Young person (up to 18 years).
              B = Student (Undergraduate or Postgraduate).
              C = Young Professional (19–29 years).
              D = Professional (30–45 years).
              E = Senior Professional (46 years+).
              F = Elderly/Retired.
              G = Unemployed.

Chart 2: A = Fan of cast/director.
              B = Fan of independent cinema.
              C = Interested in specific subject matter of film (i.e. – historical, social, geographical, or thematic content/original source material).
              D = Responded to advertising/promotional material (i.e. – trailers, posters, Internet, TV spots).
              E = Read newspaper/magazine review or article.
              F = Recommended or prompted by friend/colleague/family member.
              G = Impulse selection.

Screening 1: Gangs of New York (Saturday 25th January 2003, City Screen Cinema, York)

Film Background: With a budget reported to be in excess of $100 million, courtesy of the Walt Disney corporation under the banner of its 'independent' division, Miramax, and a cast of Hollywood stars including Leonardo DiCaprio, Daniel Day-Lewis, Liam Neeson, and Cameron Diaz, *Gangs of New York* is not what would be traditionally perceived as an 'independent' film. However, the serious subject matter and the reputation of director Martin Scorsese, who is widely credited with inspiring the independent film movement, elevate the popular perception of the film from the Hollywood popcorn picture to something more culturally significant. Scorsese's epic was shot on massive soundstages in Italy and courts Oscar gold from its opening frames, with detailed period recreations and a sense of historical importance, particularly resonant after the tragic events of September 11th since the film charts the development of New York City and its near-destruction following a devastating riot. However, this is essentially an ambitious historical framework for a central plot line that would befit a violent 'pulp' novel, in that the story follows a vengeance-seeking peasant who aims to bring down the ambitious crime boss who murdered his father.

Audience Breakdown/Selection Reasons:

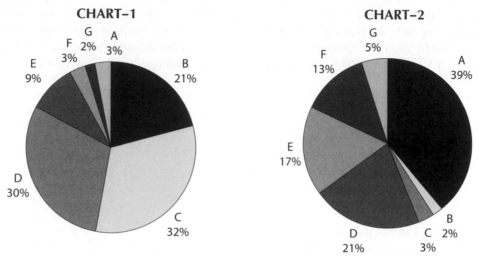

Screening Capacity: 100% (52% male, 48% female)

Although playing at a venue that is ostensibly an 'art house cinema', *Gangs of New York* appealed to audiences primarily for its Hollywood attributes – star appeal and media 'hype'. Only 2 per cent of the audience identified the film, incorrectly, as an 'independent film', although the study did not delve into their reasons for such a categorization. An overwhelming 39 per cent were enthusiastic about seeing a film with big stars from a major director, while an additional 21 per cent responded to the advertising campaign, a campaign which indicated this was both a populist blockbuster and a prestige Oscar contender. As such, the audience was divided between young people, students, professionals, and some older viewers, all of whom, given the production's industry pedigree, were most likely expecting to see a film of a certain artistic and technical standard, but not a work of 'independence'. Ultimately, *Gangs of New York* performed more like a successful Hollywood blockbuster than a successful art house title. It attracted the majority of its audience in its first few weeks, experiencing a substantial drop-off as the 'up-front' demand was satisfied and general 'word of mouth' proved to be of a mixed, rather than wholly enthusiastic, nature.

Screening 2: Lost In Translation (Saturday 24th January 2004, Cornerhouse Cinema, Manchester)

Film Background: Filmed for $4 million on location in Tokyo, with the crew often filming without permits, *Lost in Translation* is more akin to the traditional perception of the 'independent film' in that it is a lower budget effort by a sophomore director, Sofia Coppola, following her well-received debut feature, *The Virgin Suicides*, with a film that finds her evolving both aesthetically and thematically. As with the independent features of the 1970s, plot is secondary to character as *Lost in Translation* explores the platonic relationship between a fading movie star (Bill Murray) and a young philosophy graduate (Scarlet Johansson) who are both unable to sleep during their stay at a five-star hotel. Although the film is emotionally reflective and moves a languid pace, there are more conventionally comedic sequences which derive much of their amusement from the notion of strangers in a strange land. A textured soundtrack by a number of fashionable 'ambient' artists is an added selling point, helping Coppola's film to belie its low-budget origins.

Audience Breakdown/Selection Reasons:

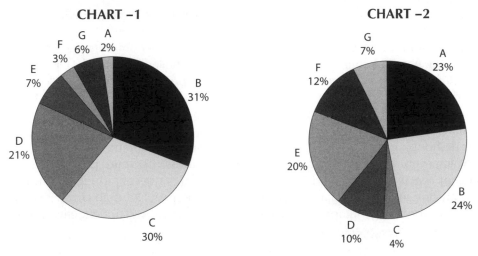

Screening Capacity: 97% (47% male, 53% female)

The results for the *Lost in Translation* screening were similar to those for *Gangs of New York*. Although the former cost $4 million as opposed to the latter's $100 million, it was almost as heavily marketed in the UK, where promotional material, the presence of a well-known Hollywood star (Bill Murray), a rising starlet with more magazine covers to her credit than actual film appearances (Scarlet Johansson), and a well-received soundtrack that had been in circulation prior to the release of the film, gave

Sofia Coppola's low-budget feature the appearance of a major Hollywood release. Once again, the audience was split almost evenly in terms of gender, with perhaps the romantic element and young female lead bringing in slightly more women than men, while male audiences with nostalgia for the commercial films of their youth were drawn by the presence of Bill Murray, who achieved his biggest successes with *Ghostbusters* in 1984 and *Groundhog Day* in 1993.

Unlike *Gangs of New York*, however, this was a film that was identified by a certain section of the audience as an 'independent film' and appealed to them for that reason, showing that there is a core audience which will either actively seek out such pictures, or respond to materials which identify them as such. Critical acclaim and the enthusiastic media coverage had clearly marked *Lost in Translation* as a 'talking point' film, as much of the audience came in either groups or couples, and 12 per cent stated that the film had either been recommended to them, or they had been encouraged to attend the screening with a friend or family member. These early indications of strong 'word of mouth' explain why *Lost in Translation*, and other well-received American independent films, proved to be enduring box office performers, spending more weeks on cinema screens than many more expensive studio titles.

Screening 3 – Fear X (Saturday 15th May 2004, Showroom Cinema, Sheffield)

Film Background: *Fear X* is a structurally challenging film that confronts the idea of the fear of the unknown within a relatively conventional thriller framework. Directed by Nicolas Refn, the film is a Danish-American-British co-production, filmed on locations in Canada, which substitute, somewhat unconvincingly, for the American state of Utah. John Turturro, a well-regarded character actor, known primarily for his supporting roles in the films of Spike Lee and the Coen Brothers, is here cast in the central role of a widowed shopping mall security guard who obsesses over finding his wife's killer, a quest which eventually leads him to a police detective in another state. The crime-related scenario of *Fear X* is a characteristic, and a cliché, of many recent independent films, as is the casting of established actors (Turturro, James Remar, Deborah Unger) who are recognizable, but not genuine 'stars' in that their names alone will not effectively 'open' a film and bring in a sizeable audience.

Audience Breakdown/Selection Reasons:

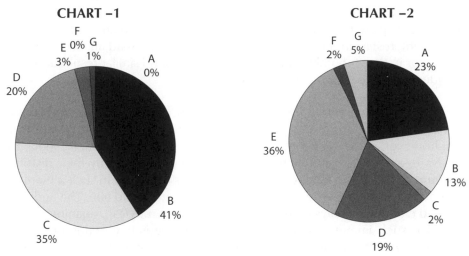

Screening Capacity: 43% (94% male, 6% female)

The audience for *Fear X* was primarily students and young professionals. Although *Fear X* is ultimately an 'art' film in that the plot disintegrates to follow the central protagonist's descent into madness, its commercially identifiable attributes are those of violence, suspense, and the universal theme of vengeance, all of which appeal to a young, mostly male, audience. The film did not benefit from much advertising, and was not the lead review of any newspaper publication on its opening weekend, although some reviews were favourable, if not ecstatic, hence the 43 per cent capacity of the screening. Most audience members surveyed had found out about the film either through advertising or reviews, while some had seen the director's previous films, *Pusher* and *Bleeder*, a pair of socially conscious crime films that have achieved cult status on DVD in the UK, a medium where *Fear X* is likely to be more widely seen.

Fear X disappeared swiftly from UK cinemas after only a few weeks, and was released on DVD shortly afterwards to capitalize on any exposure that had been generated by the film's theatrical release.

Results of Research Screenings

American independent films such as *Lost in Translation*, and quasi-independent films such as *Gangs of New York*, are as well attended as Hollywood 'blockbusters', providing they receive blanket promotion. The adult nature of the material means that they gain crowds such as students and young professionals who often attend films in couples or larger social groups. Less well attended were independent films that had only enjoyed minimal advertising and moderate press coverage, mostly in the form of reviews in magazines. Ironically, many of these films are wholly independent, in that they had not received financing or distribution from the Hollywood majors, yet they were found floundering in the environment where they should have been thriving. The Saturday evening screening of *Fear X* was less than half full in its opening weekend. The audience members that I spoke to afterwards were mostly students and chose the film because it 'sounded interesting in the reviews', or because they had read an interview with the film's director in their monthly magazine of choice. I found similar results at screenings of the independent features *Narc* and *Auto Focus*.

It could be argued that *Lost in Translation* is a superior film to *Fear X*, *Auto Focus*, and *Narc* and, therefore, attracted a greater turnout upon release. The quality of these films is, however, endlessly debatable. What is not debatable is their media profile. *Fear X*, *Narc*, and *Auto Focus* were not aggressively marketed by their distributors. *Lost in Translation* was an independent film that was marketed in such a manner that its audience awareness level was on a par with that of a studio film. The audience for Hollywood cinema is always enthusiastic about 'event movies', meaning those films that receive such immense coverage that they immediately penetrate the public conscious to become a 'must see' proposition. While some of these films drop off in large percentages following a lucrative opening weekend, they at least manage to monopolize audience interest for a small, but financially significant, period of time.

While American independent cinema does not manufacture 'event movies' in the same way, it is reliant on a certain number of features per year that will generate intense audience interest. When tabloid film magazines report on 'another great year for independent film', they are really reporting the success stories of a select few films, and ignoring the fact that most independent features fail to secure much of a following on their theatrical run and have clawed their way into profit through the ancillary markets of foreign sales and home rentals. There is a cinephile audience that will see a wide variety of films purely because cinemagoing is part of the culture of their daily lives, and if these films are there to be seen, they will see them. This is the small audience that attended screenings of *Narc*, *Auto Focus*, and *Fear X*. The audience that flocked in droves to *Lost in Translation* was a crossover crowd, ranging from cinephiles to people simply looking for a good movie to enjoy.

The audience goodwill that turns an independent film into a box office success is not driven by a desire to see the latest that Hollywood has to offer by way of spectacular visual effects. It is looking for something that is outside of the mainstream in that it is more personal and reflective, yet still tells a story that can be intriguing, amusing, and exciting. This is the audience that does not necessarily prefer low-budget over big-budget films, but is looking for something that the Hollywood mainstream is not providing. In this sense, the audience for modern American independent films is very much the same audience which lined up to buy tickets for *Easy Rider* in 1969, an audience that is looking for films which can capture the zeitgeist and encapsulate movements of popular feeling within two hour's worth of flickering celluloid.

10.5 Four Ideal Types – Why do Audiences 'Need' American Independent Cinema?

The fact that a substantial percentage of audience members actively seek out films that are at least perceived to be 'independent', and are attracted to works for their challenging subject matter, or because of the status of their directors, indicates that there is a certain 'need' within the cinemagoing public for American independent feature films. This 'need' suggests that the audience finds such films to be both socially useful and also emotionally and intellectually satisfying. This is an audience which possesses/seeks:

(1) Cultural hopefulness.
(2) Narrative enthusiasm.
(3) Individual assertiveness.
(4) Urban life expectation.

Although the sector has experienced economic fluctuations that indicate varying degrees of audience interest over the last three decades, a number of independent films have always found favour with audiences regardless of general viewing trends. This evident need for a certain type of cinema is indicative of the benefits that the audience receives from it, benefits of a primarily social nature. As a means of examining the relationship that exists between American independent cinema and its audience, this chapter will now offer four types of regular cinemagoers. The manner in which the subjects chose their cinematic viewing is of particular interest, as it is this process of selection that is indicative of their own natures as filmgoers and contributors to our social-economy. As Bourdieu states,

> Choosing according to one's tastes is a matter of identifying goods that are objectively attuned to one's position and which 'go together' because they are situated in roughly equivalent positions in their respective spaces, be they films, or plays, cartoons or novels, clothes or furniture; this choice is assisted by institutions – shops, theatre, critics, newspapers, magazines – which are themselves defined by their position in a field and which are chosen on the same principles.[6]

Each study was constructed out of interviews in which the individuals were questioned about their personal taste with regard to film, and the circumstances in which they developed an interest in the cinema. An emphasis was also placed on how film fits in with their everyday life, how it informs and enhances their life experiences outside of the art house.

Type 1 – Kevin

Age: 28, Profession: Sales Executive
Kevin is a true cinephile in that he has a wide knowledge of cinema and makes a concentrated effort to watch a number of films each week, several of which are new releases, the others being DVD rentals or repeat viewings from his own collection.

Kevin is 28 years old and works in media, following four years of higher education. He is single, lives in a major city, and enjoys social pursuits. Although he visits his local gym twice per week, Kevin's interests do not include sport, preferring instead cinema, music, literature, and selective television viewing. Cinema and the arts in general are both a mental and social stimulus for Kevin, providing him with an intellectual pursuit outside the work environment, and also a social driver for interaction with friends and new acquaintances. Kevin struggled socially at an early age and sought solace in television. Reliant on the schedules for his viewing opportunities, Kevin witnessed a wide range of films dating from the 1930s and 1940s through to more recent productions.

As his knowledge about the production of movies and the people behind, as opposed to the celebrities in front of, the camera grew and grew, Kevin became more attracted to independent cinema because of the individuality it appeared to encourage. During the 1990s, Kevin was able to witness the 'explosion' of independent cinema, with directors like Quentin Tarantino, Robert Rodriguez, and Kevin Smith emerging almost out of 'nowhere'. Early articles on the likes of Tarantino and Smith in particular portrayed them as talented tyros who had learnt everything they knew about making movies from catching re-runs of 1970s cult classics on late-night television. The daily life of these film-makers seemed to mirror that of Kevin's, leading him to feel a certain kinship with certain directors and an eagerness to see every film they released. These self-styled slackers of modern film, who wrote such dynamic dialogue, yet would be so flippant about their abilities when praised by a gushing member of the press, made making movies seem like a good alternative to getting a 'proper' job. Although he followed an academic path and is now in a well-paid position, his interest in American independent films has continued for a variety of reasons, the most obvious being that the film-makers with whom he felt such an affinity as a teenager have also matured and are now making films that are relevant to him in different ways to the ones he enjoyed so much at a younger age.

Type 2 – Emma

Age: 41, Profession: Teacher
Emma is a viewer of American independent cinema more out of an interest in a particular type of film than a particular form of film-making. As a teacher of English literature, her main interest and leisure activity is reading, and she actively seeks media that can offer a similar level of insight and stimulation, or complement her primary interest. Her own selection of favourite films from the last few years comprises such titles as *The English Patient*, *In the Bedroom* and *Master and Commander – The Far Side of the World*, all literary adaptations from Miramax, Disney's 'independent' division. She considers her interest in cinema to be something that has 'always been there', probably from the recreational viewing of films on television with her family whilst growing up, and from attending screenings of films at her University cinema whilst an undergraduate student.

She does not, however, consider herself to be a 'film buff' and was often left unmoved by the more self-conscious 'art' films that she witnessed on the student circuit. Although intelligent and informed, and more than able to offer an interpretation of the abstract work of Derek Jarman or Peter Greenaway, she found more pleasure in the discussion of such films than in the actual viewing of them. Emma is not so much a cinephile as a discerning viewer, seeking cinematic entertainment that has prior credibility from being an already established property. As such, she does not distinguish independent features from studio features, but does try to select what she perceives as 'classy' films that offer some degree of historical, sociological, or intellectual value as well as providing escapism from her daily routine. As a single professional, the cinema is a useful social-driver for Emma, providing her with an opportunity to meet up with friends, or an evening out with a potential partner. The films themselves are an easy topic for discussion, and as someone who considers herself to be a 'private person', Emma likes to be able to communicate with others through reference to a text, whether it be literary or cinematic, as a means of exchanging points whilst not being explicitly personal.

Type 3 – Adrian

Age: 30, Profession: Web Designer
For Adrian, the independent sector exhibits an aesthetic sensibility that both appeals to, and challenges, his own ideas about the assemblage of imagery, meaning that cinemagoing is an extension of his own work with regard to the communication of ideas and ideology through a visual medium. He cites such recent independent films as *Being John Malkovich*, *Eternal Sunshine of the Spotless Mind*, and *Requiem for a Dream* as his favourite works, although the earliest of the three was released in 2000, suggesting a lack of interest in films of earlier decades. Adrian's taste could be described as specific to the point of narrow-mindedness in that he is interested in particular films, rather than film itself, and did not begin to distinguish independent films from studio offerings until a few years ago, when he became more aware of different methods production through Internet articles. Previously, he was content with films from any sector, providing they offered visual spectacle or innovation, and recalls such big-budget extravaganzas as *Total Recall* and *Terminator 2* as films that impressed him at an earlier age, although he was slowly drawn to more esoteric fare such as *Lost Highway* and *Twelve Monkeys*, finding interest in how the thematic concepts of the films were mirrored in their visual tapestries.

The independent films that Adrian has sought out are of a heightened visual nature, meaning that certain films and directors appeal more than others. Quentin Tarantino, Darren Aaranofsky, and Spike Jonze stand out as key film-makers, and he generally rejects, or is simply ignorant of, the more reflective works of the sector's elder statesmen, like Altman, Sayles, and Cassavettes. Even though he will readily name directors whose work has recently impressed and excited him, Adrian is not necessarily interested in following these film-makers unless their future projects fall into alignment with his own taste. Working within the field of web design has led Adrian to form the view that art and commerce are developing at such a rate, that there is simply not enough time to look so far back as to the 1970s or even the 1980s for inspiration or insight, and that a knowledge and understanding of current work is sufficient to develop and predict coming trends in the area of visual media.

Type 4 – Chloe

Age: 21, Profession: Student
Chloe is an undergraduate student of History of Art and developed an interest in cinema through her Media Studies classes at 'A'-level. Through engaging with visual media in an educational environment, Chloe found an increased level of interest in an area that had previously been a form of escapism and found her awareness of film culture and technique growing as a result. Prior to her Media Studies course, Chloe had enjoyed cinema as a social pursuit, but meeting up with friends was the primary activity. After spending some months analysing film and studying narrative construction and intertextuality, her taste broadened to include films outside the Hollywood mainstream.

As Chloe has a keen interest in fashion and celebrity, her viewing choices are often governed by the actors and actresses who feature in films, rather than by directors or subject matter. She has a modest collection of films on DVD, although these are mostly for leisure purposes, to be enjoyed with friends and family, and therefore her collection is comprised more of mainstream fare, comedies, and romances, such as *The Notebook, Meet the Parents*, and *City of Angels*. Although it is tempting to draw correlations between film and her art degree, Chloe does not see much relation at this stage, possibly because she is primarily interested in current film releases, and any inclinations she has had to investigate the back catalogue of cinema have been interrupted by study deadlines and social activities. Much of Chloe's enjoyment of the independent sector comes not just from the films, but also from the environment in which they are screened. The city in which she studies has two art house venues, both with café-bars for socializing and book shops, while one has an exhibition of local artists. As she has made a number of friends from her degree class, the art house cinema has come to represent a social environment, a place to meet friends and fellow students for leisure and work-related activities.

Results of Analysis
These types suggest an audience that is far removed from the lives depicted in American independent cinema. While many of the characters in such films are outsiders, individuals with anti-social tendencies, tormented psyches, and obsessive natures, the audience for American independent cinema is more stable, comfortable with its position in the overarching social-economy, fixed in specific roles, usually those of 'professional' or 'student'. This audience is not so much interested in film as social representation, seeking knowledge of themselves and others through their relationship with the silver screen. As Durgnat states,

Very few spectators seek to read texts. They want to raid them for some relevance to their own interests. The study of movies undoubtedly has its place, but very few moviegoers want to study movies. They want to loot them.[7]

With the exception of Kevin, who is a true cinephile, these types do not lead lives that revolve around the cinema, but their social experience would most definitely be missing something without it. The independent sector provides them with a source of discussion, escapism, and sometimes creative inspiration, and they are inclined to seek out such films because of both the novelty of their ideology and imagery, and the prestige that comes through the cultural legitimacy of well-reviewed films or literary adaptations. Even within what Bourdieu would consider to be the more cerebral form of cinema, superficial responses to, and reasons for selection of, independent films have been noted – the appeal of actors, music, fashions, and the comfort that comes from adaptations of well-regarded novels do not suggest an audience that wants to be constantly challenged and questioned by film. However, this is an 'active' audience in the sense that it is seeking out specific films within a crowded marketplace, and maintaining an interest through the application of inter-related thoughts, philosophies, emotions, experiences, and social inclinations towards its selection of visual media.

10.6 Brutal Youth – How American Independent Cinema Has Grown with its Audience

Several of these case studies are representative of a relatively new generation of cinemagoers who were attracted to the output of American independent sector in the early 1990s, a time when the scene was largely dominated, at least in terms of media coverage, by violent urban thrillers. These were films that provoked immediate reactions from audiences and critics due to their graphic depictions of sex and violence that were at odds with the altogether more thoughtful American independent cinema of the 1970s. Less sensationalist works, such as the domestic dramas *Gas Food Lodging* and *Passion Fish*, and subtle comedies like *Johnny Suede* and *Living in Oblivion*, struggled to attract audiences, despite critical acclaim. This was largely a result of the success of Tarantino's *Reservoir Dogs*, a film that became the catalyst for an emphasis on films that documented the anti-social urges of the urban male within the context of the crime genre. Abel Ferrara's *Bad Lieutenant*, Roger Avary's *Killing Zoe*, and the Hughes Brothers' *Menace 2 Society* are just three of the more notable examples of this trend, although it should be noted that each has its own aesthetic and moral vision, and the mutual association of these films is more the result of lazy media journalism than a conscious effort on the part of their directors.

Throughout the 1990s, as this new wave of American independent films developed its audience began to age, moving from student coffee houses into the commercial workspace, and the films themselves began to make subtle shifts in emphasis, even within the confines of genre. Tarantino himself acknowledged the newfound maturity of both himself and his audience with *Jackie Brown*, a crime story which kept most of the carnage off the screen and focussed on the jaded desperation of those involved in the criminal universe, as opposed to their nihilistic 'coolness'. The fortunes of many independent directors mirrored their audience, as they also 'graduated' not from school to employment, but from small independent films where the financial risk is low and to bigger studio ventures with large budgets and corporate pressure. In doing so, they have taken some of their audience with them, creating a crossover market for smart studio films, with notable examples being Doug Linman's spy thriller *The Bourne Identity*, the Warschowski brothers' science-fiction extravaganza *The Matrix*, and David O'Russell's Gulf War satire *Three Kings*. These are films that exhibit an independent aesthetic but align that quality with the resources of a major studio with more immediate rewards in terms of box office performance.

Independent cinema is maturing almost self-consciously, as if it is aware that it needs to adjust to the needs and sensibilities of the generation which was, at a young age, intoxicated by the punch-drunk machismo of *Reservoir Dogs*, but has come to be interested in matters closer to home, hence the success of independently financed dramas like *Lost in Translation* and *In the Bedroom*, or romantic-comedies such as *My Big Fat Greek Wedding*. This is not to say that the cinephile set is no longer interested in confrontational subject matter, as potentially 'difficult' documentaries such as *Capturing the Friedmans*, *Fahrenheit 9/11* and *Dig!* enjoyed success on the art house circuit and beyond. Independently produced crime thrillers have moved away from the macho posturing and violent depictions of *Reservoir Dogs* and its grubby offspring to examine the psychological implications for characters placed in situations of physical and emotional duress. *Memento*, *Fear X*, and *Narc* all feature crime-related scenarios, with protagonists driven by a desire for vengeance and retribution, yet feature relatively little on-screen bloodshed or verbal profanity, replacing Tarantino's cine-literacy with rounded character arcs and stories that take place in a 'real' world where 'loss' refers to an individual's emotional state rather than the removal of one of his limbs by another protagonist's shotgun blast.

In the police procedural thriller *Narc*, the exploration of violence is not so much through the depiction of the act itself, but through its psychological and emotional impact. Early sequences which succinctly but effectively examine the family life of the undercover officer (Jason Patric) show him in a loving environment, taking care of his newborn son, with the cinematographer employing warm visual textures to suggest a shelter from the horrors of the outside world. Later in the film, as Patric immerses himself in a case involving drugs, murder, and possible police corruption, he becomes alienated from his wife and child, with the scenes of his home life now bathed in a ghastly green light, suggesting the social sickness that he encounters through his work has infected his home. No longer do we hear the innocent laughter of his child, only the downbeat headlines from the television news as he sits alone at the far end of the sofa, emphasizing the absence of his loved ones from his present physical state, and the verbal anger of his wife who is heard from another room.

10.7 State of Independence – A Summary of Modern American Independent Cinema

As a result of its necessary 'interaction' with the audience, American independent cinema is continually evolving, subtly reinventing itself to continuously capture the attention and imagination of its core demographic and, occasionally, a wider crowd. Those directors who have sustained careers in the sector, with little or no work for the Hollywood studios, have done so because they have acknowledged that the audience for independent cinema expects films that possess a certain level of novelty, yet also carry a cultural capital which is almost bestowed on the viewer who has selected their film, whether it be at the cinema, or on DVD, or on television, as their entertainment of choice. Through their consumption of particular films, cultural capital becomes economic capital, and the film-makers are able to produce another independent feature and continue doing so providing that their work remains socially relevant and also innovative in terms of visual and narrative approach. However, these directors are in the minority, as they are as motivated by working against the system as they are by exploring stories, characters and themes.

The history of American independent cinema studied here has been generational, covering the period from 1969 to 2006. This is a period in which a popular movement has achieved cultural prominence through its reaction to its corporate counterpart, only to be absorbed and appropriated by the industrial giants. With the production opportunities that are presented by digital video, and with the more sophisticated home computers providing the necessary post-production facilities, it is now possible for aspiring film-makers to work entirely independently, providing they have enough finance and leisure time to fulfil their cinematic ambitions. However, the Hollywood studios have secured dominance with regard to distribution, and this means that defiantly independent cinema may prove to be, if not non-existent in the coming decade, certainly hard to find, although the Internet may offer an outlet to film-makers who do not wish to compromise their vision in order to secure a distribution deal. For the audience, this means a lack of variety and, consequently, confusion with regard to the definition of 'American independent cinema'. Despite the best efforts of such film-makers as John Sayles and Jim Jarmusch to sustain a cinema that is ingrained with its own rhetoric, the term has become a label that is more applicable to the lifestyle choices of consumers than it is to a legitimate artistic community or mode of cultural production. As a marketing tool, the term has immediate implications for the cinematic consumer, suggesting a certain type of film, and a sense of cultural legitimacy that comes from being at once outside the corporate system but within an inherently fashionable social group. As a category of actual film-making activity, it is less clear, with many independent productions conforming to the practices of the Hollywood mainstream, even when operating under severe budgetary restrictions.

This analysis of American independent cinema leads us to define the sector as being a form of cultural production that is able to explore diverse themes in an intellectually and aesthetically challenging manner, providing that it does not completely ignore the rules of market and alienate its niche audience, or cross so far into the avant-garde that it eradicates any 'crossover' potential. It is largely independent in terms of theme and subject matter in that the sector is entirely reliant on the idiosyncratic personalities of its creative contributors for the novelty that is its main selling point and cultural attribute, although it is dependent on the fiscal resources of Hollywood studios when seeking to reach a mass audience and achieve the kind of social impact that can only come from wide availability. The Hollywood mainstream relies on the 'independent' sector for renewal, seeking to formulate its 'unique' successes, whilst neutralizing any radical impulses that could upset the balance of power with regard to the dominance of the mass audience that the corporate giants continue to profit from. It is clear from a discussion of the work of certain film-makers that a level of creative autonomy is possible within the system of mass production, although it is only possible if the film-maker possess the social-political ability required to skilfully navigate the institutional network of the entertainment industry, filtering their ideology through work that can be regarded as commercial product by the giants, and yet also viewed as possessing artistic legitimacy by critics and selective audiences.

American independent cinema, in the widely known, commercially viable, form in which it has been discussed within this study, could be re-imagined as 'marginal Hollywood cinema'. This could be said to be a cinema that sustains itself through the cultivation of a niche audience by exploring subject matter that is out of the intellectual reach of the summer blockbusters, but does so with the aid of recognizable Hollywood characteristics such as genre and movie stars and a reliance on industrial resources (distribution, marketing) and institutional bodies (the Academy Awards, cultural critics, film festivals). By establishing a position within the machinery of the industry of mass production, such marginal cinema achieves a connection to an audience that is so eager to accept the existence of a form of 'alternative' media, that it will largely ignore the corporate origins of such films and accept them as doctrines of independence.

Notes

1. Gripsrud, J, 'Film Audiences' in *The Oxford Guide to Film Studies* (Hill, J & Gibson, P eds), 2nd edn, p. 202, London, Oxford University Press, 1998.
2. Bourdieu, p. 230, 1979.
3. Bourdieu, p. 231, 1979.
4. Bourdieu, p. 231, 1979.
5. http://www.rottentomatoes.com.
6. Bourdieu, p. 232, 1979.
7. Durgnat, R, 'Nostalgia: Code and Anti-Code' in *Moving Places – A Life at the Movies*, Wide Angle, 1981.

BIBLIOGRAPHY

Texts

Aftab, K, *Spike Lee – That's My Story and I'm Sticking to It*, 1st edn, London, Faber & Faber, 2005.

Anderson, J, *Sundancing – Hanging Out and Listening in at America's Most Important Film Festival*, Avon Books, 2000.

Andrew, G, *Stranger than Paradise – Maverick Filmmakers in Recent American Cinema*, 1st edn, London, Prion, 1998.

Belazs, B, *Spirit of Film Volume II*, Schoken, 1931.

Benjamin, W, *Illuminations*, Schocken, 1969.

Biskind, P, *Down and Dirty Pictures – Miramax, Sundance, and the Rise of Independent Film*, 1st edn, London, Bloomsbury, 2004.

Biskind, P, *Easy Riders Raging Bulls*, 2nd edn, London, Bloomsbury, 1998.

Blumer, J, Gurevitch, M, Katz, *Uses of Mass Communication by the Individual*, 1st edn, London, Sage, 1974.

Bogdanovich, P, *Picture Shows – Peter Bogdanovich on the Movies*, 1st edn, New York, Clark Doble & Brendon Ltd, 1975.

Boorman, J & Donohue, W (ed), *Projections 3 – Filmmakers And Filmmaking*, 1st edn, London, Faber & Faber, 1994.

Bourdieu, P, *Distinction – A Social Critique of the Judgement of Taste*, Routledge & Kegan Paul, 1979.

Bourdieu, P, *The Field of Cultural Production*, Polity, 1993.

Christie, I (editor), *Gilliam on Gilliam*, 1st edn, London Faber & Faber, 1999.

Collins, H & Radner, A (eds), *Film Theory Goes to the Movies*, 1st edn, London, Routledge, 1993.

Dyer, R, *Stars (Second Edition)*, BFI Publishing, 1998.

Falsetto, M, *Personal Visions – Conversations with Independent Film-Makers*, 1st edn, London, Constable, 1999.

Fleming, C, *High Concept – Don Simpson and the Hollywood Culture of Excess*, 2nd edn, London, Bloomsbury, 1998.

Fonda, P, *Don't Tell Dad – A Memoir*, 2nd edn, London, Pocket Books, 1999.

Garnham, G, *Capitalism and Communication – Global Culture and the Economics of Information*, 1st edn, London, Sage, 1990.

Gilbey, R, *It Don't Worry Me – Nashville, Jaws, Star Wars and Beyond*, 1st edn, London, Faber & Faber, 2003.

Hill, J & Gibson, P (editors), *The Oxford Guide to Film Studies*, Oxford University Press, 1998.

Hillier, J (ed.), *American Independent Cinema – A Sight and Sound Reader*, 1st edn, London, BFI Publications, 2001.

Hoberman, J, *The Dream Life – Movies, Media, and The Mythology of the Sixties*, 1st edn, New York, The New Press, 2003.

Hoggart, R, *The Uses of Literacy: Aspects of Working-Class Life with Special Reference to Publications and Entertainments*, 1st edn, London, Penguin, 1958.

Jackson, K (ed.), *Schrader on Schrader – Revised Edition*, 2nd edition, London, Faber & Faber, 2004.

Jain, CS, *Marketing, Planning and Strategy*, 2nd edn, South Western Publishing, 1985.

Johnstone, N, *Abel Ferrara – The King of New York*, 1st edn, London, Omnibus Press, 1999.

Katz, E, Blumer, J, Gurevitch, M, *Uses of Mass Communication by the Individual*, 1st edn, London, Sage, 1974.

Kracauer, S, *The Mass Ornament – Weimar Essays*, 2nd edn, Cambridge, Mass, Harvard University Press, 1995.

Kramer, P, *The New Hollywood – From Bonnie and Clyde to Star Wars*, 1st edn, London, Wallflower Press, 2005.

Lay, S, *British Social Realism – From Documentary to Brit Grit*, 1st edn, London, Wallflower Press, 2002.

Levy, E, *Cinema of Outsiders – The Rise of American Independent Film*, 1st edn, New York, New York University Press, 1999.

Linson, A, *What Just Happened? – Bitter Hollywood Tales from the Front Line*, 1st edn, London, Bloomsbury, 2002.

Littejohn, S, *Theories of Human Communication*, 7th edn, London, Wadsworth, 2002.

Lowenstein, S (ed.), *My First Movie*, 1st edn, London, Faber & Faber, 2000.

Mattelart, A, *Multinational Corporations & the Control of Culture*, 1st edn, New Jersey, Harvester Press, 1979.

McDonald, P, *The Star System – Hollywood's Production of Popular Identities*, 1st edn, London, Wallflower Press, 2000.

McKee, R, *Story – Substance, Structure, Style, and the Principles of Screenwriting*, 1st edn, London, Methuen, 1998.

Merritt, G, *Celluloid Mavericks – A History of American Independent Film*, 1st edn, New York, Thunder's Mouth Press, 2000.

Murphy, Robert (ed.), *The British Cinema Book*, 2nd edn, London, BFI, 2000.

Murphy, Robert (ed.), *British Cinema Of The 90s*, 1st edn, London, 2001.

Neal, S (ed.), *Contemporary Hollywood Cinema*, 1st edn, London, Routledge, 1998.

Neal, S (ed.), *Genre and Contemporary Hollywood*, 1st edn, London, BFI, 2002.

Owen, A (ed.), *Smoking in Bed – Conversations with Bruce Robinson*, 1st edn, London, Bloomsbury, 2000.

Owne, A (ed.), *Story and Character – Conversations with British Screenwriters*, 1st edn, London, Bloomsbury, 2002.

Piercy, N, *Market-led Strategic Change: Making Marketing Happen in Your Organization*, Thorsons, 1991.

Pierson, J, *Spike, Mike, Slackers & Dykes – A Guided Tour Across a Decade of Independent American Cinema*, 1st edn, London Faber & Faber, 1995.

Rodley, Chris (ed.), *Cronenberg on Cronenberg – Revised Edition*, 2nd edn, London, Faber & Faber, 1997.

Rodriguez, R, *Rebel Without a Crew, Or How a 23-Year-Old Filmmaker With $7,000 Became a Hollywood Player*, 1st edn, London, Faber & Faber, 1996.

Rokeach, S & DeFleur, M, *A Dependency Model of Mass Media Effects*, 1976.

Rosenblatt, L, *Literature as Exploration*, Appleton-Century, 1938.

Salisbury, M, *Burton on Burton*, 2nd edition, London, Faber & Faber, 2006.

Sayles, J, *Thinking In Pictures – The Making of the Movie Matewan*, 1st edn, Boston, Houghton Mifflin Company, 1987.

Smith, G (ed.), *Sayles on Sayles*, 1st edn, London, Faber & Faber, 1998.

Taylor, T, *The Big Deal*, 1st edn, New York, William Morrow & Company Inc., 1999.

Thomson, D & Christie, I (ed.), *Scorsese on Scorsese*, 1st edn, London, Faber & Faber, 1989.

Umland, R & S, *Donald Cammell – A Life on the Wild Side*, 1st edn, London, FAB Press, 2006.

Walker, S, *King of Cannes*, 1st edn, London, Algonquin, 2000.

Wasko, J, *How Hollywood Works*, 1st edn, London, Sage, 2003.

Wenders, W, *The Logic of Images – Essays and Conversations*, 1st edn, London, Faber & Faber, 1991.

Williams, T, *The Cinema of George A. Romero – Knight of the Living Dead*, 1st edn, London, Wallflower Press, 2003.

Journal Articles

Acheson, K, Maule, J, 'Understanding Hollywood's Organization and Continuing Success', *Journal of Cultural Economics*, 18:0 (1994).

Albert, S, 'Movie Stars and the Distribution of Financially Successful Films in the Motion Picture Industry', *Journal of Cultural Economics*, 22:0 (1998).

Andre, C, Haacke, H, Perreault, P, Nemser, C, 'The Role of the Artist in Today's Society', *Art Journal*, 34:4 (1975).

Brookes, J, 'The Rise or Fall of the British Film Industry? A Critical Overview of UK Film Making in the 1990s', discussion papers in mass-communications, University of Leicester Press, 2002.

Caves, R, 'Contracts Between Art and Commerce', *Journal of Economic Perspectives*, 17:2 (2003).

Dalgic, T & Leeuw, M, 'Niche Marketing Revisited: Concept, Applications and some European Case Studies', *European Journal of Marketing*, 28:4 (1994).

De Vany, A, Walls, DW, 'Uncertainty in the Movie Industry: Does Star Power Reduce the Terror of the Box Office?', *Journal of Cultural Economics*, 23:0 (1999).

Durgnat, R, 'Nostalgia: Code and Anti-Code', *Moving Places – A Life at the Movies*, (1981).

Eliashberg, J & Shugan, S, 'Film Critics: Influencers or Predictors', *Journal of Marketing*, 61:0 (1997).

Guback, T, 'Are We Looking at the Right Things in Film', paper presented at the *Society for Cinema Studies* conference, Philadelphia, PA, 1978.

Haley, Stuart, & Co, *The Motion Picture Industry as a Basic for Bond Financing*, 27th May 1927.

Hills, P, '1936: Meyer Schapiro, "Art Front", and the Popular Front', *Oxford Art Journal*, 17:1 (1994).

Hirsch, P, 'Cultural Industries Revisited', *Organizational Science*, 11:3 (2000).

Hirsch, P, 'Cultural Productions in the U.S.: Do Changes in Ownership Matter?', *Organizational Science*, (1985).

Hoggart, R, 'Why I Value Literature', *Speaking to Each Other, Vol II, Times Educational Supplement*, 1963.

Jameson, F, 'Periodizing the 60s', *Social Text*, Duke University Press, 1984.

Kerr, CE, 'Incorporating the Star: The Intersection of Business and Aesthetic Strategies in Early American Film', *The Business History Review*, 64:3 (1990).

Koch, G, Hansem, M, 'Bela Balazs: 'The Physiognomy of Things', *New German Critique*, 40:0 (1987).

Kotler, P, 'From Mass Marketing to Mass Customization', *Planning Review*, September/October 1991.

Moran, J, 'Greg Araki: Guerilla Film-Maker for a Queer Generation', *Film Quarterly*, 50:1, (1996).

Perren, A, 'Sex, Lies and Marketing – Miramax and the Development of the Quality Indie Blockbuster', *Film Quarterly*, 55:2 (2001).

Unknown Writer, 'A Bigger Picture', *Film Policy Review*, 03/1998.

Unknown Writer, 'Turning An Industry Inside Out: A Conversation With Robert Redford', *Harvard Business Review*, 80:5, (2002).

Press Articles

Anonymous, 'Special Independents Issue', *The Hollywood Reporter*, 08/1996.

Biskind, P, review of *The Sundance Kids: How The Mavericks Took Back Hollywood* in *Sight & Sound*, June 2006.

Bloom, P, 'The British are Coming ', *Empire* magazine, 08/1990.

Broderick, P, 'The ABC's of No-Budget Filmmaking', *Filmmaker Magazine*, winter 1992.

Ceroe, D, 'Taking an Independent Path', *Los Angeles Times*, 03/05/1989.

Clark, J, 'The Soul of Sundance's Machine', *The New York Times*, 04/12/2005.

Dalton, S, interview with Jarmusch, J, *Uncut* magazine, 11/2005.

Fleming, M, 'Crying all the Way to the Bank', *Variety*, 02/03/1993.

Greenberg, J, 'Sex, Lies, and Kafka', *Connoisseur*, 11/1991.

Hemblade, C, interview with Modine, M, *Empire* magazine, 03/1998.

Hirschberg, J, 'His Way', *The New York Times*, 19/12/1999.

Kirn, W, interview with Redford, R, *The New York Times Sunday Magazine*, 16/11/1997.

Nelson, R, 'Safe at Sundance', *Metro Active Online Edition*, 21/02/1997.

Spines, C, 'Who Let the Underdogs Out?', *Premiere*, 10/2002.

Timberg, S, 'Fresh Blood', *New Times Los Angeles*, 08/07/1999.

Unknown Writer, interview with Harvey Weinstein, *The New York Times*, 13/12/1992.

Unknown Writer, 'Product Must Be Right for Today's Market', *Kine Weekly*, p. 13, 13/06/1970.

Winsten, A, article in *The New York Post*, 15/07/1969.

Online Articles

Caribay, L, 'The Story of Go', www.ifp.org/interviews, 01/06/2002.

Daly, S, 'Liman on Liman', www.ew.com, 14/05/2006.

Farrow, B, 'What is the Point of Film Festivals?', www.guardianonline.com, 08/12/1999.

Fischer, P, 'X2 Director Has Something to Sing About', www.filmmonthly.com, 04/07/2003.

Hanrahan, D, 'The Bourne Identity – Doug Liman interview', www.bbc.co.uk/films, 05/09/20002.

Major, W, 'To the Max', http://www.boxoffice.com, August 1997.

Nelson, R, 'Safe at Sundance', www.metroactiveonline.com, 01/02/1997.

Topel, F, 'Behind Bourne', www.actionadventure.about.com, 2002.

Unknown Writer, 'Britannia's Committee for Cool', www.news.bbc.co.uk, 01/04/1988.

Wiener, J, 'Quiet in Hollywood', http://www.thenation.com, 26/11/2002.

Wilonsky, R, 'From Major to Minor – Why the Best Films of 2004 Look Like Indies but Aren't', www.eastbayexpress.com, 22/12/2004.

Unknown Writer, 'Lord of War', http://www.cinemareview.com, 11/2005.

Websites

Action Adventure Cinema www.actionadventure.about.com

Boxofficeguru www.boxofficeguru.com

Boxofficemojo www.boxofficemojo.com

Cinema Review www.cinemareview.com

Dark Horizons www.darkhorizons.com

Empire Online www.empireonline.com

Entertainment Weekly www.ew.com

Filmmakers www.filmamker.com

Film Monthly www.filmmonthly.com

Film Threat www.filmthreat.com

Hypnotic www.hypnotic.com

Indiewire www.indiewire.com

Internet Movie Database www.imbd.com

Jam! Movies www.jammovies.com

Lions Gate Films www.lionsgate.com

Miramax Films www.miramaxcafe.com

Rotten Tomatoes www.rottentomatoes.com

Films

The Blair Witch Project

Clockers

Coffee and Cigarettes

Cold Mountain

Collateral Damage

The Conversation

Copland

Crouching Tiger, Hidden Dragon

The Crow

The Crying Game
Cube
The Day after Tomorrow
Dead Man
Dead Man Walking
Death Wish
Die Hard
Dirty Harry
Disclosure
Donnie Darko
The Doom Generation
Do the Right Thing
Driller Killer
Drugstore Cowboy
Easy Rider
El Mariachi
The Empire Strikes Back
The English Patient
Erin Brokovich
Eternal Sunshine of the Spotless Mind
The Exorcist
Farewell my Concubine
Fear X
A Few Good Men
Fight Club
Five Easy Pieces
Flirting with Disaster
Forces of Nature
Fahrenheit 9/11
Full Frontal
Gangs of New York
Garden State
Gas Food Lodging
Ghost
Ghostbusters
Ghost Dog – Way of the Samurai
Ghost World
Girlfight
Girl 6
Gladiator
The Gladiator (1985)
City of Hope
Clerks
Go

Go Fish
Gone in 60 Seconds
Good Will Hunting
The Graduate
Gummo
Halloween
Heavy
Hidden Agenda (1989)
House Party
How to Lose a Guy in 10 Days
The Hudsucker Proxy
The Hulk
I Heart Huckabees
Independence Day
In The Bedroom
Jackie Brown
Jaws
Jerry Maguire
Johnny Suede
Juice
Jungle Fever
Kafka
Kes
Kids
The Kid Stays in the Picture
Kill Bill Vol. 1
Kill Bill Vol. 2
Killing Zoe
Kingdom of Heaven
The King of New York
King of the Hill
The Kiss of the Spider Woman
La Dolce Vita
Land and Freedom
The Last Picture Show
Leaving Las Vegas
Like Water for Chocolate
Limbo
The Limey
The Living End
Living in Oblivion
Lock, Stock and Two Smoking Barrels
Lone Star
Lord of War

Lost Highway
Lost in Translation
Magnolia
The Glass Shield
Malcolm X
Mallrats
Man Bites Dog
Marathon Man
MASH
Master & Commander
The Matador
Matewan
The Matrix
Mean Streets
Medium Cool
Menace 2 Society
Metropolitan
Midnight Cowboy
Mission: Impossible
Mission: Impossible II
Memento
Mr & Mrs. Smith
Mulholland Dr.
My Big Fat Greek Wedding
My Name is Joe
Mysterious Skin
Mystery Train
Nadja
Napoleon Dynamite
Narc
Natural Born Killers
Night of the Living Dead (1968)
Night on Earth
Overnight
Ocean's 11
Outbreak
Out of Sight
The Parallax View
Passion Fish
The Passion of the Christ
Permanent Vacation
Pi
The Piano
Platoon

Public Access
Pulp Fiction
The Quiet American
Raining Stones
The Rainmaker
Rain Man
Repo Man
Requiem for a Dream
Reservoir Dogs
Ricochet
Ruby in Paradise
Runaway Bride
Schizopolis
Scream
Serendipity
Serpico
Set it Off
Sex, Lies, and Videotape
Shakespeare in Love
Shaking the Cage
Shallow Grave
The Shawshank Redemption
She's Gotta Have It
The Shipping News
Short Cuts
Sideways
Silver City
Slacker
Sleepless in Seattle
Slingblade
Solaris (2002)
Spanking the Monkey
Speed
Spider-Man
Stranger than Paradise
Summer of Sam
Swingers
Taxi Driver
The Texas Chain Saw Massacre
There's Something about Mary
Things to do in Denver when You're Dead
The Thin Blue Line
Three Kings
Trees Lounge

Twelve Monkeys
The 25th Hour
Traffic
Trainspotting
The Unbelievable Truth
The Underneath
Unforgiven
The Usual Suspects
The Virgin Suicides
The Watcher
Welcome to Collingwood
X-Men
X-2: X-Men United
The Yards
Your Friends and Neighbours

INDEX